William Ingraham Kip

The Christmas Holydays in Rome

William Ingraham Kip

The Christmas Holydays in Rome

ISBN/EAN: 9783743317475

Manufactured in Europe, USA, Canada, Australia, Japa

Cover: Foto ©Thomas Meinert / pixelio.de

Manufactured and distributed by brebook publishing software (www.brebook.com)

William Ingraham Kip

The Christmas Holydays in Rome

THE

CHRISTMAS HOLYDAYS IN ROME.

BY THE
RIGHT REV. WM. INGRAHAM KIP, D. D.,
BISHOP OF CALIFORNIA.

—— rerum pulcherrima, Roma.
VIRG. *Georg.* ii. 534.

E. P. DUTTON AND COMPANY.
BOSTON: 135 WASHINGTON STREET.
NEW YORK: 762 BROADWAY.
1869.

Entered according to Act of Congress, in the year 1865, by
E. P. DUTTON AND COMPANY,
in the Clerk's Office of the District Court of the District of Massachusetts

RIVERSIDE, CAMBRIDGE:
STEREOTYPED AND PRINTED BY
H. O. HOUGHTON AND COMPANY.

To

THE COMPANION OF THESE WANDERINGS,

HER HUSBAND

INSCRIBES THIS VOLUME.

"Why, wedded to the Lord, still yearns my heart
  Upon these scenes of ancient heathen fame?
  Yet legend hoar, and voice of bard that came
Fixing my restless youth with its sweet art,
And shades of power, and those who bore their part
  In the mad deeds that set the world in flame,
  To fret my memory here — ah! is it blame
That from my eye the tear is fain to start?
Nay, from no fount impure these drops arise;
'Tis but the sympathy with Adam's race,
Which in each brother's history reads its own."
— *Lyra Apostolica.*

PREFACE.

To have seen Rome is a great fact in an individual's life. So it appeared to the writer of these pages, when wandering among her mighty ruins, finding everywhere the bright pictures of youthful imagination surpassed. Cicero in his day declared, — "We are surrounded by the vestiges of history." How then should we feel when, standing on the same spot, we realize that eighteen centuries have since added their relics!

The title of this volume does not perhaps, give an adequate idea of its contents. The writer was led to adopt it, because his primary object in visiting Rome at that season, was to witness the Christmas services. His residence there was, however, prolonged through the greater part of the winter, all of which time was occupied in diligent study of the inexhaustible objects around him. To attempt a description of one half, in a work of this size, would be in vain; he has therefore only selected from his notes written on the spot, some of those things which excited the greatest interest in his own mind.

It will be seen that while he has paid some attention to the antiquities of the city and the classical associations connected with them, he has dwelt particularly upon Ecclesiastical matters relating to the Church of Rome. And in this respect, he thinks the work will differ from most of those on the same subject. Travellers seem generally to have given only a one-sided view of the Papal Church. Some were ready to commend everything, and others, on the contrary, saw nothing good in the whole system, — no rite or service which did not shock some violent prejudice. Now in this, as in everything else, there is a proper medium. The Church of Rome is indeed deformed by many fearful errors, which often strike at the very cardinal doctrines of our faith, but she has also retained much that is Catholic. Were it not so, that mighty Hierarchy could not have subsisted for so many centuries, through every change and convulsion; winning to its spiritual sway, the crowds of northern barbarians which swept over the city; and even at the present day, drawing to itself proselytes in lands, where intellectual and spiritual freedom give every opportunity for the thorough discussion of this subject. These are the very things which render the system so dangerous, enabling it to charm the imagination and retain its hold upon the human mind, while its influence is withering to the best interests of our race. The writer has, therefore, endeavored to look at the Church of Rome without prejudice, and while his investigation strengthened the unfavorable view he before had of the practical working of that system, he still has not withheld his tribute of praise from anything he saw which was truly Catholic.

He has been obliged to write this volume entirely during the last three months, amidst those engrossing cares of parish duty which necessarily gathered around him after the absence of nearly a year from his field of labor. He mentions this, not to deprecate criticism, but to account for mistakes which may exist. To him, however, the labor has been a pleasant one, reviving associations which he would always wish to cherish. Beautiful Italy! thy old traditions lingering around each crumbling fane, and consecrating each fountain and grove, are inspiration to the mind! thy very language is melody to the ear! Thy bright and sunny clime; thy land so richly dowered with loveliness; thy antique and solemn ruins; how will the recollections they furnish mingle with the stern realities of coming days, and soften the carking cares of this working world! They will return to us like the glorious visions which ever after floated before the eyes of the Arabian shepherd, when — as Eastern fable tells us, — while wandering in the wilderness, he had caught a single glimpse of the gardens of Irim, and then lost them again forever.

Albany, *Christmas*, 1845.

PREFACE TO PRESENT EDITION.

More than twenty years ago, after a winter spent in Rome with the enthusiasm of early days, the author published this volume. It was shortly after reprinted in London, edited by the Rev. Wm. Sewall, of Exeter College, Oxford, and in successive editions has retained its place, with the reading public in England, to this day. In this country, however, it has been long out of print, and the author has, therefore, yielded to the requests of friends to have a new edition issued.

In revising it, after another visit to Rome and with the wider experience which these years have given, he finds no necessity to modify a single opinion or alter any conclusion which he then expressed. Rome sits unchanged upon her Seven Hills. Gregory XVI. indeed sleeps with his predecessors, and Pius IX. reigns in his stead, but the system is unchanged. All things there continue as they were.

Even the outward features of the city are unchanged. A score of years has left no impress on her hoary ruins. The Railway indeed now winds across the desolate Campagna, from Civita Vecchia to the city, but it stops without the walls. Within them no innovations of the nineteenth century are allowed. When the author was asked, — "Do you see changes in anything here since your last visit?" — he was obliged to answer, — "In nothing but myself!"

October, 1868.

CONTENTS.

I.
CIVITA VECCHIA. — JOURNEY TO ROME. — THE "ETERNAL CITY" BY MOONLIGHT 1

II.
VIEW FROM THE TOWER OF THE SENATOR 8

III.
ST. PETER'S CHURCH 21

IV.
THE CHRISTMAS SERVICES 41

V.
THE CAPITOLINE HILL 53

VI.
THE VATICAN 67

VII.
PRESENTATION AT THE PAPAL COURT. — THE POPEDOM . . 81

VIII.
A DAY'S RAMBLE IN ROME 90

IX.
THE EPIPHANY SERVICES 105

X.
THE TOMBS OF THE LAST STUARTS 115

XI.
The Coliseum. — Palace of the Cæsars. — Baths . . . 122

XII.
Dramatic Character of the Church Services. — Sermon by a Vicar-General. — Capuchin Cemetery 149

XIII.
Christian Art. — Overbeck 151

XIV.
Excursion on the Appian Way 159

XV.
Cardinals. — Mezzofanti 179

XVI.
The Protestant Burial-ground 188

XVII.
The Palaces of Rome 199

XVIII.
Excursion to Tivoli 223

XIX.
The Churches of Rome 236

XX.
Exhibition at the Propaganda. — Funerals. — Vespers at the Convent of Santa Trinita 258

XXI.
The Roman People. — The Civil Government of the Papal Court 270

XXII.
The Papal Church 281

XXIII.
Farewell to Rome 301

THE
CHRISTMAS HOLYDAYS IN ROME.

CHAPTER I.

CIVITA VECCHIA. — JOURNEY TO ROME. — THE " ETERNAL CITY " BY MOONLIGHT.

IT was in one of the most lovely nights ever seen under an Italian sky, that the steamer in which we had embarked from Genoa came within sight of the coast of the Papal dominions. The moon had risen in her queen-like beauty, and as she rode high above us in the heavens, every wave of the Mediterranean seemed tinged with her radiance. Felucca, polacre, xebec, and other strange looking craft, were floating lazily on the sea, while our own vessel, as she glided through the blue waters, left a track of molten silver to mark her way. The cool, fresh breeze which came sweeping over the sea was far more grateful than the heated air of the cabin, and we remained long on deck, seeing as we passed, on the one hand, Napoleon's miniature kingdom of Elba, and on the other, the long line of the main-land, which owes submission to his Holiness Gregory XVI.

At sunrise the next morning we entered the harbor of Civita Vecchia, the nearest approach which can be made by sea to the city of Rome. The remaining distance, fifty-two miles, must be travelled by land. Ostia, the ancient port in which, during the days of the republic, her galleys rode, where Scipio Africanus embarked for Spain, and Claudius for Britain, is indeed but sixteen miles from the city, and was formerly much nearer, but the gradual accumulation of sand has entirely destroyed its harbor. After it was sacked by the Saracens in the fifth century, no attempt was made to restore it. The salt marshes, which Livy mentions as existing in the days of Ancus Martius, gradually encroached on the one side, and the sand was drifted over it from the sea on the other, until this city, which once contained eighty thousand inhabitants, now has only about fifty souls living in wretchedness among its ruins. We passed it in the steamer some months afterwards on our way up from Naples; but the site is only marked by the remains of a temple and theatre almost concealed by brambles, and a picturesque old fortress erected during the Middle Ages, with two solitary pine-trees standing in front of it. And yet, this place was once a suburb of imperial Rome: from thence the old consuls went forth to victory, and there they landed to commence their triumphs as they entered the city.

Civita Vecchia, with its fortress erected from plans furnished by Michael Angelo, and its long ramparts, presents a striking view from the sea, which you find, on landing, the reality by no means justifies. It has, however, some traces of antiquity, for the massive stone-work of its port was built under the direction of Trajan (the younger Pliny describes it as the "Trajani Portus"); and here, as at Terracina, the bronze rings by which the Roman galleys were made fast to the quays still remain. The immense prisons lining the basin have a bright appearance, which contrasts strangely with the gloomy object to which they are devoted. When we came on deck at dawn, the galley-slaves, in their parti-colored dresses, were just marching out to work, attended by a strong guard of soldiers. Their number is said to be nearly twelve hundred, and the clanking of their chains as they walked was the first sound which greeted us from the States of the Church.

The manner in which we were fleeced on all sides at this port of his Holiness was a foretaste of what we were to expect in Italy. You first pay sundry pauls[1] for being rowed ashore from the steamer; several porters (*facchini*) seize your baggage, and, unless you can squabble in Italian, you must bestow some more pauls on each for carrying it to the custom-house — more pauls to the officials there, for weighing it, to see whether or not it is beyond the allowable weight for the carriage — more for plumbing it (that is, cording it up, and fastening it with a lead seal, which is not to be taken off till you reach Rome) — more for the printed permit to pass it through the gates when you leave — more for hoisting it up on the top of the carriage; and so you go on, paying away on the right and on the left, until your small change and patience are both exhausted. In this little catalogue is not included the fee to the custom-house officer, whose inspection was a mere *pro formâ* business. He lifted the covers of our trunks, made a great flourish about the examination, in the course of which he opened a book (happening to be a controversial one on the Romish Church), and looked into it as curiously as if there was

---

[1] A *paul* or *paulo* is about *eleven cents.*

any probability of his understanding what it was, and then closed the trunks again. He next whispered to us, that "he should be happy to receive something, as we had been well served," turned his back, put his open hand behind him with a great affectation of secrecy, closed it as the expected pauls dropped in, and the farce was over. Add to this about a dollar for the *visé* of each passport, and you have the history of the blackmail levied on us at Civita Vecchia in about two hours.

At noon we set out in a carriage drawn by three horses. "And so we went towards Rome." The road for one half of the distance skirts the Mediterranean, through a region dreary and often uncultivated, though the last part, where it turns eastward into the country, becomes more hilly. One who looked only to the present, would pronounce it a ride without interest, except where his curiosity was, at times, excited by some massive ruins near the road, or a lonely tower hanging over the sea, reminding him of days of feudal strife. But, as Walpole says, "our memory sees more than our eyes in this country." The classical scholar, therefore, looks upon it as a land seamed and furrowed by the footsteps of past ages. He is in the midst of places of which Strabo and Pliny wrote. He crosses the Vaccina, the Amnis Cœretanus of his old school days. He passes through Cervetere, once one of the most important cities of ancient Etruria, where Virgil tells us Mezentius reigned when Eneas entered Italy; and the paintings in whose tombs, Pliny says, existed long before the foundation of Rome. It is supposed, indeed, that the Romans were first initiated in the mysteries of the Etruscan worship by the priests of Cære; and, when Rome was invaded by the Gauls, it was here that the vestal virgins found an asylum, and were sent for safety with the sacred fire. Every scene, indeed, has its separate story; and old memories of the past are crowding back on the traveller's mind, as he hears names which are associated with all he knows of classical interest.

It is something, too, to be riding along the shores of the Mediterranean. Its waves are haunted by the spirit of the past. We see them sparkling at our feet, or stretching out to the horizon, blue and beautiful in the sunlight, and we remember what countries they lave. Opposite to us is Africa, where St. Augustine once ruled, and hundreds of temples reared the Cross on high; then comes Egypt with its hoary antiquity, by the side of which Italy is young and childlike; then that holy land which our Lord " environed with his blessed feet," and where Paradise was Lost and was Regained. On we pass to old Tyre, where, as prophecy foretold, the nets are drying on the rocks; and onward again, till we behold the waters breaking in the many bays of Greece. There was the last foothold of the " faded hierarchy " of Olympus; and now, though songs are hushed and dances stilled in that land, yet beauty has everywhere left the wonderful tokens of her presence. And to the shores, too, where we are, the waves of this sea have borne one race after another from the far East, and seen the feeble colonies expand into greatness, until their children went forth to inherit the earth. What wonderful memories then linger around this mighty " valley of waters ! " [1]

The last few miles were over the silent and desolate

---

[1] " The valley of waters, widest next to that
Which doth the earth engarland."
Dante. Il Paradiso, c. ix. l. 80.

Campagna — low stunted trees only at times were seen, and not a habitation gave notice that we were drawing nigh to a mighty city. Far as the eye can reach is an unbroken waste, and the mistress of the world stands encircled by a melancholy solitude. Yet is it not appropriate that it should be so? About fair Naples are lovely vineyards, lining the road with the rich festoons they have hung from tree to tree; and from whichever side you approach beautiful Florence, whether from the smiling fields of Tuscany, or "leafy Valombrosa," or the woody heights of Fiesole, where Milton mused and wrote, there is still the same rich and lively scenery. All things are in unison with the gay and poetical character of these cities. Should not Rome, then, the fallen metropolis of the earth, majestic even in ruins, be surrounded only by barrenness and decay? Every object should inspire thoughts of awe and melancholy, as we approach this "Niobe of nations," standing thus —

"Childless and crownless in her voiceless woe."

It was late at night when we reached the neighborhood of "the Eternal City;" but the moon was up, shedding its light over the whole landscape, and we waited with eager impatience for our first view of the mistress of the world. At length it came. "ROMA!" shouted the postilion, and at once all heads were thrust through the carriage windows. Towers and turrets, columns and cupolas, rose before us, and high above all, the majestic dome of St. Peter's mounting in the air. We were approaching the Porta Cavalliggeri, immediately in the rear of that miracle of architecture. A few moments more and we reached it — our passports were inspected by the guard — we entered, and were within the walls of Rome. Our carriage drove round close to the mighty colonnades of St. Peter's, stretched out far on both sides as if embracing the vast arena they inclose; then rose before us, with its massive towers, the Castle of St. Angelo, once the mighty tomb—

> ——"which Hadrian rear'd on high,
> Imperial mimic of old Egypt's piles."

We crossed the Tiber, as it sluggishly wound along in the calm moonlight, by the ancient Pons Ælius, and around us on every side was the magnificence of which we had heard from our earliest years,—a magnificence which still survives the wrecks of wars and violence, and rapine and earthquake, and conflagrations and floods. All was the more grand and solemn because not seen in the glare of day. The delusive visionary light and deep, broad shadows enlarged every portico, increased the height of every dome and tower, and left the imagination to fill up the gigantic outline they revealed. And thus, we felt, should Rome be seen for the first time!

CHAPTER II.

VIEW FROM THE TOWER OF THE SENATOR.

IT takes some time for one to become accustomed to the thought that he is in Rome. To be actually living within its walls — to be treading on the same spot where the old consuls walked — where the Scipios and Cæsars played that mighty game which bequeathed their names to all posterity — this is the fulfillment of our early dreams, which it is difficult for a long while to realize. We find ourselves insensibly exclaiming, "This is Rome!" as if these little words contained a meaning we were unable fully to grasp, and which we were endeavoring, therefore, to impress upon our minds. And these feelings are natural. Servius Sulpicius, "the Roman friend of Rome's least mortal mind," could be won from a remembrance of his own griefs, by a sight of the time-worn ruins of ancient days. As he gazed upon Megara and Ægina, Corinth and the Piræus, he forgot his private sorrows, merging all other feelings in his sympathy for fallen greatness.[1] May not we then, wanderers from a distant continent, of whose very existence the old Roman was ignorant, when we stand for the first time in the home of his ancient glory, feel as if haunted by a memory of the mighty deeds which have been there achieved?

[1] Middleton's *Cicero*, v. ii. p. 371.

Our first object was to gain a clear knowledge of the situation of Rome and the localities of the surrounding country. This morning, therefore, we took our way through the Corso (or Via Lata), passing the beautiful columns of Trajan and Antoninus, with the spiral line of sculpture winding from the base to the capital of each. They are perfect, except that the statues of the emperors have been removed, and those of St. Peter and St. Paul substituted in their place. At the distance of a hundred and twenty feet from the ground, it is of course impossible to distinguish an apostle from an emperor, although the former seems very much out of place above these sculptured representations of Eastern wars and heathen sacrifices. We ascended to the Capitol, and, from the lofty tower of the Palace of the Senator, beheld the country spread out around us like a panorama. It was a clear and beautiful day, so that in the transparency of an Italian atmosphere, the most distant points were easily visible. But where on the wide earth can a single spot be selected, which will command a view of so much historical interest! The Capitoline Hill stands between the ruins which remain of old Rome and the new city which has sprung into being on the other side — between the ancient Capitol of the Republic and the Empire, and the modern city of the Popes, which has grown up in the last few centuries. It seems, therefore, to look down, as it were, upon the living and the dead. On the one hand, stand lonely and grand those majestic ruins — the Forum, with the lofty pillars of its temples — the Coliseum — the triumphal arches of the emperors — all, indeed, which eighteen centuries of war and rapine have left us. Their venerable forms bear not alone the furrows of age, but are marked also by the traces of destruction and Gothic violence. We turn from them, and on the other hand are the narrow, crowded streets, and faintly there ascend to us the tumult and noise of busy life among the thousands who have inherited the name of Roman, without being heirs to any of the stern virtues which distinguished their ancestors.

Let us then place ourselves for an hour on this hill, and "begetting the time again" out of the recollections of history, summon back the two thousand years which have gone. On this spot stood the humble cottage of Romulus, long preserved with pious care as a relic of their rude forefathers. Here and on the neighboring Palatine Mount were gathered his little band of colonists, while the surrounding hills were yet tangled wildernesses of trees, and the low grounds were marshes formed by the overflow of the Tiber. About their habitations they had erected a wall, which, if we credit the traditionary stories of Livy, could have offered but little resistance to the many enemies who lived almost at their gates. Years went by, and one hostile nation after another was conquered, and sometimes, as in the case of Alba, the population removed and incorporated among the victors. Thus the city grew, and extended over "the Seven Hills," whose outline we can yet easily trace, though the accumulation of soil in the valleys has much diminished their height. It was not, however, till the days of Aurelian that it attained its extent, and by him the walls were erected the same in circumference that they are at this day. Then too the ancient Campus Martius was taken in, which from the time of Servius Tullius had been without the city. Where the Roman youth had been for ages accustomed to practice their martial exercises, Augustus commenced the erection of magnificent buildings. The population has since travelled northward, and gradually encroached upon it, until now it is the most thickly settled district.

Thus it is that the old landmarks connect the past with the present, and ancient Rome was the same in the circuit of its vast and antique walls that the city is now. Yet within them how different does everything appear! The population has gradually diminished, until it has become thinly scattered over this wide space. Look over it, and you behold wild fields mingled with its habitations, and here and there grassy lanes winding among ruins, or some hill-top rising up lonely and bare, apparently deserted by the foot of man. The "yellow Tiber" sweeps onward, among hoary monuments which bend over its waters. Heathen temples and the domes of Christian churches — the stately palaces of her ancient nobility, with around them garden terraces rising one above the other, glittering with pillars and statues, on whose snowy whiteness the climate produces no change: smiling orange groves, their rich green and gold gleaming in the sunshine; the tall cypresses, with their dark foliage; the stone pines, with their broad flat tops, so oriental in appearance; and, diffused over all, the many tinted, colored atmosphere of this delicious clime; such is Rome as we gaze upon it to-day.

We said in the last chapter that the Campagna encircled the city, and from the elevated place on which we stood, we saw its flat, unbroken surface stretching out, until it was bounded, like the frame of some mighty picture, by the Sabine hills, about sixteen miles distant. It is a waste of fern, with here and there a withered pine-tree breaking the dull uniformity; yet generally treeless, and often shrubless. The roads of ancient Rome — such, for example, as the Appian Way — pass over it, lined with the remains of tombs, which, though now in ruins, are so beautifully picturesque that they are the admiration of the painter, and form always the finest feature in his landscape. At a distance, too, may be seen the long line of arches of the Claudian Aqueduct, the most massive ruin without the walls. But from the surface of the ground, the noxious malaria is constantly rising, and malignant sickness cuts down the shepherds who have made their home in the old ruined tombs.

And yet it is evident that this dreary waste must once have been covered with cities, and inhabited by a busy population. Among the fifty nations enumerated by Pliny as belonging to Latium in an early day, and which had entirely disappeared, he places no less than thirty-three towns within the compass of what are now the Pontine Marshes.[1] The Fidenæ were only five, and the Gabii ten miles from Rome, and yet so few vestiges of their existence remained, that when Horace wishes to convey an idea of perfect desolation, he says [2] —

> "Gabiis desertior atque,
> Fidenis vicus." ——

Ancient writers tell us, indeed, that from Rome to Ostia, a space of sixteen miles, the whole road was lined with buildings; and Florus calls Tibur, which is about the same distance over the Campagna, a suburb of Rome. "Whoever," says Dionysius, "wishes to ascertain the size of Rome, will be led into error,

---
[1] *Hist. Nat.* iii. 5. [2] *Epis.* i. xi. 7.

and have no certain mark to decide how far the city reaches, or where it begins not to be city; the country is so connected with the town, and gives those who see it an idea of a city infinitely extended."[1] This certainly presents a very different picture from Rome as it is at the present day, hemmed in by its walls, and all without them a desolate solitude. Tacitus, however, states that in the reign of Claudius the inhabitants amounted to nearly six millions;[2] a population which could not have been contained within the walls, and must have been widely spread over the Campagna itself.

The causes of this change, however, are obvious. As long ago as the days of Strabo, the marshes on the coast rendered that part of the country unhealthy. These must gradually have encroached on the interior, their poisonous exhalations been borne farther and farther by the sea-breeze, and the evil of course gone on more rapidly, when a place became uninhabited. Now the Campagna was wasted by successive hordes of invaders to the very walls of Rome. We can see to this day the traces of their progress. The northern side of the city, from which direction they came, is more ruinous than the rest, while the antiquities on the southern part are in the best preservation. When, therefore, the population was driven within the walls, and the open country became deserted, a few seasons would transform all without into a desolate wilderness, and then the rank herbage would gradually conceal the ruins.

And so it has remained for centuries, becoming each age more dreary, and, except the tombs, and here and there a mound of loose stones, there are no traces of the

[1] Lib. iv.   [2] An. lib. xi. c. 25.

nations which once inhabited those extensive tracts. In winter, you may see upon it thousands of the large gray Tuscan oxen, with their mild eyes and long horns; the descendants of the white cattle of whom Virgil speaks. At intervals, a herdsman, one of the gaunt *massari*, is watching them, and in his picturesque costume — a broad hat flapped over the eyes, sheepskin cloak, and carrying a long lance, while the gun is slung at his side — he seems wilder even than the fiery horse on which he dashes about. Vast herds of buffaloes, too, of a dingy color, introduced from foreign lands into Tuscany by Lorenzo de Medici, but since naturalized all over Italy, roam on the Campagna, and with their wild, red eye, bent neck, and lowering aspect, they seem to warn the passer-by not to approach too near their short curved horns.

But when the summer comes, the cattle are driven to the pastures of the Sabine hills, or even the more distant mountains of the Abruzzi. Then each day the heat increases, until the air seems like a sea of fire. Even the shade of night brings no relief, and the only breeze which blows through the sultry atmosphere is the hot sirocco. The grass is burnt up, the stagnant water infects the air, and even the Tiber seems to have shrunk from its banks to half its usual breadth. No cloud, no rain, no cooling wind; nothing but the hot rays of the sun beating down on the parched ground. Every breath from the sulphurous atmosphere seems to kindle a scorching fever in the blood, and the wild buffaloes are roused to madness by the myriads of stinging insects which swarm the heated air. Thus for months on the wide Campagna, life seems almost insupportable. But even at this season, when the heats are so terrific and the malaria is most deadly, there are materials there from which death can reap his harvest. About once in four years certain portions of this desolate tract are planted, and the summer is the time of harvest. "The peasants from the Volscian hills, and from beyond the frontier, come down into the plain to earn a few crowns for the ensuing winter; they work in the harvest-field all day under a scorching sun, and at night sleep on the damp earth, from which the low, heavy vapor of the pestilent malaria begins to rise at sunset. Even the strongest and healthiest are often struck down in a single week: before the harvest is gathered in, hundreds of hardy mountaineers have perished on the plain, and those who survive either die on their return home or bear the mark of the pestilence for life." Such is the Campagna, which has usurped the place where the busy thousands of Imperial Rome once dwelt. How invaluable to us would be a view of the city as it was in those its palmy days! Charlemagne, we are told, had "faire silver tables" made, on which were engravings of Constantinople and *Rome*. The one which contained the plan of Rome was given by him to the Church of Ravenna. If this could be recovered, what a treasure would it be to the historical student!

But let us resume the map and continue our view. Beyond the Campagna rises the chain of richly wooded mountains of which we have already spoken. But of what changing scenes have those heights been the mute observers, since first the land around them lay silent and untenanted, when the waters of the deluge had gone! They beheld one race after another come from the East, and strange rites and sacrifices performed on those Seven Hills, and the wide plain between. The Etruscans laid deep their massive architecture, and then passed away so entirely that even their language has perished, and the inscriptions they recorded on the solid rock, later generations cannot interpret. Then came a wilder race, which gradually rose to power, until the Roman name filled the earth. One by one their enemies fell before them. On that long ridge once stood Alba Longa, whose ruin Livy has immortalized. There dwelt the Samnites, and that little stream, the Anio, which still goes murmuring on its way to join the Tiber on the plain, then separated their country from Latium. The Gauls came, and on that crest of rocks is the Arx Libana of Livy, to which they were driven back when attacking the city. The Carthaginians, too, entered the arena of conflict; and there, to the left of the Alban Mount, is still pointed out the small, open plain, on which they were encamped while they besieged Rome. What consternation must have been felt around the Capitoline Hill, while these events were going on! What noise and busy note of preparation were heard, as the armed legions of Rome marched down its sides, and went forth to fight for their homes and altars! How different from the stillness which now rests upon this spot, where nothing is seen but these old and hoary ruins.

But all these nations were crushed beneath the iron tread of the conquerors. Then the whole landscape became crowded with works of art. The inhabitants of the city crossed the wide Campagna, and even the Sabine hills were transformed into the seats of Roman luxury. Every valley and peak was consecrated by

Roman genius. That lofty mountain in the dim distance, now covered with snow and so dazzling white as the sunbeams play upon it, Horace celebrated as the "gelidus Algidus." That height he speaks of as "Lucretilis;" and that opening of the plain between the hills is his "frigidum Præneste." How often, too, in his lyrics, does he sing the beauties of the ancient Tibur; that little place which you can just perceive almost buried in its woods and olive groves!

Cicero has also left his name associated with those hills, for there was the site of his far-famed Tusculum. He purchased the villa, which had once belonged to Sylla the Dictator, filled it with all the magnificence which art in that age of luxury could devise, and to its library — adorned, we are told, with statues of the Muses — or to the cool groves which surrounded it, he retired from the strife of the busy city. From its noble portico he could look over the wide landscape, until the view was terminated by the splendors of Rome itself; and here he has laid the scene of some of his philosophical works, the "De Divinatione," and the "Tusculan Questions." Beyond his retreat, on the highest point in the chain of hills, was the sacred grove of the Alban Mount; and towering above it, in sight not only of the surrounding country but of Rome itself, stood the magnificent Temple of Jupiter Latiaris. How often must the patriot and consul have turned to it with the deepest reverence! There, once in each year, the Latin tribes assembled to hold their sacred festival, and together they offered common sacrifice to the tutelar deity of the nation.[1] The Roman generals

---

[1] Eustace, *Class. Tour.* vii. p. 94.

repaired thither in the hour of their triumph, to return thanks for victory; and on one occasion, when Cicero himself was pleading for Milo, he turned his eyes to that temple, in full view from where he stood in the Forum, and burst forth with the eloquent apostrophe, " Tuque ex tuo edito monte, Latiaris Sancte Jupiter, cujus ille lacus nemora finesque," etc. From that mount, too, Virgil represents the Queen of Heaven as watching the changing fortunes of the battle, when the Latin and Trojan forces were arrayed on the plain beneath. With new interest, indeed, we read the last books of the Æneid, when we have before us the hills, the groves, the winding Tiber; the very scenes which the poet has there described.

Thus it is that the spirit of the past broods over every portion of this haunted land. Men may change, one race after another pass away, the very monuments they have left perish; yet still the features of nature remain the same. The mountains are there, and the streams, and the Seven Hills, and the wide plains, into whose bosom, through the silent lapse of centuries, the ancient cities have gradually been sinking, until now the Spring, with her flowery veil, conceals their ruins entirely from our eyes. The valleys are unaltered, and the cliffs look down upon them as of old, except that the long ages as they went by have written there the chronicles of their flight. These pass not away, and, therefore, every old historic association can find its home. And so it is in every part of this land, which Poetry has consecrated and made her own. The very forms of vegetable life, the trees and fragile flowers, carry us back two thousand years into the bosom of the past. The ilex yet waves upon the heights of Mount Alburnus, as when Virgil wrote his Georgics; about the site of Tusculum, the plane-tree blooms as luxuriantly as it did when Cicero, in his introduction to " De Oratore," speaks of its " overshadowing the spot with its spreading boughs;" and twice in each year, when May and December come round, " the roses with their double Spring" (*biferi rosaria Pæsti*) still blossom among the ruined temples of Pæstum, with that renewing sweetness which attracted the attention of Ovid, and furnished a beautiful simile to grace the writings of Propertius.

The last few pages have scarcely enumerated the objects of interest which crowd upon us, as we gaze this morning from the lofty tower of the Palace of the Senator. To the reader they may, perchance, present only a dull catalogue of names; but to us, with the scenes themselves before our eyes, there is a life and a reality in everything. From the cloudy past, twenty-five centuries rise up to meet us, as we look upon those places which are " familiar in our mouths as household words." It is at such times, too, that the spirit of our own early days returns, and passages of Virgil and Horace, which we studied at the school-desk, call up again the friendships of our boyhood. The present is forgotten. The weary cares of manhood fade away, and " the heat and burden" beneath which we are now laboring, is unfelt. The Spring of life returns in all its freshness. Friends, whose faces we can never more see in the flesh, gather about; familiar voices fall upon the ear with a startling distinctness; and scarcely realizing that all this is only of the imagination, we bless the associations which can produce the change. For a brief and sunny interval we even doubt the truth of that melancholy song of the German students, —

— " the gladness of our youthful prime, —
It cometh not again, — that golden time!"

CHAPTER III.

ST. PETER'S CHURCH.

THE first thought in Rome is of St. Peter's. We have, of course, often been there, for when there is nothing else immediately to occupy our attention, we can repair to this mighty temple, and find a subject for study which is inexhaustible. Instead, however, of vainly attempting a description — for every effort of this kind for centuries has proved that no words can give any idea of this unrivaled edifice — we would rather note down a few of the impressions left upon the mind.

The way which led to it was through a series of narrow, winding streets, crowded with a miserable population, deeply demoralized, and crushed to the earth by indigence. At length we reached the Castle of St. Angelo, and from this spot a broad avenue opened before us to the massive colonnades of St. Peter's. Our first view of the exterior by daylight disappointed us, for when seen from this point it is certainly not imposing. The façade is allowed to be disproportioned to the building, and too much conceals the dome. We have since examined, in the library of the Vatican, a copy of Michael Angelo's original plan, in which this defect is avoided, and the whole front appears more grand and striking. His drawing of the façade closely resembles the portico of the Pantheon.

In the open square in front, stands an ancient obelisk, which points up to heaven, tapering away as if it seemed to lose itself in the air. Caligula brought it from " old hushed Egypt" to adorn his baths, and a Pope placed it in front of St. Peter's. On each side of it is a fountain, which flings up its column of water, as if into the clouds, where it seems to pause for a moment, reflecting back the changing colors of the sky, and then falling into its porphyry basin, the thousand hues are lost in one dazzling sheet of foam. But who pauses to dwell on these when the temple itself is before them! We ascend the broad marble steps, put aside the heavy curtain which veils the entrance, and the sensations of the next few minutes are worth a year of commonplace life.

The first effect on every one must be bewildering. He sees gathered before him treasures of art of which before he could scarcely have conceived, and all enshrined in a building which mocks any comparison with the gorgeous Temple of Jerusalem, or those magnificent fanes which the worshippers of the old mythology raised to their fabled deities. For more than three centuries, the energies and wealth of thirty-five Pontiffs were devoted to this work, and the aid of the whole Christian world was invoked to render it a temple worthy of the Most High. Eustace estimates that the building itself cost twelve millions sterling. Everywhere, indeed, we see marbles, bronzes, and precious materials, which were gathered in Rome during the luxurious days of the Empire, but are nowhere else to be found in such profusion. We realize, indeed, that here man has exhausted the treasures of his genius and his worldly wealth.

Almost every traveller states that his first impressions were those of disappointment. The interior did not appear as vast as he expected. The reason of this, undoubtedly, is, because we have no received experience by which to judge its proportions. The eyes are "fools of the senses;" and here occurs a case in which they have not been trained to convey a correct estimate.[1] But with me, I confess, this was not the case. Having been told so often that I should be disappointed, I was prepared for it, and, therefore, expected too little. Slowly we passed up the nave, until we found ourselves opposite to the High Altar. Above it rises a canopy, more than a hundred and thirty feet in height, its twisted columns of Corinthian brass covered with golden foliage, while beneath rests the body of St. Peter, around whose tomb a hundred lamps are burning day and night. We stand under the dome and look up, when an abyss seems to open above us. We can scarcely believe that its top is four hundred feet from the marble pavement. The inscription on the frieze does not seem very large, yet each letter is six feet high, and the pen in the hand of St. Mark is of the same length, although from where we stand the whole figure of the saint does not appear to be much beyond the ordinary stature. The mighty dome ex-

[1] "Our outward sense
Is but of gradual grasp — and as it is
That what we have of feeling most intense
Outstrips our faint expression; even so this
Outshining and o'erwhelming edifice
Fools our fond gaze, and greatest of the great,
Defies at first our nature's littleness,
Till growing with its growth, we thus dilate
Our spirits to the size of that they contemplate."

Childe Harold.

pands above us like the firmament, and within are pictured in rich mosaic the saints and celestial spirits looking upward and worshipping towards the throne of the Eternal, which, encircled with radiance, crowns this dizzy height.

At our first visit we spent almost the whole day going over each part in detail, and every little while stopping, and vainly endeavoring by one effort of the mind to grasp the mighty proportions of the building. The figures which occasionally moved across the marble pavement seemed dwarfed into pigmies, and we could scarcely realize that this vast structure, with its gorgeous profusion of paintings, and marbles, and gilding, could have been erected by those who, in comparison, appeared so insignificant. This Church has, indeed, a spirit within it, which is possessed by none other that we have ever entered. It is sufficient to preserve a faith in existence centuries after its life has gone.

The very temperature of the building is remarkable, being always uniform; mild and pleasant in winter, and cool in summer, when the heat of the sun is so intense above as almost to melt the lead. Professor Playfair accounts for it on the supposition, that the immense edifice absorbs so much heat during the summer, that it never wholly discharges it throughout the winter. However this may be, the atmosphere is always delightful; no damp air is perceived; nothing but the slight perfume of the incense which is wafted from some side chapel where service is performing.

We passed around, and wandered from aisle to aisle, and from chapel to chapel, finding on all sides the same lavish magnificence. Everything is in perfect keeping, the statues themselves being gigantic to harmonize with the building. Around us were the gorgeous monuments of the Popes, on which the ablest sculptors of the last three centuries had exhausted their skill: the masterpiece of Canova, erected to the memory of Clement XIII., with its Genius of Death, holding the inverted torch, and the sleeping lion below, the finest efforts of the modern chisel; and the marble group of the Virgin supporting "The Dead Christ," a most touching work, which first established the fame of Michael Angelo. There was one before which we particularly paused, because it bore, sculptured on the enduring marble, so plain a record of the high-handed oppression of the Papal power during the Middle Ages. It was the tomb of the celebrated Countess Matilda, who, in the days of Hildebrand, was the powerful ally of the Church, bequeathing to it also at her death her valuable patrimony in Tuscany, a portion of which is still held by the Papal See. Living in the very crisis of that conflict between the feudal system and the power of the Church, so well did she aid the latter in gaining its triumph, that she deserved her burial-place in its noblest temple. Five centuries after her death, Urban VIII. removed her body from the Benedictine Monastery, near Mantua, and deposited it beneath this stately monument. Does that statue, which Bernini has placed above her tomb, represent her as she was in her living day? We may believe so, for it embodies our own idea of that stern woman, as she sits there frowning in the marble, holding in her hands the keys and the Papal tiara. But it is on the sides of the sarcophagus below, that we see portrayed the scene she aided to bring about, and which she considered her chief glory.

When Henry, the young Emperor of Germany, had been excommunicated by Gregory VII., to obtain an interview with his rival and rescue himself from the anathema, he was obliged to cross the Alps in the depth of winter, over fields and precipices of ice which could only be traversed on foot. His object was, to throw himself at the Pontiff's feet and obtain absolution; but he found this spiritual autocrat in Matilda's strong mountain fortress of Canossa in the Apennines, and for a time every avenue was barred against him. At length Gregory consented that the Emperor should enter the fortress in the garb of a penitent, to receive his sentence. Then was witnessed, what we may well consider the most extraordinary scene in the annals of the Papacy. It was on a morning in January, 1077, when the cold was intense, the mountain streams frozen, and the ground white with snow, that earth's greatest monarch of that day was seen, barefooted, and clothed only in a thin linen penitential garment, toiling mournfully and alone up to the rocky castle of Canossa. He passed two gateways, but found the third closed against him. It was at sunrise that he appeared in this humiliating state, and there he remained hour after hour, cold and faint, the object of wonder to the crowds which had gathered to the spectacle. But the gates opened not, and at sunset he was forced to retire, the object of his bitter penance still unaccomplished. Again the dawning day found him at his post, humbled and dispirited, while within the castle the proud Pontiff who was trampling him to the ground, held his regal court with princes gathered around him. Yet the second day passed like the first, and the third followed it, while the wretched king was suing in vain for admittance, and Gregory was prolonging, what has been well termed, "this profane and hollow parody on the real workings of the broken and contrite heart." But human endurance could bear it no longer, and the monarch rushed from this scene of suffering to a neighboring chapel, to beseech on his knees the intercession of his kinswoman Matilda, and the venerable Abbot of Cluni. For several days all within the castle, even with tears, had entreated the Pope to end this painful scene, and reproaches of wanton tyranny were heard from his own adherents; but he remained inexorable. At length, when Henry had reached the fourth day of his penance, Gregory consented that, still barefooted and in his penitential garment, he should be brought into his presence.

This is the point of time which the artist has chosen. The youthful King — for he was only twenty-six — reduced at last to vassalage to the Church — his fiery spirit utterly crushed by the misery of the last three days, and the shame that weighed him down — crouches abjectly at the feet of his oppressor, as if submitting his neck to be trodden on. The Italian Court are around, the witnesses of his degradation, while above him stands Gregory, proud and haughty in his mien, — the very incarnation of mitred tyranny. Matilda is there, rejoicing in her kinsman's indignities; and Hugh, the Abbot of Cluni, who had administered to Henry in his infancy the rite of baptism; and Azzo, Marquis of Este; and Adelaide of Susa, and her son, Amadeus, all calmly beholding these acts of spiritual despotism and relentless severity, performed by one claiming to be the Vicar of Him who was "meek and lowly of heart."

Is this a scene which it is well to perpetuate in the unchanging marble? On one occasion at least it would have been better for the Papal power if this record of its triumph had not been quite so prominent. We are told, that on the visit of the Emperor Joseph II. to St. Peter's, when he came to this monument, he regarded it for a moment with fixed attention, and then turned away with a blush of indignation and a bitter smile. We all know the Kaiser's future course; but might not the remembrance of that hour in St. Peter's have strengthened his purpose of a philosophical reformation, to depress and curb, in his own dominions, a power which could become so tyrannous?

"There is but one painting in St. Peter's: see if you can find it!" said a friend to me the day before our first visit. As we looked round the Church, his words recurred to us, and we wondered what he could have meant. There was an immense picture over every altar, and in every chapel, and we recognized copies of the noblest masterpieces on sacred subjects. It was not until we had been there some hours, that we discovered, with one exception, they were mosaics, — the colors, and lights, and shades being all so admirably imitated, that they rival the choicest works of the pencil. And probably centuries after the hues on the canvas have faded, these brilliant copies will preserve to the world a true record of the artist's genius. Time has already wrought its changes in the "Transfiguration" of Raphael; yet here is a duplicate in the unchanging stone, which even now begins to convey a truer idea of that great painter's conception, than the much cherished original in the Vatican. How deeply is it to be regretted, that among them we have not Da

Vinci's "Last Supper," which exists now only as a fresco at Milan, the damp fast obliterating its colors, so that to the next generation its beauty will be entirely gone! "How long will that picture last?" Napoleon once asked, as he was looking at a beautiful painting. "Perhaps five hundred years," was the answer. "And such," said the Emperor, with a smile of scorn, "is a painter's immortality!" The builders of this magnificent pile seem to have shared these feelings, and to have determined that nothing should be here which, in the lapse of time, might perish.

But in the wide transepts is a sight which cannot but arrest the attention of every one who is sighing for Catholic Unity, and remind him of those days when every nation acknowledged the same faith, and with one voice professed the same creed. There are arranged the boxes for the confessional, in every language. Not only are those of Europe to be seen inscribed over these places, but also its various dialects, and the strange tongues of the East. Thus, the wanderer from every land, who worships in these rites, beholds provision made for his spiritual wants. "There is one spot where the pilgrim always finds his home. We are all one people when we come before the Altar of the Lord." [1] Such are represented as the words of Marco Polo, in the thirteenth century, and here, to the member of the Church of Rome, they are realized. He comes to what he regards as the Mother Church of Christendom, and learns that he is not a stranger or an alien. He can unburden himself to a priest of his own land, and the consolations of his faith are doubly sweet, when conveyed to him in the familiar words of

[1] Sir Francis Palgrave's *Merchant and Friar*, p. 138.

"his own tongue, wherein he was born." With the errors of Rome, we have no sympathy; we feel and realize how much she has fallen from the simplicity of the faith; yet Catholic traits like this, none but the most prejudiced can refuse to admire. They show the far-reaching wisdom of that Church; that overlooking the distinctions of climate and country, and recognizing her field of labor to extend wherever there is a degraded being to listen to her message, she is resolute to "inherit the earth."

But this vast edifice is never filled, not even, we are told, upon the coronation of a Pope. It is only, indeed, on a few great festivals that service is performed in the body of the Church, for ordinarily one of the side chapels is used, and the High Altar stands lonely and deserted. Even Eustace, though a priest of the Church, inquires why "the Pontiff, surrounded by his clergy, does not himself perform every Sunday the solemn duties of his station, presiding in person over the assembly, instructing his flock, like the Leos and Gregorys of ancient times, with his own voice, and with his own hands administering to them 'the bread of life,' and 'the cup of salvation?'" Such a sight would indeed be one both affecting and sublime.

There is much, however, to detract from our pleasure in the survey of this unrivaled temple. The very inscription on the front, instead of dedicating it to Him who alone should be worshipped here, states that it is consecrated by Paul V., IN HONOREM PRINCIPIS APOSTOLORUM. We pause to inspect the *bas-reliefs* on the magnificent bronze doors, and are transported back to the days of heathenism. The artist drew his inspiration from no source more hallowed than the "Metamorphoses" of Ovid; and Ganymede and the Eagle, with Leda and the Swan — the latter group more spirited than chaste — figure on the doors of this Christian temple. Advance to the High Altar, and near it, on a pedestal about four feet high, stands an old bronze statue, which the skeptical antiquary will tell you was once a Jupiter, by a slight change transformed into an undoubted St. Peter. However this may be, it is now a mere instrument of superstition, and through the whole day crowds may be seen kneeling before it in earnest prayer. Their devotions ended, they approach, kiss the extended foot, — which is almost worn off by this constant friction, — press their foreheads to it, and the process is ended. Has the Romanist any reason to laugh at the poor Mussulman, who performs a pilgrimage to Mecca, to kiss the black stone of the Caaba? On St. Peter's day this image is clothed in magnificent robes; the gemmed tiara placed upon its head; the jeweled collar around its neck; soldiers are stationed by its side, and lighted candles burning about it. A clergyman of the Church of England, who was present on this occasion last year, told me that the effect of the black image thus arrayed was perfectly ludicrous; and with the people all kneeling before it, had he not known he was in a Christian Church, he should have supposed himself in a heathen temple, and that, the idol.

In the massive columns which support the dome, are preserved some holy relics, which are only shown with much ceremony from a high balcony, during Passion Week. A portion of the true Cross, the head of St. Andrew, the lance of St. Longinus (with which our Saviour was pierced), and the *Sudarium*, or handkerchief, containing the impression of our Lord's features, form a part of this sacred treasury. Unfortunately, there are divers other lances of similar pretensions,— one at Nuremberg, and another in Armenia. With the *Sudarium* it is still worse, there being six rival ones shown in different places, namely, Turin, Milan, Cadoin in Perigort, Besançon, Compiègne, and Aix-la-Chapelle; while that at Cadoin has fourteen bulls to declare it genuine, and that at Turin four. The learned, however, solve the difficulty by saying, that the handkerchief applied to our Lord's face consisted of several folds, consequently the impression of the countenance went through them all, and they are all genuine![1]

One more item, and I have done with this disagreeable portion of the subject. Pass the High Altar, and at the farther extremity of the Church is a magnificent throne of bronze and gilt, surmounted by a canopy, and supported by four colossal gilt figures of St. Augustine, St. Ambrose, St. Chrysostom, and St. Athanasius. Within is a chair, which tradition tells us is the identical one in which St. Peter sat when he officiated as Bishop of Rome. Some twenty years ago, Lady Morgan gave to the world another story of this wonderful relic. She states that when the French held Rome, their sacrilegious curiosity induced them to break through the splendid casket for the purpose of seeing the sacred chair. Upon its mouldering and dusty surface were traced carvings, which bore the appearance of letters. The chair was quickly brought into a better light, the dust and cobwebs removed, and the inscription faithfully copied. The writing is in Arabic characters, and is the well known confession of

[1] Burton's *Rome*, vol. ii. p. 156.

Mahometan faith, — "There is but one God, and Mahomet is his prophet." The story, she adds, has since been hushed up, the chair replaced, and none but the unhallowed remember the fact, and none but the audacious repeat it.[1] Dr. Wiseman takes *miladi* to task with great severity, and asserts that it is an ancient curule chair, evidently of Roman workmanship, and may therefore reasonably be supposed to have been used as an Episcopal throne when St. Peter was received into the house of the Senator Pudens at Rome. The truth probably is, that it was brought from the East among the spoils of the Crusaders; presented to St. Peter's at a time when antiquarian research was not much in fashion; and now, its origin has been forgotten.

But to continue the account of our visit. The hours went by, and we could not leave this spot which had been thought and dreamed of for so many years. We realized the feelings of the imaginative author of Vathek, when he wrote, "I wish his Holiness would allow me to erect a little tabernacle within this glorious temple. I should desire no other prospect during the winter; no other sky than the vast arches glowing with golden ornaments, so lofty as to lose all glitter or gaudiness. We would take our evening walks on the field of marble; for is not the pavement vast enough for the extravagance of this appellation? Sometimes, instead of climbing a mountain, we should ascend the cupola, and look down on our little encampment below. At night I should wish for a constellation of lamps dispersed about in clusters, and so contrived as to diffuse a mild and equal light. Music should not be wanted:

[1] *Italy*, vol. ii. p. 227.

at one time to breathe in the subterranean chapels, at another to echo through the dome."

But the melody which Beckford desired, we were soon to hear. A side door opened; forth came a procession, — a Cardinal and long array of priests, — and we followed them to see what service was at hand. They swept across the Church, paused for a moment in the centre, and sunk upon their knees, with their faces turned to the High Altar, and then entered the chapel called the *Capella del Coro.* It was the hour for Vespers, which at once commenced. There were perhaps twenty in the choir, by whom the principal part of the service was performed, while nearly two hundred more — prebendaries, canons, clerks, and choristers — were seated in the chapel, and joined in the responsive parts. It was the first time we had heard the Pope's choir, so celebrated throughout the world, and yet our expectations were more than realized. They still use those old austere chants of surpassing beauty, which have been handed down to them through centuries, — the Lydian and Phrygian tunes, first introduced into the Western churches by St. Ambrose. St. Augustine listened to them in the Church of Milan, when he represents himself as being melted to tears, and even expressed the fear lest such harmonious airs might be too tender for the manly spirit of Christian devotion.[1]

[1] "Sometimes, from over jealousy, I would entirely put from me and from the Church the melodies of the sweet chants which we use in the Psalter, lest our ears seduce us; and the way of Athanasius, Bishop of Alexandria, seems the safer; who, as I have often heard, made the reader chant with so slight a change of note, that it was more like speaking than singing. And yet, when I call to mind the tears I shed when I heard the chants of Thy Church in the infancy of my recovered faith, and reflect that at this time I am affected, not by the mere music, but by the subject, brought out, as it is, by clear voices and appropriate tune; then, in turn, I confess how useful is the practice." — *Confessions,* x. 50.

Mingled with these were the richer Roman chants which were collected by Gregory the Great, and bear his name. They sang the Psalms for the evening, and I rejoiced that I knew they were uttering inspired words; for the music, as it swept by us in a perfect flood of harmony, seemed too sweet and heavenly to be addressed to any but God alone. The organ mingled its rich, mellow tones with the voices which were thus pouring out their melody; sweet incense filled the chapel as they flung high their golden censers; and we remained listening to the delicious sounds, until the whole was over, and the procession once more took its way through the Church.

As we followed them out, we found the sun was setting, and we stayed to watch the effect of the gathering darkness. The Church was untenanted, save by some solitary worshipper kneeling apart, and no sound was heard except now and then the light tread of a sacristan as he crossed the marble pavement. Gradually the shadows deepened; the building appeared more vast and solemn; the hundred lights which are ever burning around the tomb of St. Peter seemed like distant, twinkling stars; the statues on the monuments grew more wan and phantom-like; and we departed, repeating to ourselves those striking lines of the pilgrim poet : —

> " But thou, of temples old, or altars new,
> Standest alone — with nothing like to thee —
> Worthiest of God, the holy and the true;
> Since Zion's desolation, when that He
> Forsook His former city, what could be,
> Of earthly structures, in His honor piled,
> Of a sublimer aspect? Majesty,
> Power, glory, strength, and beauty — all are aisled
> In this eternal ark of worship undefiled."

Yesterday it rained, and the sun this morning rose with that cloudless beauty which is so often seen when the atmosphere has just been cleared by a storm. The air was perfectly still and clear, and we determined to avail ourselves of the opportunity to ascend the dome of the Church. Having procured the necessary permit from the Cardinal Secretary of State, we were admitted, and commenced the ascent by a broad stone staircase, so slightly inclined that mules walk up it with their loads. After a time it narrows, and winds around between the inner and outer domes, until passing through a door, we find ourselves on a light gallery in the interior, more than three hundred feet above the pavement. The brain becomes dizzy as we look down, and see men appearing like insects crawling far below. The mosaic pictures which line the dome, and from the pavement looked so fair and beautifully shaded, here seem coarse, and the figures are gigantic. Nowhere else can we realize the unparalleled vastness of this edifice, and for a time we stood and looked down in silence, while from one of the side chapels there came faintly and fitfully the swell of voices and the music of the organ, as some priests were performing there the morning service.

From thence we ascended to the exterior gallery on the top of the dome. Here was spread out before us the same glorious prospect which we had already seen from the Senator's Tower on the Capitoline Hill. The morning sun was pouring down its beams, flooding the whole landscape with brightness. White, fleecy clouds still lingered about the distant Apennines, while a line of mist stretching far over the Campagna, showed the course of the Tiber. There, everything spoke of repose and desolation, and the country spread out like a prairie with none to occupy it. We felt, as did Rogers, when he asked, —

> " Have none appeared as tillers of the ground,
> None since *they* went — as tho' it still were theirs,
> And they might come and claim their own again?
> Was the last plough a Roman's? "

Below us were the formal gardens of the Pope, with their sparkling fountains, and orange groves loaded with fruit; while a palm-tree growing near, and the stony pines, with their flat, dark tops dispersed about, seemed to increase the oriental illusion of the scene. We walked over the stone roof of this mighty building, which covers an extent of several acres. How strange it seems to find at this dizzy height the habitations of human beings! Yet here are the houses of the workmen who are always employed in the repairs of the edifice, so that we seem to be in the midst of a little village. A fountain, too, is playing by our side, throwing its water into a marble basin; and while the lofty parapet cuts off all view beyond, we can scarcely realize that we are not treading on the ground. About us were traces of countless pilgrims, who during the last two centuries had climbed to the same lofty elevation, and left there their names and the dates of their visits. Among them was an Italian name carved deeply into one of the bronze balls of the railing around the gallery, with the date 1627. Perhaps this is the only trace the individual has left of his existence on the earth.

From this highest gallery at the foot of the stem which supports the ball and cross, a small iron ladder enables visitors to ascend into the ball itself. It is of bronze gilt, seven and a half feet in diameter, and will accommodate a small party. There is something, however, in the idea of being inclosed in a ball four hundred and thirty feet from the ground, which gives the visitor an uneasy feeling. It seems to vibrate and tremble; he remembers how small is the metal stem which sustains it; and being, in addition, almost roasted by the rays of the sun on the thin copper, he is generally contented with a very short sojourn at this aërial height. Instead of a cross, the ball was once surmounted by a large pine of bronze, which had before ornamented the top of the tomb of Hadrian. Being thrown from St. Peter's by lightning, it was transferred to the gardens of the Vatican, where it now stands by the side of the great Corridor of Belvidere. It was here in the days of Dante, for when describing one of the monsters in the Inferno, he says, —

> " His visage seem'd
> In length and bulk, as doth the pine that tops
> St. Peter's Roman fane."

We descended again to the church, and finding one of the sacristans, proceeded to visit the crypts beneath it. He conducted us down a stairs under one of the side altars, and at its foot, fixed in the wall, is a marble slab, the inscription on which states that females are not permitted to descend into these vaults except on Whitsunday, — on which day men are excluded, — and if any infringe this regulation, they are anathematized. The reason of this absurd rule we could not discover. We have here below us, probably, the most ancient church pavement in existence; for when the present sumptuous temple was erected over the first church, the pavement was left untouched. This spot, indeed, was chosen by Constantine for the first religious edifice he erected, because it was a part of the Circus of Nero, and consecrated by the blood of numberless martyrs who were slaughtered in the arena.

Immediately below the High Altar is what is called the tomb of St. Peter. As we stood beside it, we thought what would be the feelings of the humble fisherman of Galilee, could he rise from his martyr-grave, wherever it may be, and behold the gorgeous ceremonies of the temple which is called by his name. The purity of the faith for which he died, perverted; the simplicity of ancient worship deformed by countless rites, partaking of the "pride and pomp and circumstance" of Pagan rituals; the gospel mingled up with strange legends from the old mythology; his own name, which he only wished to be "written in heaven," now exalted above all human fame, and made an argument for blinding superstition, — how would his lofty rebuke startle the thousands kneeling here, and echo even through the halls of the Vatican, as he summoned all away from the "cunningly-devised fables" which are taught in this glorious shrine, to those changeless and immutable truths which are to last while "eternity grows gray!"

As we passed around, we beheld on all sides small chapels where lights are kept ever burning, and which are regarded as places of peculiar sanctity. Wherever we turned, we saw the tombs of those who for their services in the cause of the Church, or their extraordinary holiness, had been thought worthy of a resting-place in this unequaled temple. Here, covered with bass-reliefs, to illustrate Scripture history, is the rich sarcophagus of Junius Bassus, Prefect of Rome, who died A. D. 359.

Here lie buried, Otho II. of Germany; Charlotte, Queen of Jerusalem and Cyprus; the last members of the royal family of Stuart, and many of the Popes. Unlike most vaults of the kind, there is no dampness in the atmosphere, nor that chilliness which speaks so plainly of the grave; and it seemed as if the very balminess of the air took from us all thoughts of the tomb. When we again ascended, and dropped the fee into the hand of the smiling young priest, we found it difficult to realize that we had been treading on a spot where, for fifteen centuries, the great and noble had found their burial-place.

CHAPTER IV.

CHRISTMAS EVE AT THE SISTINE CHAPEL. — THE SERVICES IN ST. PETER'S ON CHRISTMAS DAY. — THE BRITISH CHAPEL.

THE Christmas Holydays are at hand, and on every side we hear the note of preparation. The shops are decorated with flowers, while the altars of the churches are arrayed in their most splendid ornaments. The images of the Virgin in particular are seen in their gayest dress, and all the jewelry which the treasury can furnish is brought out to give them an elegant and fashionable appearance.

At this time, too, in addition to the varied population of the city, — its priests, soldiers, and beggars, who together form the great proportion, — a new accession is pouring in from the surrounding country. The peasants who live in the deserted tombs on the Campagna; the natives of the Alban mountains, fierce, banditti-looking fellows, who gather their cloaks about them with a scowling air which would not be at all pleasant to encounter among their own hills; and the Trasteverini, in their picturesque costumes, boasting themselves to be the only true descendants of the ancient Romans, and as proud and haughty in their bearing as if they had also inherited the heroic virtues of their ancestors, — these are to be met roaming about every street, and in the churches, gazing in wonder at their magnificence.

The most singular, however, are the Calabrian minstrels, the *pifferari*. Their dress is wild and striking, consisting of a loose sheep-skin coat, with the wool left on it, and a high peaked cap, decked with gay ribbons and sprigs of heather, while the huge *zampogne* of goat-skin is formed like the bagpipes of Scotland, and resembles them too in its shrill music. These interesting characters arrive during the last days of Advent, and consider themselves the representatives of the shepherds of Judea, who were the first to announce the news of the Nativity. Their usual gathering-place is on the steps of the *Piazza di Spagna*, where they lounge and sleep in the warm sun. Every little while a party sets out on a tour through the city, blowing away with the most desperate energy. At the next corner is one of the shrines of the Madonna, and this is their first stopping-place, to salute the Mother and Child. Lady Morgan says, it is done "under the traditional notion of charming her labor-pains on the approaching Christmas." They turn down the *Via Frattina*, and a short distance further come to a carpenter's shop, which must also be favored with a tune, — " per politezza al messer San Giuseppe," — " out of compliment to St. Joseph." The owner hands them out a *bajoccho*, and they continue their march until the circuit is completed.

At sundown, on Christmas Eve, the cannon sounded from the castle of St. Angelo, to give notice that the Holy Season had begun. We were advised to attend service in the Sistine Chapel, and accordingly at an early hour repaired to the Vatican, in which it is situated. Gentlemen are only admitted in full dress, and ladies are also compelled to appear in black, their heads covered only with a veil. The entrance was guarded by the Pope's harlequin-looking guards, in the ridiculous uniform said to have been designed by Michael Angelo; and the company all gathered round them until the doors were opened, when they pushed in as best they could, jostling and being jostled. Half way up the chapel there is a grating, beyond which the ladies are not permitted to go, so that for once the gentlemen were best accommodated. At the upper end of the large area above is the altar, while on the sides are raised seats for the Cardinals, and to these we struggled up, until all further advance was cut off by the halberds of the guards. Here we took our stand, and waited with the most exemplary patience for the service to begin.

Nearly an hour passed while the Cardinals were collecting. One by one they came into the area, their long, red trains supported by two priests in purple dresses, and after kneeling for a moment on the floor, facing the altar, ascended to their seats. Their brethren, already there, rose and greeted them with a stately bow, and the attendants placed themselves humbly at their feet. At length the music began, but I confess I was disappointed. It was too loud for the size of the chapel, and we missed the sweet sounds of the organ, which formed so noble an accompaniment at Vespers in St. Peter's. In the middle of the chapel stood a lectern, and to this at different parts of the service, a priest would be escorted, who, after going through his portion in a kind of recitative manner, was again in form escorted back to the door. These modulations, we are told by Roman Catholic writers, were first introduced to raise and support the voice, to extend its reach and soften its cadences, because its common tones cannot adequately be heard when the service is performed in a large church. They vary, however, in number and solemnity in the different parts of the service. "In the lessons and epistles, the interrogations, exclamations, and periods only are marked by a corresponding rise or fall: the Gospel had its variations more numerous and more dignified: the Preface is rich in full melodies and solemn swells, borrowed, as it is supposed, from the stately accents of Roman tragedy. The Psalms, or to use an expression more appropriate, the anthems that commence the service, precede the Gospel, usher in the Offertory, and follow the Communion, together with the *Gloria in excelsis* and Creed, were set to more complicated and more labored notes."[1] The priests who officiated this evening seemed to have been selected for their voices, and we certainly never heard anything superior to them in compass and richness of tone. As with their faces turned to heaven, they sang from the large, golden-clasped volumes, it seemed to be the very perfection of the human voice. There could, however, be no devotion except for those well acquainted with the service, and as there was great sameness in the singing, the audience evidently soon began to grow weary. For a time, therefore, I scrutinized the Cardinals, some of whom have magnificent heads — keen, intellectual looking men, well worthy to be pillars of the Vatican. Then I tried to make out the frescos on the ceiling, and the great painting of the "Last Judgment" by Michael Angelo, which occupies the end of the chapel, and is more than sixty feet high. But the paintings were too far off to be seen even by the bril-

[1] Eustace, vol. ii. p. 81.

liant lights around us, and the brightness of their colors has been sadly dimmed by the smoke of the candles and incense during the last two centuries.

The audience seemed to be almost entirely English, and I suppose were Protestants. Such at least is the complaint of the Italians, that they can never gain admittance to the services of their own Church, but every place is occupied by foreigners. This formed the subject of one of the satirical witticisms of Pasquin. One night the question was affixed to his statue, "How shall I, being a true son of the Holy Church, obtain admittance to her services?" The next night the answer which appeared was, "Declare that you are an Englishman, and swear that you are a heretic." After a while, the rumor began to spread round among the spectators, that the Pope was not to be present this evening, and therefore there would be no High Mass after Vespers. The news apparently made them more restless, and they began to thin out. One party after another passed down the line of guards, as they stood like statues, and departed. Many went to the Church of St. Maria Maggiore, to see at midnight *the true cradle in which our Lord was rocked* carried in procession. Having, however, little taste for such exhibitions, we did not join them. I found indeed, from the account of a friend who witnessed it, that we did not lose much. After standing for some hours in a dense crowd, listening to the singing of the choir, a procession of priests carried the Holy Relic across the Church from the sacristy to the altar. It was inclosed in a splendid coffer of silver, with a canopy of gold cloth elevated over it. Banners waved; the lighted tapers were held up; incense rose in clouds about it; the guard of soldiers, and the crowd which filled the Church, dropped on their knees; it passed, and the whole show was over.

Near midnight we took our course homeward, beneath as splendid a moon as ever shone, even through the transparency of an Italian sky. In the square before St. Peter's, the obelisk raised its tapering point up to heaven, and the fountain on each side flung high its waters, which fell in silver spray as they reflected back the clear light of the moon. We stood for a while on the bridge of St. Angelo, looking at its beams play upon the Tiber. That mighty fortress — Hadrian's massive tomb — was frowning darkly above us, and the statues which lined the bridge looked pale and wan in the clear night, till they appeared like pallid phantoms, steadfastly watching the current of time, by which they could be influenced no more.[1]

Christmas morning fulfilled in its beauty the promise of the night before. It is the great festival of the winter. The Papal banners are displayed from the Castle, and the streets are filled with crowds thronging up to St. Peter's. The guards, in their strange white and red costumes, were stationed around the body of the Church, while at the lower end a body of troops were drawn up, who remained there on duty during the whole service. With the audience the same formality of dress was required as the evening before. At the upper end of the Church was the magnificent throne of the Pope, raised quite as high as the altar which it

---

[1] "Les rayons de la lune faisoient des statues comme des ombres blanches regardant fixément couler les flots et le temps qui ne les concernent plus." — *Corinne.*

fronted, and decked out most splendidly with its cloth of crimson and gold, and the gilded mitre suspended above. Next to it on the sides were the seats for the Cardinals; then the boxes for ambassadors and their suites; and then high platforms covered with crimson cloth, to afford seats for the ladies. The altar has no chancel around it, and the great area between its steps and the Papal throne was left vacant for the performance of the services. As my stand happened to be close to the ambassadors' boxes, I had an excellent view of everything which took place.

After waiting for at least an hour, suddenly there came a burst of music from the lower end of the Church. It was a loud chant, which, softened by the distance, floated sweetly through the building. Every eye was strained towards the spot from which it proceeded, and there, raised high on the shoulders of men clothed in violet-colored robes, we beheld the Pope borne above the heads of the kneeling multitude in his crimson chair, the falling drapery from which half concealed those who carried him. The gemmed tiara was on his head, and his robes sparkled with jewels. On each side of him were carried high, fan-like banners of ostrich feathers, such as we see in pictures of the processions of an eastern rajah. Before him marched a guard of honor, consisting of some sixty Roman noblemen, who always form his escort on great festivals. Around him was his brilliant court: the Cardinals; the Bishops of the Greek, Armenian, and other eastern churches, in their most gorgeous array; the heads of different religious brotherhoods, in ash-colored garments; priests in purple and white, some bearing the Great Cross and lighted tapers, and some flinging in the air their golden censers,—thus the procession came slowly on to the sound of anthems,—the most gorgeous show which probably ever entered a Christian church. The Pope passed within six feet of where I stood. His eyes were closed; his whole countenance seemed dull and lifeless; and the constant nodding of his head, as the bearers walked with unsteady step, gave him the appearance of a mere image, splendidly decked out to form part of a pageant.

At length, amid his kneeling train he was deposited on the pavement in front of the altar, and the guard of nobles ranged themselves on each side of the area up to the throne. He knelt for a few moments; parts of his dress were changed, the tiara being put upon the altar and a mitre substituted in its place; he joined in the psalms and prayers which precede the solemn service, and was escorted in state to his lofty seat, while the choir sang the *Introitus*, or Psalm of Entrance. Then one by one the Cardinals swept across the Church, their long, scarlet trains borne up behind them as they walked, and spread out so as to cover a surface of yards in extent when they stopped, and ascending the steps they kissed the Pontiff's hand and the hem of his garment.

The service of High Mass now began, in which he at times took part. He read the Collect; gave his benediction to the two deacons kneeling at his feet with the Book of the Gospels; commenced the Nicene Creed, which the choir continued in music; and returning to the altar, fumed it with incense from a golden censer, offered the usual oblations, and washed his hands, in token of purity of mind. When the elements were consecrated, two deacons brought the Sacrament to the

Pope, who is seated. He first revered it on his knees, and then received it sitting.

But it would be impossible for me to describe the long and complicated service. A Cardinal officiated at the altar; rich and solemn music swelled out from the choir, and filled the mighty building in which we were; sweet incense floated through the air; thousands and thousands were gathered under that golden dome; and no single thing was omitted which could add to the magnificence of the pageant. In this respect it is probably unequaled in the world. Yet to most who were present it could have been nothing but an empty show. The priests crossed and recrossed; censers waved; candles were lighted and put out; dresses were changed and rechanged; the Cardinals walked back and forth, until the mind became utterly bewildered. All things about us indeed — the vastness of the edifice, the works of art, the rich dresses, the splendid music — contributed to heighten the effect; yet, with all this, the seriousness of devotion seemed to be wanting.

Had I known nothing of Christianity, I should have supposed the Pope to be the object of their worship. His throne was far more gorgeous than the altar; where they knelt before the latter once, they knelt before the former five times;[1] and the amount of incense offered before each was about in the same proportion. He was evidently the central point of attraction. The entrance of the old man, so gorgeously attired, among kneeling thousands, and the splendor of

---

[1] " Never, I ween,
　　In anybody's recollection,
　Was such a party seen
　　For genuflection."

the whole service, showed more fully than ever before how far the Church of Rome had wandered from the simplicity of the faith, and how much of ceremony it had substituted for the pure worship of the early Christians. The day before I had gone over the service for Christmas with an ecclesiastic of the Romish Church, received from him every explanation, and I now followed it through with the Missal in my hand. I wished to form an opinion for myself, and after investigating as far as possible the meaning of the many ceremonies we have witnessed, I could not but feel the truth of the remark I have somewhere seen, that " the Romanist has been the Pagan's heir." The most interesting part to me was, to hear the Nicene (or rather, Constantinopolitan) Creed chanted in Greek immediately after it had been chanted in Latin. " It is to show the union of the two Churches," a priest most gravely told me. I thought that whereas the Latin Church has for centuries anathematized the Greek, and the Greek in turn repudiated the Latin, this service had about as much meaning as the title " King of Jerusalem," which the King of Naples still uses.

At length the service ended. The Pope was once more raised on his lofty seat and carried down the Church; the Roman nobles formed around him; his body-guards shouldered their halberds; the Cardinals, with their train-bearers, fell into their places, and the gay procession went as it came. While it passed down, the Pope gently waved his hand from side to side to dispense his blessing; the immense multitude sunk upon their knees as he went by, until the train disappeared through the door, and the successor of St. Peter departed to his dwelling in the Vatican. The released ecclesiastics proceeded to pay their respects to the ladies; violet and scarlet stockings appeared in the crowd among the brilliant uniforms; "nods, and becks, and wreathed smiles" were visible on all sides; compliments in French and Italian mingled into one chaos of sound, — and the whole broke up like a gay pleasure party.

For some time I lingered under the colonnades to see the immense multitude pour out and disperse. As they passed down the steps and by the massive pillars, they seemed pigmies in size. Before the Church, the whole square was alive. The crimson and gold carriages of the Cardinals, with their three liveried footmen hanging on behind, were dashing away; the troops were pouring out; military music was sounding, — and I went home with scarcely a feeling to remind me that I had been at church.

From this gorgeous and unsatisfactory show I was glad, at a later hour of the day, to repair to the pure worship of our own Church, for I felt that thus far I had been doing nothing to keep the solemn festival of the Nativity. The Papal power, which in our own land talks so loudly of toleration, here will not allow the worship of a Protestant within the bounds of " the Eternal City," and almost supported as its people are by the money which the thousands of English scatter among them, it does not permit them even to erect a church in which to meet. Without the walls of the city, just beyond the *Porta Del Popolo*, a large " upper room " has been fitted up for the British Chapel, and there *on sufferance* they gather each week. There is no organ, no singing; everything is as plain and simple as possible. Yet never did I so much enjoy the services of the Church as on this occasion. Never did I feel so grateful to the Reformers of the Church of England, that at the cost of their own lives they had bequeathed to us primitive purity. I thought of the time when, eighteen centuries ago, while the magnificence of a Heathen Ritual was going on in old Rome, perhaps some little band of Christians had met beyond its walls, in seclusion to offer up their simple worship. How great must have been the contrast between the two scenes — the splendor of those forms and ceremonies with which thousands bowed around the altars of the Capitoline Jupiter, and the simplicity and purity with which a few disciples of Christ prayed to their crucified Master!

"Did you receive much spiritual benefit from the services at St. Peter's this morning?" said a friend to me as we were leaving the British Chapel. "Yes," I answered, "indirectly, I received much; for it taught me to realize the value of our own services as I never did before, and I trust therefore to use them for the rest of my life with greater benefit. It is the contrast between the Church in the days of Leo X. and in the time of Constantine."

CHAPTER V.

THE CAPITOLINE HILL.

WE have devoted this morning to antiquities; and as strangers in winter all congregate about the *Piazza di Spagna*, — which, by the way, is the site of the old Circus of Domitian, — we were obliged to pass through the whole extent of the city to reach the Capitoline Hill, which was our first point. We went through the Corso, and by the old Venetian Palace, and then threaded our way among the labyrinth of narrow, filthy streets, until we found ourselves at the base of the Hill. On its top once stood the pride of Rome, the Temple of Jupiter Capitolinus, which was filled with the offerings of princes and kings, and the treasures of a conquered world. The whole earth was ransacked to add to its glory, and even the columns of Pentelic marble, which adorned its front, were brought from the distant plains of the Ilissus, where Grecian genius had placed them to form the portico of one of its own beautiful temples. But it has passed away so completely, that its very site is a subject of antiquarian dispute.

A magnificent flight of marble steps, broad enough for an army to mount with its ranks unbroken, leads up to the Hill. At its base stand two basalt lions — old Egyptian monuments, brought from some ancient temple whose faith has long since perished, and bearing the impress of everything which comes from that mysterious land. Colossal and frowning, with that strange, unearthly expression of countenance which Egyptian sculptors seem always to give, conveying the idea of something mystic and awful, these solemn antique figures remain, age after age, gazing fixedly and severely forward, as if the silent witnesses of all the deeds of darkness and fear which are going on in the changing city below them. They are fit guardians of "the Staircase of the Lion," at the head of which so much noble blood had been shed, when it was the spot on which for ages state criminals paid the forfeit of their lives. The broad platform at the summit — "the Place of the Lion" — where these tragedies were enacted in the view of all Rome, while the bell from the Capitol above tolled mournfully and slow to show that a soul was passing away, is now filled with antique statuary, the colossal forms which have been preserved from the wreck of the Republic and the Empire. In its centre once stood a gigantic image of Jupiter Capitolinus, made from the armor taken from the Samnites in the fifth century from the building of the city, and so lofty that it could be seen from the Mons Latialis, near Albano, a distance of twenty miles.[1] Its site is now occupied by the magnificent equestrian figure of Marcus Aurelius, the finest in existence. In the fourteenth century the place of the statue was in front of the Lateran, and it bore a prominent part in that gorgeous show, when Rienzi the Tribune cited to appear personally before him the kings of Bavaria and Bohemia, to plead their own cause and prove their claim to the title

---

[1] Pliny, lib. xxxiv. c. 18.

of Emperor of Rome — a proud challenge in behalf of the liberties of Italy, which his opposers have always ridiculed as the splendid folly of an enthusiastic mind, while his friends have lauded it as the sublime daring of a noble nature. When the historians of the day describe that royal banqueting, they cite, in proof of its lavish profusion, that from morn till eve, wine poured out like a fountain from the nostrils of this horse.

The summit of the Hill, around the three sides of "the Place of the Lion," is occupied by palaces, built by Paul III., from the designs of Michael Angelo. The centre is the Palace of the Senator, which we have before mentioned, — a vast, unoccupied building, where some inferior courts of justice at times are held, and whose great bell hangs silent in the tower above, being never rung except on the death of a Pope, or to proclaim that the Carnival has begun. The proud initials, S. P. Q. R., are placed over the entrance and still carried in processions, recalling as if by a sort of mockery the palmy days of the Republic. The Senator, too, — for that august body has dwindled down to one man, — is still appointed, and the Romans say, "the Senator represents the people." His office, however, is a mere shadow; its most weighty duty being that of carrying the sacramental vessels between the High Altar and the Pope on the great festivals of the Church, and its highest privilege that of standing in a picturesque dress on the second step of the Papal throne during some great ceremony.

The palaces on the other two sides of the square are used as museums, principally for the works of antique art. It is places like these, indeed, which enable Rome to preserve her supremacy over the world, ruling now in the realms of taste as she once did in those of arms and religion. Within her walls are gathered most that the wreck of time has left of beauty, from the creations of Greece or ancient Rome, or the still older attempts of Egypt and Etruria. And all these are freely opened to the pilgrim to this land. The labors of Art are before him, from its achievements in far distant ages, when men dimly imagined a grace which they were not able to embody, down to its perfect triumph in creations which more than realize his brightest dreams. Here are forms steeped in an atmosphere of beauty, and he can dwell upon them until his own taste has grown into faultless purity.

Let us enter then these palaces, and at once we have the realization of what we have just written. Sculpture has preserved the heroes of all times and countries, and they are before us with the life which characterized them, when the artist so admirably arrested and fixed, in enduring marble, the passing expression. These halls are crowded with their busts and statues, and now there is gathered on this Hill a nobler assemblage of Consuls, and Princes, and Dictators, than ever trod its temples in their living day.[1] When the sunlight plays on them, you are dazzled by the reflection of the white marbles, as the animated figures seem

[1] It is curious to mark how faithfully the marble has transmitted to us the difference between the early Romans and the late Emperors. The former have something noble and elevated in their looks; while those who, in the last ages of the Empire, were called to the throne from the seraglio, or the ranks of a barbarian army, show in every lineament their mixed blood and vicious habits. A similar change may be seen in the busts of the Medici in the vestibule of the *Galeria Imperiale* at Florence. In every generation you can mark the deterioration. There is a regular series of stages, from the stern countenance of Cosmo I. and the magnificent head of Lorenzo, down to the silly face of Gaston, the profligate buffoon, with whom the family expired in 1737.

often starting from their pedestals. But nobler even than these life-like copies of "men of like passions with ourselves," are the forms of beauty which the artist created when he gave himself up to his worship of the Ideal. We meet with group after group, which realizes the dreams we had over the studies of our boyhood, and calls up again the bright legends of the Grecian faith. Here is the heroic beauty of the "Apollo," while the shrinking loveliness of many a fabled goddess contrasts with the austere and majestic lineaments of "the cloud-compelling Zeus." And mingled with them is that antique sacerdotal sculpture, the only memorial of the vanished faith which once prevailed on the banks of the Nile. Thus the spoils of art have been widely gathered, from the Temples of old Egypt, from the Porticoes of Athens, and the Forum of ancient Rome.

We passed a morning among these treasures, which the past has bequeathed to us; but when we now look back upon them, all seem dimly remembered, or rather almost effaced by the vivid recollection of one single statue — the "Dying Gladiator." Standing in the centre of a hall to which it gives the name, it is the gem of the whole collection. We had often seen casts of it, but they are utterly wanting in the effect produced by the great original. They fail entirely in conveying any distinct idea of its excellence.

The figure is a little larger than nature, and represents him as wounded in the fight, with life just ebbing away. He is reclining on his sword and shield, which have fallen beneath him, and has raised himself languidly on one arm, as if to try how much strength remains. The limbs seem to be gently yielding from languor, as weakness creeps over him, and he is gradually falling to the ground. He is evidently insensible to all that is passing around, and absorbed with his own situation. The countenance is deeply sorrowful and expressive of agony, but we see that it is more than mere physical suffering. There seems to be a conflict going on within, which is shown in the despair of the eye, the bitter writhing of the lip, the wrinkled brow, and the abstracted air of the whole visage. Melancholy emotions insensibly creep over us as we look upon him; and herein was shown the artist's skill, that he should excite these feelings by the mere touching display of a fellow-being in conflict with death. Its power, indeed, rests on nothing but an appeal to our common interests in humanity, for there are no adventitious circumstances to call forth our sympathies. There is no heroic interest about the Gladiator. It is not the fall of one whose name is written in history, or whose fate can at all affect the world. It is nothing but the death of a slave, as the cord round his neck proves him to be; yet we are forced to gaze with sympathies which can be awakened by no other statue in existence. The Gladiator's last fight is over; the sweat is yet upon his brow, clotting together the thick locks of hair; his exhausted strength is just suffering him to sink to the earth; and it seems as if in a few moments more he would pass away, and be at once forgotten among the thousands who thus fall in the arena. Yet he is a man, in the solemn hour of death, and so well has the artist told this fact, that he appeals at once to every kindly feeling in our common nature. And as genius has always an affinity with genius, we find that one of the noblest passages in "Childe Harold" is the embodiment, in the language of poetry, of what this ancient and unknown sculptor has so well expressed in marble:—

> "I see before me the gladiator lie:
> He leans upon his hand; his manly brow
> Consents to death, but conquers agony,
> And his droop'd head sinks gradually low —
> And through his side the last drops, ebbing slow
> From the red gash, fall heavily, one by one,
> Like the first of a thunder-shower; and now
> The arena swims around him: he is gone,
> Ere ceased the inhuman shout which hail'd the wretch who won.
>
> "He heard it, but he heeded not: his eyes
> Were with his heart, and that was far away;
> He reck'd not of the life he lost, nor prize,
> But where his rude hut by the Danube lay,
> There were his young barbarians all at play,
> There was their Dacian mother — he their sire,
> Butcher'd to make a Roman holyday.
> All this rush'd with his blood. Shall he expire,
> And unavenged? Arise, ye Goths, and glut your ire!"

Was this the idea which the artist intended to develop? We know not, nor does it matter. We are satisfied with the interpretation of the pilgrim-poet. But after examining most of the noblest masterpieces of antiquity which remain, we find none on which the memory dwells with the interest it does on this single statue, which, as we gaze, calls back eighteen centuries, and transports us to the arena of Roman sports. The "Apollo," noble as it is, appeals only to the imagination. Even the "Venus de Medici," the glory of fair Florence, touches not the deepest feelings. You seem indeed, as you stand at its pedestal, to inhale an atmosphere of beauty, until you are forced to confess the power of antique art, and realize that the old poetical mythology must have furnished inspiration to genius. You turn away at last, "dazzled and drunk with beauty;" but this is all. There is no appeal to the heart, and therefore we give the preference to the "Dying Gladiator," and remember it as the very perfection of what can be wrought by the chisel.

Leaving the Museum, we passed around the base of the Hill, and came to the side which formerly overlooked the ancient city. But where all this magnificence once stood, nothing is now to be seen but ruins. One tide of desolation after another swept over it, until finally, what remained was ravaged by the Normans under Robert Guiscard, when the Capitol, the Coliseum, and all the surrounding antiquities, seem to have been hopelessly shattered. He had been summoned to the relief of his ally, Gregory VII., besieged by the Emperor Henry in the Castle of St. Angelo. The German army having been forced to retire, the Pope was led in triumph to his ancient Palace of the Lateran. It was, however, a rescue dearly purchased by the Roman Pontiff. On the third day the people rushed to arms, and commenced the indiscriminate massacre of their invaders. Overpowered by numbers, Guiscard at last gave the order to fire the city; and when the sun set behind the Tuscan hills, Gregory looked out from his windows on a scene of woe, of which Rome was for centuries to bear the traces. The whole sky was reddened by flames, while the fierce Saracens — who composed a part of the Norman army — gratified their hatred of Christianity by plundering every church and altar. The fires swept on until two thirds of the city were destroyed, and the noblest monuments of Mediæval Rome had perished. Then, at last, Guiscard reigned unopposed amidst the smoking ruins of this ancient splendor; but Gregory — fearful of a population more hostile to him than ever — fled from the city, shortly after to die in exile.

The whole of the Esquiline seems at that time to have been laid waste, and no attempt has since been made to restore its monuments. The modern city grew up on the other side of the Hill, and the site of Ancient Rome was abandoned to desolation, as if a spell rested over it. As we gazed down upon its hoary ruins, all seemed silent and lonely; not a living creature visible but a solitary artist, who, sitting on the base of a fallen column, was sketching some of the time-worn monuments.

Here was the site of the old Forum, " the field " in which — Lord Byron tells us — " a thousand years of silenced factions sleep." It was evidently once surrounded by a colonnade, which must have given it somewhat the form and appearance of the Palais Royal in Paris, or the Piazza San Marco in Venice. We stood within it, where Cicero had pleaded, and countless schemes of ambition run their wild career. Above our heads towered high on the one side eight granite columns, which once formed the portico to the Temple of Vespasian; while on the other side stand three lofty fluted Corinthian columns, the sole remains of the Temple of Saturn. How strange they look as they are seen in contrast with the deep blue of the Italian sky, so tall and solitary, supported by no wall and with no roof above, nothing near but the ivy which wreathes itself around and falls in graceful festoons from their sculptured capitals! Round and round the ruined Forum pass their lonely shadows, as if this was Time's dial, and he had placed them there to mark his ages as they went by. Before us was the magnificent triumphal arch of Septimius Severus, its statues still remaining, and its inscriptions uneffaced; while at the lower end of the Forum, near the Portico of Vespasian, rises in lonely grandeur that solitary pillar to which Byron refers in the line, —

"The nameless column with a buried base."

It would have been well, perhaps, for our interest in this monument, if its origin had always remained thus mysteriously concealed. Later excavations, however, have proved that it was erected in honor of the Emperor Phocas, one of the most despicable of mortals. He was a sanguinary usurper, whom his own people having abandoned to the Persians — whose envoy he had burned alive — he was taken by them and put to death. And yet the base of this column bears the inscription, — "To the most clement and felicitous Prince Phocas, Emperor, the adored and crowned conqueror, always august," &c.

Leaving the Forum, we stood beneath the Arch of Titus. More than fifty generations have passed away since this monument was reared to commemorate the destruction of Jerusalem; yet on its worn and broken compartments we can still trace the story it recorded. In the distance are imagined in relief, the fearful accompaniments of a city taken by assault, — old men and women and children gathered into groups, and around them an enraged and brutal soldiery. On one side are seen the Temple walls riven by fire, and just tottering to their fall, while in the foreground is the triumphal procession of the victors as once it swept over this very spot, and, amidst the shoutings of the Roman populace, ascended to the Capitol. Slowly and sadly walk the captive Jews, bearing in their hands the spoils of their holy worship. The tables of shew-bread, the seven-branched golden candlestick, the Jubilee trumpets, and the incense vessels, are there, copied from the originals.[1]

---

[1] It is interesting to inquire what became of these sacred relics. Josephus says (*De Bello Jud.* lib. vii. c. v.) that the veil and books of the law were

On the opposite side of the Arch is seen the triumphal chariot of Titus, drawn by four horses. He is standing within it, while Victory is crowning him with laurel, and around are the crowds of his rejoicing army, lictors carrying the fasces, and the captives dragged in chains. Even to this day, the crushed and stricken Jew will not walk under this monument of his country's fall, but passes round it, and winds his way by the ruins of the Temple of Peace, or else among the crumbling relics of the Palatine Mount. Yet time has brought its retribution, and now the persecuted Israelite, as he stands by this monument of Hebrew desolation, may see the palaces of the Imperial family one mountain of ruins.

It is from this spot, indeed, that we have the noblest view of these ancient remains. Here, all around are the monuments of the past. Behind us is the Forum and the scene we have described; before us, the Arch of Constantine, and the Coliseum, the noblest relic of old Rome; on the one side are the massive ruins of the Temple of Antoninus and Faustina, that of Venus and Rome, and the Basilica of Constantine; on the other side is the Palace of the Cæsars, covering the whole Palatine Mount like the wreck of a mighty city,— walls, and arches, and porticoes, mingled with the vineyards,

placed in the palace at Rome, and the candlestick and other spoils in the Templo of Peace. The golden fillet is mentioned as late as the time of Hadrian. When Genseric entered Rome, among other spoils which he carried to Africa were the Hebrew vessels. On the conquest of the Vandals by Belisarius, A. D. 520, they were recovered and taken to Constantinople. Procopius states, that a Jew advised the Emperor not to put them in his palace, as they could not remain anywhere else but where Solomon had placed them; and this was the reason why the palace in Rome had been taken, and afterwards the Vandals conquered. The Emperor therefore, alarmed, sent them to the Christian churches at Jerusalem. (Burton, vol. i. p. 236.) From that time all trace of them is lost.

and massive columns peeping up through the long grass, or dimly seen among the ivy which hangs in thick festoons about them.

On our return we came to the entrance of the old Mamertine prisons, which are built under the base of the Capitoline Hill. Livy tells us they were begun by Ancus Martius: and we know that in these gloomy chambers, Jugurtha was starved to death; the accomplices of Catiline were strangled by order of Cicero; and Sejanus, the minister of Tiberius, was executed. Sallust, in describing it, says, — " The appearance of it from the filth, the darkness, and the smell, is terrific; " and such, we can well believe, must in that day have been the case. Tradition has consecrated this prison as the one in which St. Peter was confined, and in the sixteenth century a chapel was therefore erected over it, the walls of which are now covered with votive offerings from those who ascribe their cure to prayers offered at its altars.

Here we procured a guide with lighted tapers, and commenced our descent into the dungeons. A flight of twenty-eight stone steps led us into the upper cell. It is about twenty-seven feet by twenty, constructed of large masses of peperino, without cement, and showing by its very construction its high antiquity and Etruscan origin. From the first chamber a still farther descent brought us into the lower one, which is only about nine feet wide, and six high. The massive stones of the roof, instead of being formed on the principle of an arch, point horizontally to a centre. There was formerly no entrance to either, except by a circular aperture above, through which the prisoners were lowered, and a corresponding aperture in the floor of the upper cell to lead into the lower. A more horrible dungeon could not well be imagined. There is a stone pillar on one side, which our guide — a young priest — pointed out to us as the one to which St. Peter was chained, and in the centre, welling up through an opening in the stone floor, is a fountain, which is said to have miraculously sprung up, to enable him to baptize his jailers, Processus and Martinian. The story is, of course, intended to be an improvement on the baptism at Philippi. Our guide also pointed out to us in the hard rock, the impression of a man's face. His story was, that when the soldiers thrust St. Peter into this gloomy dungeon, it was done with such violence that he fell against the wall. The hard stone immediately yielded, as if it had been soft, received the impression of the Apostle's face, and there it is to this day. It may have been a freak of nature, but we should think it was artificial. We asked the young priest if he believed the legend, but could get no definite answer. He only laughed and evaded the question. It was evident to us that, like the ancient philosophers, he had an *esoteric* and an *exoteric* doctrine.

From this spot commenced the *Via Sacra*, where Horace tells us he was accustomed to walk, — "Nescio quid meditans nugarum, et totus in illis." Centuries of rubbish had gathered over it, so that the surface of the ground was here many feet higher than formerly, half burying the columns which stand around. When the French held Rome, they commenced excavations, which have since been constantly carried on, until the old pavement under the Arch of Severus was uncovered, and we may now tread the same causeway which formerly echoed to the step of the warriors and poets of old Rome. Had we some magic wand to wave back the triumphal processions which in "the purple days" of the Empire passed over these stones, what a gorgeous picture would they form! Captive kings; princes from the far East, of strange language and costume; wild beasts dragged from the forests of Africa, to grace a triumph or contend in the Coliseum with men scarcely less savage; cars and chariots, loaded with the spoils of rifled cities; and the armed legions of Rome in all the bravery of their conquests, — these would swell the long array which swept before us.

We passed once more around the Hill, to find the Tarpeian Rock, down which, in the days of the Republic, traitors were hurled and dashed to pieces at its base. Though surrounded with buildings, and the soil accumulated below, yet it is still plainly visible on the southern side of the Capitoline, facing the Tiber. We threaded our way among the narrow streets beneath, and ascending, passed through a garden, when we found ourselves standing on the brink of an abrupt precipice, at least seventy feet in height. It needed not the "Ecco! Rupe Tarpeja!" of our ragged guide, the *custode* of this classical spot, for we recognized it at once as the place described by Seneca, when he says, — "It is chosen that the criminals may not require to be thrown down more than once." And here, in the ancient days of Rome, suffered those who forgot their allegiance and plotted against her liberty!

> "The steep
> Tarpeian, fittest goal of Treason's race,
> The promontory whence the traitor's leap
> Cured all ambition."

CHAPTER VI.

THE VATICAN.

WE have spent several days in different parts of the Vatican. The gardens, at some seasons of the year, are very pleasant, although arranged too much in the dull uniformity which was the fashion a century ago. When we visited them in the month of January, the oranges were ripe upon the trees, and flowers were blooming around us. They contain some beautiful fountains, and some which are tortured into the most grotesque shapes, as if to deviate as far from nature as possible. Like every other part of Rome, we find here, also, some antiquities — vases, columns, and statues, which have been dug up from the ruins of the ancient city. It was in these gardens that Pius VII. was accustomed to give audience to ladies, a custom which his successor has abandoned, having transferred his presentations to the apartments of the Vatican.

The manufactory of mosaics is also an interesting place to visit, particularly after seeing the magnificent pictures in St. Peter's. It is under the government of the Court, and few of its works are allowed to be sold. The greater part are intended for the adornment of churches, or else as presents to different crowned heads. The number of tints used amounts to about ten thousand, and some of the large pictures take from twelve to twenty years to complete. It requires, therefore, not only care and patience, but also a high degree of artistical skill. These little *tesserœ* are put in rough, and the full effect cannot of course be seen until the whole surface is polished, when alterations cannot well be made.

We passed one morning in the halls containing the Library of the Vatican, which is well known as being, in some respects, the finest in the world. It was probably formed at a very early period, as it is not likely that men like St. Damasus (in the fourth century), who was celebrated for his learning, would have been unprovided with the means of study. We find, however, no express record of it before the days of Hilary (A. D. 467), who established two libraries in the Basilica of the Lateran Palace. In the sixth century we first hear of the Bibliothecarius of the Apostolical Library, an office which has been filled to the present day. In the eighth century, the collection begun by Hilary was transferred to the Basilica of St. Peter's, and received constant additions. Then follow several centuries in which we find nothing but casual allusions to the Papal Library, though scattered through this period are the works of Roman writers, which could not have been composed without the aid of many books, and particularly those of ancient authors. We consider this, therefore, one proof that the Library must not only have then been in existence, but also extending its influence.

During the vicissitudes and troubles of the Papal See, in the days when rival Popes were contending for the tiara, it seems to have been well preserved. When Clement V. removed to Avignon, he took with him the literary treasures of the See. At the end of the secession, Martin V. restored them to Rome, and they have since been constantly increasing. During the revival of literature under Leo X., that Pontiff sent learned men through the whole East to purchase oriental manuscripts, to add to this collection. Its number of printed books is much smaller than is usually supposed, not exceeding thirty thousand. It is in manuscripts that the Library is so particularly rich, numbering nearly twenty-four thousand; some of them as old as the fifth century, and others richly illuminated with pictures and miniatures, to execute which must have been the labor of many years.

We found the anteroom filled with portraits of the librarians, and immediately inquired of the *custode* which was the picture of Assemanni? But he told us, alas! that the collection was limited to those who had attained the dignity of Cardinal, and as such had not been the case with either of the Assemanni, both were excluded; and yet the fruits of the researches which they sent forth to the world, will preserve their names long after most of the cardinals, whose portraits grace these walls, have been forgotten. In the long list of librarians, indeed, we doubt whether any were as conversant as Joseph Assemanni with the rich treasures of the Vatican. Scarcely stirring beyond these precincts, he explored them year after year, suffering no other earthly interest to mingle with his literary dreams, and so absorbed in the pursuit that the remembrances of early youth faded away, and he forgot even his own distant Syrian home. And when at last he was laid in the cemetery at Rome, his biographer tells us that he sorrowed as much to part from the treasures of the Vatican, as from his decaying life.[1]

There is little, however, to be seen by a mere visit to this stupendous collection. The manuscripts cannot be examined except by an express order, while the books are inclosed in wooden presses, so that not a volume is seen. There is nothing, therefore, of a literary air about it, as in the *Bibliothèque du Roi* in Paris, or the Bodleian in England, where you see the walls crowded to the ceiling with the labors of the learned. You may pass through these long halls without a suspicion that you are in a library. Nothing is to be seen but painted cabinets, Etruscan vases, and pictures of the early Councils of the Church. In one of the last galleries are collected all the objects of interest belonging to the early Christians, which were found in the Catacombs. Here are their personal ornaments, the sepulchral lamps, paintings, and the instruments of torture by which so many suffered martyrdom. A sight of these things transports us back to the early ages of persecution. We look upon the very hooks and pointed instruments which tore the flesh of those who " counted not their lives dear unto themselves " when they were to be preserved by apostasy from Christ.

It would be useless to attempt to describe the differ-

---

[1] Pasquin made the appointment of Assemanni the subject of one of his witticisms. His two predecessors had been Holstenius, who had abjured Protestantism, and Leo Allatius, a Chian. When, therefore, a Syrian was next appointed, the following distich appeared: —

" Præfuit hæreticus. Post hunc, scismaticus.
At nunc
Turco præest. Petri bibliotheca, vale! "

We believe, indeed, that Assemanni was never so complete a Romanist as to overcome his Syrian prejudices, and that his church, therefore, regards with much more favor the oriental researches of Renardot.

ent parts of the Vatican. It is almost a city in itself! Murray tells us, that "it has eight grand staircases, two hundred smaller staircases, twenty courts, and four thousand four hundred and twenty-two apartments." We will select, therefore, only a few of the principal parts.

We succeeded one morning in obtaining admission into the Sistine Chapel at a time when there was light enough to see the paintings. In the large saloon which leads to it, the walls are covered with frescoes, one of which, representing the "Massacre of St. Bartholomew's," might as well have been omitted, it not being a triumph of which the Church of Rome should be particularly proud. In the Papal mint, however, can be seen a medal which was struck in honor of the same occasion. The glory of the Sistine Chapel has always been the great fresco of the "Last Judgment," by Michael Angelo, which entirely covers one end. It is chiefly remarkable for the boldness of its drawing, the great number of figures introduced, and, of course, the anatomical details.[1] The blessed are there, rising from their graves, ascending into heaven, and received by angels; while demons are seizing the condemned and dragging them down to the pit. It of course gave opportunity to the artist to display his great power, as every possible passion was to be delineated; but the picture is half heathenish. In the foreground is Charon, in his ferry-boat, rowing the groups over the Styx, and striking the refractory with his oar. This, however, was in accordance with the spirit of the age;

---

[1] In 1841, the favorite ballet at the French Opera in Paris was called *The Infernal Gallopade of the Last Judgment*, all the attitudes of which were taken from this picture.

and Michael Angelo only painted the retributions of Eternity as Dante had described them.

It may be a great want of taste, yet the pictures of Michael Angelo are not those on which we could ever look with pleasure. They seem more intended as a study for artists, who can dwell with delight upon the skill of the fore-shortening and the grandeur of the design, than they do to excite the admiration of the unlearned. This very picture is a fair illustration of his style. It is full of sublimity, yet there is nothing to touch the heart. We shrink back from the stern and terrific Being who is hurling down his foes to the torments of the condemned. We recognize not the Son of God as we have always thought of Him. He is here only the terrible Minister of vengeance. The artist, too, seems to take a savage delight in delineating the miseries of the lost, and even uses the divine skill with which Heaven had endowed him, to minister to his revenge. The inspiration he had imbibed was not lofty enough to enable him to forget the strife and bitterness of private life, and therefore he condemns his enemies to immortality by painting their portraits among the damned.[1]

Look, too, at his pictures of the "Holy Family," even the most celebrated of all, which is in the Tribune at Florence. It possesses no characteristics of grace or beauty. His Madonna is a noble looking woman,

---

[1] This seems to have been somewhat the fashion of the age. Dante records in his poems his partialities as a partisan, and places his enemies in the *Inferno*, while Da Vinci, in his "Last Supper," gives Judas the likeness of one who had offended him. How different from our own Milton, who, bitter as he was as a politician, when he had "his garland and his singing robes about him," seemed to shake from his wings all the entanglements of earth, and to soar into a purer, holier region!

fitted to be the ancestress of a race of heroes, but that is all. There is nothing soft and attractive in the countenance — none of that touching loveliness which we should wish to recognize in the Mother of our Lord. For these traits we must look to the pictures of Raphael and Poussin. His infant Saviour, too, only suggests to us the idea of a young Hercules. We should pronounce him a "a noble boy," but seek in vain in his lineaments for anything divine. There is, however, one painting by Michael Angelo, which belongs to the class of subjects he should always have chosen. It is "The Parcæ," in the Pitti Palace at Florence, a strange looking picture, with very little coloring, so that it seems unfinished. It is a bold design of the Three Fates, — grave, thoughtful, and severe, — spinning and cutting the thread of human life. The conception is Dante-like, and one well suited to the character of the artist's mind. Lord Byron has somewhere recorded his admiration of this picture.

In truth, the mind of Michael Angelo was too fiery and impetuous to enable him to execute the high finish of painting, and he therefore always prided himself most on being a sculptor. His signature generally was, *Michel Agnolo Buonarotti, Scultore*, and in one of his letters to Varchi, he says, that "Sculpture is to Painting what the sun is to the moon." We are told that he often struck and hewed at the block of marble with a desperate energy, as if struggling to extricate the form which in his imagination he saw concealed. For a noble evidence of his talent, we should look at his statues of the gloomy Lorenzo and the armed Julian, in the Church of San Lorenzo at Florence, — as Rogers describes them, — "two ghosts, sitting on their sepulchres." His own family seem to have taken the same view of his characteristics; and when his fellow-citizens were raising his splendid monument in the Church of Santa Croce, and, according to the original design, Painting was to have stood in front of the sepulchre, his relatives remonstrated most urgently. As they considered his peculiar excellence to have been manifested in Sculpture, they contended that it should have the post of honor, and the whole arrangement of the statues was accordingly altered.

But to return to the Vatican. We passed, on our way, through the *Loggia of Raphael* — open porticoes covered with fresco paintings from the Old Testament. The first — the " Creation " — is one of those pictures so often attempted in the Church of Rome, in which all reverence seems to be forgotten. It represents the wildness of chaos, — clouds, and darkness, and the war of elements, — and above is a venerable old man, throwing himself upon it, to reduce to order the materials of the universe, and to separate light from darkness. It is a vain attempt to convey, by sensible objects, an idea of that scene which the words of Inspiration bring before us so sublimely in the single sentence, — " And God said, Let there be light: and there was light."

On every Monday and Thursday the Museum of the Vatican is open, and filled by eager hundreds, who are gathered in groups through every part of its marble galleries, studying these triumphs of human genius. Here, and in the Museum on the Capitoline Hill, are to be found all that survive the wars and devastations which have swept over Rome, all that her ancient conquerors brought from Greece, and all that her own artists learned to create, with these lifelike forms of Athenian sculpture as their models. And year after year, as new treasures were discovered among the buried ruins of the old city, this collection has been increasing, till it now has become well worthy of an artist's pilgrimage from any quarter of the earth. Here he will see, in some shape embodied, all those forms of beauty which have been flitting, like dim phantoms, through his brain.

It takes a morning merely to walk through this collection. Long galleries, sometimes a thousand feet in length, are each devoted to a particular subject. One is filled with Greek inscriptions from the old tombs; another with busts; another with sculptures of animals; another with vases; another with antique candelabra; while at every turn are sarcophagi, and altars, and Roman baths, which have been dug up among the ruins. The names of some of these halls — "the Cabinet of the Masks," "the Hall of the Muses," "the Hall of the Biga" — may convey some idea of their contents. Old Egypt is represented here, ever the same, with her strange, uncouth figures, melancholy sphinxes, and gods mingling the monster with the man. The influence of intellectual Greece, too, is everywhere visible, and we see how her worship of beauty softened and refined the stern grandeur of her conquerors.

Here, in a circular hall by itself, as if nothing else was worthy to stand by its side, is the "Apollo Belvedere," and around its pedestal are always collected a group, studying its matchless beauty. It is not the mere development of a human form, but rather the gathering into one of some poet's unearthly conceptions — the expression of some ideal beauty that never really existed. In looking at it, we forget everything physical, in comparison with *the soul* which beams forth in every feature. He stands, with arm extended, as if the arrow had just parted from the bow, and secure that it would reach its mark, he is tracking its course. "Childe Harold" speaks of the "beautiful disdain" visible in "the eye and nostril." It is stamped, indeed, on the whole countenance, as if he felt an immortal's contempt for the object of his vengeance.

> "But in his delicate form — a dream of love
> Shaped by some solitary nymph, whose breast
> Long'd for a deathless lover from above,
> And madden'd in that vision — are express'd
> All that ideal beauty ever bless'd
> The mind with, in its most unearthly mood,
> When each conception was a heavenly guest —
> A ray of immortality — and stood
> Starlike, around, until they gather'd to a god!"

But the mere beauty of the execution is not all. Could a modern statue be formed, no way its inferior, it would not by any means possess the same interest. It is the thought that this has united the suffrages of three centuries. The intellectual and the cultivated of ten generations have stood before its pedestal, and no dissenting voice has been heard denying its claim to admiration. Michael Angelo, and Canova, and Thorwaldsen, and sculptors from all lands, have studied it, receiving new inspiration as they gazed. Countless writers, too, whose names are familiar in the annals of literature, have delighted to pay their tribute to its surpassing beauty, and thus, as we look upon it, there is added also the charm of a thousand associations.

Here, too, in another hall by itself, is the group of

"The Laocoön"—the father and his two sons in the serpent's coil and strain. We see them struggling with the desperate energy of those who strive for life, —seeking to unlock the living links which are wound around them, "the long, envenomed chain,"—yet striving in vain. The serpent tightens and deepens its coils, and rivets them more firmly, while each moment it is driving its fangs deeper into the old man's side. And yet with this group we were disappointed. The single figure of the father, so expressive of mortal agony, if it could be seen by itself, would be all that we could desire. The sons, however, are not youths. There is nothing juvenile about their forms or features. They are merely miniatures of the father. Parts, too, are restorations, and evidently not in accordance with the original outline of the group, injuring the effect of its intense action.

As we traverse these halls we cannot but realize the superiority of sculpture to painting. Zeuxis and Apelles were in their day what Raphael and Guido are in ours, but there remains not a single work which they executed; and yet here are the beautiful creations of Grecian sculpture, as fresh as they were twenty centuries ago. The marble has faithfully retained its trust, and we gaze upon it now as when it came from the artist's hands.

But Rome is still a sepulchre of beauty, and it is impossible to tell what treasures may yet be hid beneath its ruins. Pliny informs us, that the number of statues was equal to that of the inhabitants, and many are now doubtless covered by the heaps of rubbish which have fallen above them. The elevation of the ground throughout the city, is from fifteen to twenty feet above its original level, and no excavation ever is made without disinterring some remains of antiquity. Several of the ancient baths are still unopened; and, could the Tiber be for a time diverted from its course, there is no doubt but that in its bed would be found many treasures of art, which were buried beneath its waters when the city was so often plundered by barbarous enemies. The offer to undertake this work has several times been made to the Papal government, but was always declined. Raphael proposed in his day a plan for a thorough exploration, but the authorities had not energy enough to adopt it. Had Napoleon conquered in Russia, he intended to have made a triumphal entry into Rome for the purpose of being crowned in St. Peter's, and then the scheme of Raphael would have been put in execution.

There are but fifty pictures in the Vatican, but one of them is a painting allowed to be the first in the world, — "The Transfiguration," by Raphael. I know not why it was, but my first impressions were those of disappointment, perhaps because my expectations had been raised too high. The colors, too, are said to have somewhat changed since it came from the hand of its great master. After seeing in France and Italy the *chef d'œuvres* of the first artists of different ages, and realizing that Raphael was the noblest of them all, I expected, perhaps, when I looked upon his masterpiece, to see more than human genius can ever execute. But every moment since, it has grown upon me, until I felt ready to subscribe to the decision which pronounced it the greatest triumph the pencil ever has achieved. No words can describe the aërial lightness with which the figures of the Saviour and the two

Prophets seem suspended in the air. They appear floating on the clouds, while around them is spread an effulgence of glory, which nowhere else have colors been able to produce. The Apostles are on the ground below, veiling their faces, as if smitten down, and "dazzled with excess of brightness." But it was on the head of the Saviour that Raphael lavished all his power, attempting to invest Him with a majesty and beauty — to array Him with an air of Divinity — which would make this the very perfection of art. There is but one that can compare with it, and that the countenance of our Lord in Leonardo da Vinci's "Last Supper" at Milan. There, indeed, the artist left the head imperfect, because he could not realize his conception of the celestial beauty it ought to possess. Yet, unfinished as it is, it expresses all we can imagine.

We have already in this chapter spoken of the characteristics of Michael Angelo; Raphael we regard as his perfect contrast. It has been well remarked, that the former seemed to have imbibed the spirit of the Old Testament, and the latter that of the New. Everything recorded of Raphael appears to develop a loveliness of disposition most foreign to the stern character of his great rival. Idolized by his friends, he seemed formed for the fullest display of every social affection. Beauty was the element and atmosphere in which he lived, and his most pleasant occupation was to transfer the loveliness of woman to his almost breathing canvas. There it still awakens our admiration as no other productions of the pencil can, for the centuries which have passed sent forth no rival to eclipse his fame. And when he portrayed subjects of a sacred character, his work appeals at once to our affections. With the spirit of St. John he painted the Saviour of the world, and we recognize in the portrait which he has drawn, One who can be "touched with the feeling of our infirmities." His pictures therefore teach the lessons of our faith.

"The Transfiguration" was Raphael's last work, and before it was completed he was cut off, at the early age of thirty-seven. But seldom for centuries past — if we may credit the account of those who saw it — had Rome witnessed a scene like that which took place on the sweet April day, when this divinest painter of the age was borne to his rest in the Pantheon. Yet before that solemn march began — that march which knows no return — his body was laid in state, with this his masterpiece suspended over it, the last traces of his hand still visible on the canvas.

> "And when all beheld
> Him where he lay, how changed from yesterday, —
> Him in that hour cut off, and at his head
> His last great work; when, entering in, they looked
> Now on the dead, then on that masterpiece —
> Now on his face, lifeless and colorless,
> Then on those forms divine that lived and breathed,
> And would live on for ages, — all were moved,
> And sighs burst forth, and loudest lamentations."

CHAPTER VII.

PRESENTATION AT THE PAPAL COURT. — THE POPEDOM. — PRIVATE LIFE OF THE POPES.

TO-DAY we were presented to his Holiness Pope Gregory XVI. by our Consul, through whom, as we have no minister at the Papal Court, all the necessary arrangements are made. So many holydays and other public festivals are continually occurring, that it is necessary to make application some time before, and we had been for several weeks waiting his Holiness' leisure. The required costume is the same as on other occasions, — the ladies in black, with black veils over their heads, the gentlemen also in full dress of black. The only difference is that boots are forbidden, — a very disagreeable arrangement, as passing in thin shoes and silk stockings through the cold galleries of the Vatican, and over the marble floors, an invalid would be very apt to take a cold, for which his introduction to the successor of St Peter would hardly be considered a sufficient compensation.

Twenty-two hours of the day,[1] that is, three o'clock

---

[1] The Roman day counts its hours from 1 to 24, beginning at sundown. As this is rather indefinite for a starting-point, and from its daily change would be very inconvenient, the Cardinal who presides over this department, issues a public ordinance, decreeing at what hour the sun ought to set. At this season of the year he places it at 5 P. M. Three o'clock in the afternoon, therefore, is twenty-two hours of the day.

in the afternoon, was the time appointed, and punctual to the hour, we assembled in a little room adjoining the Sistine Chapel, where we remained till our company had all arrived. Here hats and cloaks were deposited, and the Consul drilled us after a few instructions, as to how we were to bow when we walked in, and how we were to bow when we backed out, and other matters of equal moment in the etiquette of the Papal Court. Presently a servant in livery appeared, to conduct us to the anteroom; the procession formed and marshaled by him, we were led up-stairs, and on — on through the long halls and corridors, till we reached the Hall of Maps, so called because its walls are covered with huge maps, painted in fresco in 1581 by an Archbishop of Alatri, and which are now curious, as showing the geographical knowledge of that day.

Here we were left for nearly an hour. These vast galleries are always cold, even in the mildest weather, and as this happened to be one of the most severe days we had experienced while in Italy, and we were not exactly in costume for such an atmosphere, we were anything but comfortable. A large brazier filled with coals (the usual method here of warming an apartment) stood at one end, round which the ladies gathered; the gentlemen walked about to keep themselves warm; while some of the younger members of the party, having no fear of the Pope and the Vatican before their eyes, to keep their blood from congealing, most irreverently ran races up and down the gallery. This, by the way, being four hundred and twenty feet long, seemed admirably adapted for such purposes.

At length the usher in attendance walked in and announced that *Il Padre Santo* was ready to receive us. The presentation was very differerent from what I had expected, having lately read the account of one in which there was much ceremony — the guards at the doors — the anteroom filled with officers of the Court — and the mace-bearers heralding the way. Everything with us was very informal, and with the exception of the usher and two servants at the door, we saw no attendants. In we marched in procession, headed by the Consul in full uniform; the ladies next, the gentlemen bringing up the rear, and found ourselves in a long room, at the upper end of which, leaning against a table, stood the two hundred and fifty-eighth successor of St. Peter. We bowed as we entered the door — again when we reached the middle of the room — and a third time when we came opposite to the Pope. This at least is all that is required of those who " worship God after the way which they call heresy." The true members of the Church of Rome, instead of bowing, kneel three times, and end by kissing either the hand or the embroidered slipper of his Holiness. It is said, that when Horace Walpole was presented to Benedict XIV. he stood for a moment in a posture of hesitation, when the Pope, who was remarkable for cheerfulness and humor, exclaimed, " Kneel down, my son; receive the blessing of an old man; it will do you no harm!" upon which the young traveller immediately fell on his knees. Kissing the Pope's foot is not so easily justified, although the usual explanation given is, that it is to the cross on the slipper that the homage is paid. But what business has the cross in such a situation? It is curious, too, that a somewhat similar reason was given for this ceremony under the old Roman Emperors. Caligula was the first who offered his foot to be kissed by those who approached him, and we find Seneca declaiming upon it as the last affront to liberty, and the introduction of a Persian slavery into the manners of Rome. Those, on the contrary, who endeavored to excuse it, asserted that it was not done out of insolence, but vanity, that he might, by this means, display his golden slipper set with jewels.

After we were presented and had ranged ourselves in a semicircle around him, he commenced at once an animated conversation with the Consul, which gave us an opportunity of quietly studying his appearance and manner. He was dressed in his every-day costume: a white flannel robe, with a cape buttoned down before, and very similar to that worn by some orders of the monks; a little white skull-cap on his head, and red morocco slippers, on the instep of each of which was wrought the gold cross. His snuff-box (another cross on its lid) was in constant use, while he laughed and talked in the most sociable manner. Notwithstanding his age — being over eighty — he seems a hale, hearty old man, whom I should not have imagined to be more than sixty. He looked very differently from what he did in the public services of St. Peter's, when I supposed him to be feeble, and it is probable that the Cardinals whose heads are aching for the Tiara, will have to wait some years before the aspirations of any one of them is gratified. There is, however, nothing intellectual in his countenance — nothing which marks him as one worthy in this respect to sit in the seat of Hildebrand. His features are exceedingly heavy — the nose too large and drooping — and the general expression of the eyes one of sleepiness. The impression produced upon my mind was that of good-nature. During the whole audience there was nothing to remind me that he was the head of so large a portion of the Christian world — still less, that he was a temporal prince to whom many millions owed subjection.

After inquiring what parts of the country we came from, and whether all things had become quiet in Philadelphia (alluding to the riots of last summer), he suddenly turned to us, and asked, — "What do you intend to do with Texas?" It was certainly a curious place in which to hear a discussion of this question, but the Pope seemed to feel as much interest in the matter as if he had been one of our own Southern politicians. His knowledge of the geography of our country rather surprised me at the time, but I afterwards learned that he had formerly been for many years Prefect of the Propaganda, during which time the whole foreign correspondence was submitted to him, and he is therefore somewhat acquainted with those parts of the United States in which there are Roman Catholic Missionaries.

After about twenty minutes there was a pause in the conversation, when he bowed to us — rang a small bell on the table, I suppose to summon the usher — and we commenced, according to etiquette, backing out of the room. The Pope, however, immediately walked into the recess of a window near him — his usual custom, I am told, to relieve strangers from the awkwardness of so singular a mode of exit — and we were thus enabled to turn our backs to him and leave the apartment in the ordinary way.

At the close of a presentation it is customary for the Pope to bless the rosaries, crucifixes, medals, etc., which have been brought for that purpose. An attendant, therefore, was at hand to receive them, and some of the party having come well provided, the articles were carried in to his Holiness, and in a short time brought out again with the additional value they had received from their consecration.

Nothing can be so joyless as the life of the Sovereign Pontiff. Weighed down as he is by cares and business, with no means of recreation, the quiet and seclusion of the cloister would be a happy exchange. They who only think of him as a temporal monarch, or witness his splendor amidst the ceremonies of the Church, know little of the dull uniformity in which his days are passed. Four centuries ago, the Popes, in consideration of their temporal sovereignty, displayed in their palaces the same magnificence and festivity which are witnessed at other courts. The old chronicles describe to us fetes, and pageants, and tournaments, which certainly displayed more of the spirit of this world than of the next. But now a character of austerity seems outwardly, at least, to mark the Pontifical Court. The vast and gloomy apartments of the Vatican are deserted, and as you pass through them you meet no one but the officials of the Palace, or some ecclesiastic gliding along with a subdued look and noiseless step. You might imagine yourself in a monastery of Carthusians. The Pope, indeed, is at all times the slave of the most rigid etiquette. The heavy robes of his office trammel his steps, and he leads a life of restraint and confinement. A walk in the formal gardens of the Vatican or Quirinal; a quiet ride among the mournful ruins of former ages; or a visit to some church filled perhaps with monuments which announce how short were the reigns of his predecessors, are his only sources of relaxation without the walls of his own palace.[1]

In the days of Leo X. the hours which were spent around the table of the Pontiff were devoted to the highest social enjoyment. While literature was reviving, it was there that its progress was discussed, and plans were canvassed and hints given, which constantly suggested to this Sovereign of the House of Medici, new schemes for restoring its former glory. Philosophers, orators, and artists, gathered there; genius was encouraged to attempt its loftiest flight; and the poet sang his noblest verses to the music of the sweet lyre, certain of a favorable audience. The deep mysteries of science, and the lighter graces of literature found equal favor with the princely Leo, and in his presence the subtle alchemist from the far East and the gay troubadour of Provence, were seen side by side. There seemed then to be an inspiration in those saloons, and from the halls of the Vatican the new Augustan age first dawned upon the world. So it had been before at Avignon, and as we explored the ruined palace of the Popes, we thought more of Petrarch who came thither from Vaucluse to recite his sweet sonnets, than we did of the Pontiff and Cardinals whose applause he sought to win. But now this too is changed, and custom requires that the table of the Pope should be occupied by himself alone. His repasts are solitary, unenlivened even by friendly converse. In many respects, indeed, this change is a

[1] Eustace, *Class. Tour*, vol. iii. p. 346.

favorable one, and the austerity of the present day far better becomes the head of the Roman Church than the gay pageantry of the former centuries, yet it necessarily makes his life solitary and cheerless.

Elected as the Popes are at an advanced age, they must of course follow each other in rapid succession. Gregory XVI. therefore, having been elected in 1831, has had a longer reign than usual. He is not a man of great talents or remarkable for any particular traits which pointed him out for the office, but was elected, as is frequently the case, amidst the strife of parties. On such occasions, some inoffensive, unexceptionable person, generally of advanced age, is chosen. He seems to share fully in all the antiquated prejudices of his Church, and has lately issued an edict forbidding all railroads within the Papal dominions. It was proposed to construct one from Rome to Naples, and the King of Naples was very anxious to have it undertaken. In fact, during the winter he arrived at Rome and it was stated that this was the object of his visit; but the Pope was inexorable. The Court fears its subjects having too great facilities for travelling, lest a further acquaintance with the world might shake their faith. And yet Rome is supported almost entirely by the money of foreigners, and should all visitors abandon it for three years, the city would be given up to famine.

What a strange spectacle does this history of the Popedom present! Aged men, reigning but a short time — insulated individuals, deriving no claim from relationship to those who went before them, and yet, amidst all the changes of the world, bequeathing their authority to those who came after them. The unbroken line stretches back from him whom we saw to-day in the Vatican, to those Bishops " appointed unto death " who ruled the Christians of the Imperial City when they met in the Catacombs of St. Sebastian, or died as martyrs in the Flavian amphitheatre. Perhaps seventeen centuries ago some of the predecessors of Gregory XVI., as they saw in the distance the smoke of heathen sacrifice ascend from the temple of the Capitoline Jupiter, were unconsciously standing on the very spot where their own magnificent St. Peter's was afterwards to be founded. Yet great as is the change in their situation, is it not equally so in the manner in which they bear the Apostolic office? Would Clemens, " whose name " — St. Paul tells us — " was written in the Book of Life," have recognized as his successors, the lordly prelates of the Middle Ages — trampling on the necks of kings, and crushing thrones with a rod of iron? Alas! before the days of Christian unity return, Rome must go back to earlier principles, remembering the heritage of suffering which once she received, and by which she grew to greatness. Laying aside her diadem, and resuming once more her ancient crown of thorns, the world must see her, sitting no longer so lordly, but rather ready to rejoice if again she should be counted worthy to suffer. Then, when purified by trial, she goes forth to her holy work, poor Humanity will greet her with joy, as she comes preaching the gospel of peace. Yea, the Churches of the world will make answer to her call, as they welcome her to their fellowship, feeling that again, after long centuries of warfare, with one mouth and one heart they can all profess the "faith which was once delivered unto the saints."

CHAPTER VIII.

A DAY'S RAMBLE IN ROME.

WE have been out to-day, rambling about from one scene of interest to another, with no fixed plan, but wandering in accordance with the suggestion of the moment. There is one advantage in Rome, which is, that from our childhood we have been familiar with pictures and models of its antiquities, so that we recognize them at once. A guide-book is scarcely necessary. We are already acquainted with the story of each old ruin, and want nothing but a map to conduct us to the spot.

We first sought for the Pantheon, through the narrow, dirty streets which have been built up around it. So crowded indeed are the modern habitations, that it is impossible to find a spot from which this unrivaled edifice can be properly viewed. Eighteen centuries ago it was looked upon as faultless, and criticism since has been unable to urge an objection. In the reign of Augustus there were gathered within its walls statues of the gods, in gold, silver, bronze, and precious marbles. Since then it has been plundered of all that could be carried off, — the statues that graced its cornice, the bronze which adorned its dome, and the silver that lined the compartments of its roof within; yet its faultless proportions remain, the wonder of every age. The original inscription on the front still records that it was erected by Agrippa, and when we enter, we stand on the same marble pavement once trodden by Augustus. Its rotunda was so well adapted to the change, that with scarcely an alteration it passed from heathen worship to be used as a Christian church. Not only was Michael Angelo proud to copy it in the dome of St. Peter's, but even Constantinople is indebted to it for the plan of St. Sophia. Its spoils too are dispersed about the city. Its bronze forms the *Balacchino*, or grand canopy over the altar in St. Peter's; the basaltic lions which guarded the entrance now adorn the *Acqua Felice*, fountain of Sextus V.; and the beautiful porphyry sarcophagus which once stood in the portico, has been removed by the Corsini to their chapel in St. John Lateran, and instead of the ashes of Agrippa, now holds that of Clement XII.

Above is a circular opening, through which alone the light is admitted, and the interior therefore reflects every change in the atmosphere. The flush of morn, the golden radiance of noon, the purple hue which fills the air as the sun is going down, the gray twilight, and the passing shadow of the darkening tempest, all are repeated and mirrored on the antique marbles within. At night, too, it is strange to stand in this solemn temple, and see the stars shining brightly in the deep azure above, and the moon flooding the whole firmament with her glory, or seeming to chase the clouds which are rapidly flying past. And although the rain pours in year after year, and the Tiber at times in its overflow reaches the pavement, yet this beautiful relic of antiquity seems to defy alike the elements and the inroads of time. We see it indeed in its " disastrous twilight," for the ages which have gone have dimmed its brightness; yet it may well be questioned, whether the deep and mellow tints it has received from passing centuries do not impart a majesty it did not possess in the time of its early glory. It has too in our day a nobler consecration than when it was devoted to the gods of the old mythology. The niches which once their statues filled, are now occupied by the busts of those who were distinguished for genius or talent. "The dearest hope," says Corinne, "that the lovers of glory cherish, is that of obtaining a place here." Yet the visitor will pass the tombs of Winkelman, Metastasio, Poussin, and Annabal Carracci, to pause before a plain inscription on the wall, which tells us that Raphael is buried below. What a fit sepulchre for him, the divinest painter of his age, who died — not in the fullness of his years, but in the fullness of his powers — just living long enough to show the world how much it had lost!

But of such a building all descriptions are useless. The words of poetry seem more appropriate, and Childe Harold has summed up everything in a couple of stanzas: —

> "Simple, erect, severe, austere, sublime —
> Shrine of all saints and temple of all gods,
> From Jove to Jesus — spared and blest by time;
> Looking tranquillity, while falls or nods
> Arch, empire, each thing round thee, and man plods
> His way through thorns to ashes — glorious dome!
> Shalt thou not last? Time's scythe and tyrant's rods
> Shiver upon thee — sanctuary and home
> Of art and piety — Pantheon! — pride of Rome!

> "Relic of nobler days, and noblest arts!
> Despoil'd yet perfect, with thy circle spreads
> A holiness appealing to all hearts —
> To art a model; and to him who treads
> Rome for the sake of ages, glory sheds
> Her light through thy sole aperture; to those
> Who worship, here are altars for their beads:
> And they who feel for genius may repose
> Their eyes on honor'd forms, whose busts around them close."

We turned from it, looking back often to its Corinthian columns, and entering once more the labyrinth of narrow alleys, sought for the ruins of Pompey's Theatre. But a few massive fragments and arches now remain, and the circular shape of the building is principally traced by the manner in which we find the houses standing, as they were erected upon its foundations. Having been seized by the Orsini during the troubles of the twelfth century, while their strong hold, it was entirely leveled by feudal violence. Yet in its magnificent portico, which once contained an hundred columns, Appian tells us, Brutus sat in judgment on the morning of Caesar's death, and close by was the Senate House, in which —

> "Even at the base of Pompey's statue
> Which all the while ran blood, great Caesar fell."

From this spot so rich in historical recollections, we wound our way through the narrow and dirty Ghetto, which is allotted to the Jews. "Sufferance is the badge of all their tribe," and here the despised and oppressed Israelites must indeed realize it. In the midst of filth and noisome smells they are crowded together, restricted to this section of the city, while soldiers mount guard at the gates, which are every night closed and kept locked till morning. Even during a great inundation of the Tiber, when all this quarter of the city was under water, their petition for a change of residence was denied. As there happened to be no danger of their drowning, they were not permitted to escape until the regular time of opening the gates in the morning, nor at night were they allowed to seek refuge in any other place. Some of them are wealthy, but the meanest beggar who sleeps in the sun on the *Scala di Spagna*, if he pretend to be a Christian, thinks himself at liberty to spurn them from his path, nor does the smitten Jew dare even to remonstrate. With the Carnival comes their more public degradation. When the bell sounds to announce the beginning of the Festival, a deputation of their oldest members ascend to the Capitol, and there kneeling bareheaded before the Senator, ask permission for their people to reside for the ensuing year in Rome. This is granted them, on condition that they pay the expenses of the Carnival, and furnish the prizes, which are generally pieces of gay velvet. Even this is an improvement on their former state; for in old times they were obliged at this season themselves to run in races through the Corso, while the people shouted in derision as " the Jew dogs " exerted themselves for their amusement. Now they perform this by proxy, and hire the horses which exhibit. They are compelled also once in the year to be present in one of the Churches at a service which is intended for their express conversion. Where it is held we did not learn, though just without the gates of the Ghetto is a Church, having on its portal in Hebrew an inscription from Isaiah lxv. 2, " I have spread out my hands all the day unto a rebellious people, which walketh in a way that was not good, after their own thoughts." The situation of this Church would be convenient for the purpose, though the inscription is by no means complimentary or inviting. The Saturday before Easter is appointed for the baptism of the new converts, who have the honor of receiving that rite at St. John Lateran, in the porphyry vase which is said to have been used for the Emperor Constantine in the same service. Subjects are always found, although the unbelievers in Rome whisper, that one proselyte has appeared so often on this occasion, that he is now regarded as a regular part of the pageant.

We went through their quarter, where the lofty houses seemed bending over to meet each other from opposite sides of the narrow street. The shops were filled with the usual miscellaneous assortment of goods characteristic of the children of Israel — rags, old clothes, scraps of iron, worn-out umbrellas, and household utensils of all kinds. Every part was swarming like a perfect hive; men and women looking out of the windows, and children of all ages sprawling about the doors. Their countenances would anywhere have proclaimed their descent, as they screamed and gibbered to us, offering their petty wares for sale, and with the most forcible gesticulations inviting us to enter their shops. But with them how strangely different do the two extremes of life appear! The black-haired, black-eyed children grow up into beautiful maidens, and then change again to be perfectly hag-like in age, as if Nature was thus revenging herself for the prodigality with which her early favors were lavished.

As we left the Ghetto, we passed the ruins of the Theatre of Marcellus, its Doric columns still standing, embedded, as it were, in the neighboring houses, when suddenly we found ourselves in front of the old Palace of the Orsini. We knew it at once by the gigantic bear — the crest of the family — sculptured in stone on each side of the portal, and it reminded us of their old war-cry, "Beware the bear's hug!" which for ages sounded so often through the streets of Rome, as they met in conflict the adherents of the rival house of Colonna. Their old baronial Castle of Bracciano, twenty-five miles from Rome, is the finest of the kind in Italy. Vast in extent, lighted by Gothic windows, still containing the family portraits, the silk hangings, the antiquated furniture, and the armorial bearings of the Orisini, it is a complete picture of a feudal residence in the fifteenth century. It was the first place in the vicinity of Rome which Sir Walter Scott expressed any anxiety to visit, and he spent a day there listening with interest to the history of the turbulent lords of this ancient fortress. In the beginning of this century it was sold to Torlonia, the Pope's banker, who commenced life as a peddler, and whose son now holds it, deriving from the estate the old feudal title once borne by the Orsini — Duke of Bracciano.

We were looking, however, for the Temple of Vesta, and found its situation to agree with the description of Horace in the Ninth Satire, where he represents it as lying in his way from the *Via Sacra* to the Gardens of Cæsar *trans Tiberim*. But, when we reached it on the banks of the river, it needed no guide to inform us that this was the object of our search. There it was, so small, and light, and beautiful, that it seemed as if it might have been borne through the air by angels, as the legend tells us was done with our Lady's Holy

Chapel at Loretto. The wonder is, that it could have remained for so many ages, when massive buildings around were swept away. Yet, of its twenty Corinthian columns, only one is gone, and the little circular temple, with the pillars round it, is as graceful and elegant as when first erected. It was, indeed, worthy of its purpose; for among all the rites of ancient heathenism, there were none so pure and poetical as these. Here watched the consecrated virgins, whose care was only to tend the sacred fire. Noble by birth, the true fulfillment of their vow entitled them to loftier honors than mere nobility could claim; while, if they erred, theirs was a fearful death by which they paid the penalty of sin. There is more romance still lingering about this little temple than all the other antiquities of Rome.

Near the Temple of Vesta is that of Fortuna Virilis, whose Ionic columns, half buried in the earth, still show what it must have been in the beauty of its early day. While we were looking at it, one of the crowd of ragged young guides, who had been running round us with the most profuse offers of their services, pointed out a house in the neighborhood as that of Rienzi. The name attracted our attention, and upon examining the building, we found that it was the one which tradition has always marked out as the residence of "the last of the Tribunes,"[1] — he of whom Lord Byron speaks as "the hope of Italy — redeemer of dark centuries of shame." The edifice is a strange mixture of all kinds of architecture. A long inscription is deciphered by antiqua-

---

[1] "The first stars of night shone down on the ancient Temple of Fortuna Virilis, which the chances of time had already converted into the Church of St. Mary of Egypt; and facing the twice hallowed edifice stood the house of Rienzi. 'It is a fair omen to have my mansion facing the ancient Temple of Fortune,' said Rienzi, smiling."—Bulwer's *Rienzi*.

rians as setting forth the pompous titles of Rienzi, while another on the architrave of one of the windows is ascribed to Petrarch. He was in Rome during the Jubilee, and may at that time have caused it to be affixed. We know that his admiration of Rienzi was great, and he was the "Spirto Gentile" of his beautiful Canzone, "Italia mia." The friendship, however, of the poet for the Tribune was the source of many trials to the former. In his distant retreat at Vaucluse he heard of the revolution which had been effected at Rome, and, animated by his love of freedom, addressed to the bold reformer an epistle, in which he exhorts him to complete the good work faithfully, remembering that the world and posterity were his judges. But, unfortunately, the old Cardinal Colonna was Petrarch's great patron, and when in the struggle which ensued at Rome, between the barons and the new power, six of the Colonnas perished, the poet seems scarcely to have known with which party to side. At length he wrote a tardy letter of consolation to the Cardinal, in which we can see most clearly the struggle in the mind between his gratitude to the family, and his sense of higher obligations to Italy.

In full view of this building stands the massive Arch of Janus Quadrifons, which in the Middle Ages underwent the usual fate of these monuments, and was transformed into a fortress by the Frangipani family. The remains of the battlements of brick work, which they erected on its top, are still visible. It is, indeed, strange, when we remember the use to which these buildings were then put by the great Roman families, that so many of them have survived to our day. Besides this Arch, the Frangipani seized on the Coliseum; the Orsini on the Tomb of Hadrian and the Theatre of Pompey; the Colonna family on the Mausoleum of Augustus and the Baths of Constantine; the Tomb of Cœcilia Metella was converted into a fortress by the Savelli and the Gætani; the ruins of the Capitol were held by the Corsi; the Quirinal by the Conti, and the Pantheon by the garrison of the Popes.

Nor is much greater respect for antiquities shown in the present day. The magnificent remains of the Temple of Antoninus Pius are now converted into the Dogana, or Custom House, while its portico — one of the noblest of ancient Rome — is walled up to form magazines. The Mausoleum of Augustus is degraded into a wretched Circus, where the spectators sit round on wooden seats as in an amphitheatre, while beneath them are the vaults in which once rested the remains of Augustus, and Livia, and Tiberius. In the wall is inserted a slab of marble, which their grateful fellow-citizens have placed in honor of divers actors and equestrians, who there covered themselves with immortal glory in the presence of admiring thousands! And yet, this is the tomb hallowed by the touching lines of Virgil, which he wrote when the young Marcellus became its first occupant! But a still more curious scene may be witnessed by one who will take the trouble to wind his way through the narrow streets and alleys which lead to the fish-market. There, almost every stall has for its counter a slab of marble, taken from some antique monument or temple, and sprats and gudgeons are flouncing about upon old Latin inscriptions, which elsewhere would be a treasure to the antiquary. Here, however, their very abundance deprives them of interest. About the market-place, too, are ancient columns, the inscriptions on which show that they were of the age of Antoninus.

Every place, indeed, teems with the relics of old Rome's magnificence. Pillars and cornices, richly sculptured, are seen masoned into the walls of the most common houses. Granite and porphyry pillars are so plentiful that they cease to have any value. In the churches are ornaments torn from Pagan temples, which there produce often a most incongruous effect. That of St. John Lateran is filled with marble columns, from the tomb of Hadrian and the Capitol, on which the old emblems still remain. Some have carved upon them the geese which preserved the city, others Gothic and Arabic ornaments. In St. Agnes, *bas-reliefs*, turned for convenience face downward, are used to form a staircase. These are the sights which meet us on every side.

But to return to our excursion. We were now upon the verge of the modern city, and before us was the more open country, with the scattered ruins of ancient Rome. We had already advanced further than we first intended, yet induced by the beauty of the weather we still went on, one object of interest leading us to another. We found ourselves near the *Cloaca Maxima* — those immense sewers said to have been built by Tarquinius Priscus, the fifth king of Rome, only one hundred and fifty years after the foundation of the city. Livy, Strabo, and Dionysius, all describe them as evidences of Roman greatness. Pliny, nearly eighteen centuries ago, recorded his admiration, and expressed surprise that they had lasted eight hundred years uninjured. Ancient authors tell us that a cart loaded with hay could pass under the arch; and when Agrippa cleansed them in the reign of Augustus, he went through them in a boat, to which Pliny probably alludes in the expression, "urbs subter navigata."

To my mind, however, the existence of these works is one proof that there was a city on this spot long before the days of Romulus. I number them with those traces we here and there find of earlier ages of a mysterious civilization which in Italy preceded the birth of Rome — a period when the massive Etruscan tombs were built, and those temples were reared in Pæstum, which two thousand years ago the Romans were accustomed to visit as antiquities. And I am happy to find that such is the view which Ferguson has given in his history. "These works," he says, "are still supposed to remain; but as they exceed the power and resources of the present city to keep them in repair, they are quite concealed, except at one or two places. They were, in the midst of Roman greatness, and still are, reckoned among the wonders of the world, and yet they are said to have been works of the elder Tarquin, a prince whose territory did not extend, in any direction, above sixteen miles; and on this supposition they must have been made to accommodate a city that was calculated chiefly for the reception of cattle, herdsmen, and banditti. Rude nations sometimes execute works of great magnificence, as fortresses and temples, for the purposes of war and superstition; but seldom palaces, and still more seldom works of mere convenience and cleanliness, in which, for the most part, they are long defective. It is not unreasonable, therefore, to question the authority of tradition in respect to this singular monument of antiquity, which so greatly exceeds what the best accommodated city of modern Europe could undertake for its own convenience. And as these works are still entire, and may continue so for thousands of years, it may be suspected, that they were even prior to the settlement of Romulus, and may have been the remains of a more ancient city, on the ruins of which the followers of Romulus settled, as the Arabs now hut or encamp on the ruins of Palmyra and Balbeck. Livy owns that the common sewers were not accommodated to the plan of Rome, as it was laid out in his time; they were carried in directions across the streets, and passed under buildings of the greatest antiquity. This derangement, indeed, he imputes to the hasty rebuilding of the city after its destruction by the Gauls; but haste, it is probable, would have determined the people to build on their old foundations, or at least not to change them so much as to cross the direction of former streets." [1]

At this day, these massive works are as entire as when the foundations were first laid, and are a lasting memorial of the solidity of Etruscan architecture. The huge blocks, put together without cement, still stand unmoved, and the archway, fourteen feet high by as many broad, expands before us as it did to the view of the Romans, twenty-five centuries ago. Yet above it is a bright, clear spring, the Acqua Argentina, or Silver Water, which comes bubbling forth and disappears under the old arch, while its beautiful stream is the more delightful, because we scarcely expect to meet with it in a spot intended for such different purposes.

We were now near the ruined palace of the Cæsars, but passed it, winding around the base of the Palatine Mount, attracted by the gigantic arches of the Baths of

[1] *Progress and Termination of the Roman Republic*, bk. i. ch. i. note.

Caracalla, which lie still further beyond. They are situated on the eastern slope of the Aventine, and next to the Coliseum are the most massive remains of ancient Rome. More than a mile in circuit, they are a perfect labyrinth of magnificent ruins. They consisted originally of six enormous halls, above two hundred feet in height, the crumbling walls of which alone remain, while the deep blue sky above is their sole canopy. The interior stretches out like vast lawns, on which some elms have grown up, spreading their branches till they touch the ruined walls. In one of the ancient buttresses still remains a winding staircase, by which you can ascend to the top of these lofty arches, and there pass around among the broken masses which rise like mountains, sometimes treading on the very verge of a deep chasm, and then climbing some crag, whose rough masonry is entirely overgrown with foliage and vegetation. Yet in all this there seems to be no air of desolation. Everything is softened down and veiled by the luxuriance of nature. Wherever the stones are reft asunder, a perfect wilderness of flowering shrubs has filled up the chasm, covering the roughness of the shattered sides. The myrtle, the bay, and the white blossoms of the laurustinus, are entwined with the profusion of creeping vines, which are produced in this luxuriant soil.

We sat down on a block of marble, and thought of the past. What a scene of splendor was this in its early day — in those years when the Romans, enervated by luxury, sought out daily new pleasures, and were fast preparing for their "decline and fall!" And yet to-day we were treading on the mouldering ruins of all this old magnificence, and except the *custode* appearing occasionally through some shattered arch, not a living creature was seen to break in upon the solitude. Lofty arches, with ivy clinging to them in every direction, and hanging in deep festoons; wide saloons, where formerly the gay thousands of Roman citizens gathered; mosaic pavements, as bright and beautiful as they were seventeen centuries ago, and representing still the *athletæ* of that day; fragments of ancient sculpture,— these were around us, covering the hill in strange confusion.

Among these ruins, too, Shelley was accustomed to linger, and here were shaped into being those noble creations which he has given us in his " Prometheus Unbound." In the preface he says, — " This poem was chiefly written upon the mountainous ruins of the Baths of Caracalla, among the flowery glades and thickets of odoriferous blossoming trees, which are extended in ever-winding labyrinths upon its immense platforms, and dizzy arches suspended in the air. The bright blue sky of Rome, and the effect of the vigorous awakening Spring in that divinest climate, and the new life with which it drenches the spirits, even to intoxication, were the inspirations of the Drama."

CHAPTER IX.

EPIPHANY SERVICES. — GREEK RITUAL. — THE BAMBINO. — VESPERS AT THE PROPAGANDA.

THE Festival of the Epiphany seems to be one much honored here, indeed quite as much so as that of the Nativity. The churches are all thronged, and the day is celebrated by their most splendid services. The Pope himself performs High Mass in the Sistine Chapel; but as we had already witnessed that service in St. Peter's, we preferred being present at one which takes place only on this single day in the course of the year.

Among the dignified ecclesiastics residing in Rome, are many foreign bishops, such as the Greek, Armenian, etc. They are to be seen in grand ceremonies, forming a part of the processions, and by the variety of their costumes, adding to the splendor of the pageant. A few days before, in a long conversation with an ecclesiastic of the Church of Rome, I endeavored to discover the precise position of the Greek Bishop, with whom I found he was intimate. He admitted that the Bishop had no jurisdiction at the East, no fixed diocese, but said that his duty was to ordain the Greek missionaries sent to those parts from Rome. "Is his authority acknowledged by the Greek Church?" I inquired. "Yes," said he, "by the Catholic portion of that Church, but not by the schismatics." I saw, of course, that he meant by "the Catholic portion," the few Romish missionaries scattered through the East, and by "the schismatics," the great body of that Church; and therefore said,—" Then, to put it in plain language, he is looked upon by the Greek Church in the East, as Bishop Hughes is regarded by our Church in New York, we acknowledging the jurisdiction of another bishop?" He looked at me for a moment with a smile, and then replied, — " Exactly."

In truth, these foreign bishops, with dioceses which they have never perhaps seen, are merely retained here as parts of the pageants of the Church. They appear at the Court of Rome as the spiritual heads of millions in the East, who entirely disown their authority and have no connection with them, but at the same time, with the many strangers here, they strengthen the idea of the perfect Catholicity of this Church. They give the appearance of a visible unity extending through the world, which in reality has no existence.

In the *Via Babuino* stands a church, which, daily as I passed it, attracted my attention, from the fact that it seemed always to be closed. While every other church in Rome has its doors open for any transient worshipper who may wish to offer his devotions, morning, noontide, or evening, this was the solitary exception. Week days, and festivals, and even Sundays passed, and still it was entirely deserted. We now, however, found an explanation of the mystery. It is the Church of St. Athanasius, subject to the jurisdiction of the Greek Bishop, and as there is no one to attend it, is only open on a single day in the year. This is on the Festival of the Epiphany, when High Mass is performed according to the ritual of the Greek Church. We saw it announced in the "Diario di Roma," and having determined to avail ourselves of what might be the only opportunity which would ever occur of witnessing this service, we repaired at an early hour to the Church. It is quite small, without anything in the architecture or paintings to attract attention, and from being so little opened, had the damp and chilly feeling of a vault. The congregation seemed to be composed almost entirely of English, drawn like ourselves by curiosity.

The Greek Bishop entered with a procession, and the choir at once commenced their anthem. He is not more than forty-five years of age, with a coal-black beard covering his breast, and has one of the the most noble voices I have ever heard. The costumes were all different from those of the Roman Church; the Greek cross instead of the Latin was embroidered on every part; the features and long beards of the attending priests plainly showed their eastern origin; and every thing united to give the service a peculiarly oriental appearance. The Bishop himself came in clothed in purple, and after being escorted to his seat, robes of white and gold were brought, and his attendants commenced arraying him in them. This process occupied nearly half an hour. Whenever he took part in the service, a priest knelt before him with a large open volume, bound in white and gold, from which he chanted his part.

The service was much longer than the Mass of the Roman Church, but composed of the same kind of ceremonies, — kneeling, crossing, chanting, the waving of censers, and processions of lights. There is, however, an evident significancy and meaning in some of the ceremonies, which requires but little explanation to be understood even by a careless spectator. For example, the Bishop frequently held up before the people branches of lights, that in his right hand containing three, and that in his left, two. This has been adopted to express their faith in the doctrine of the Trinity; heresies on this subject being those by which the Greek Church has been most troubled. The three lights signify the Three Persons in the Trinity; and the two lights, the Two distinct Natures of our Lord. The High Altar was behind a screen, the part immediately in front of it being open. At the consecration of the elements, when the Bishop was standing before the altar, this was closed by a curtain, and for some time his voice only was indistinctly heard, while he himself was unseen. This is a custom which has been for ages adopted in the Greek Church. It was at first commenced as a measure of precaution, because the rite of Baptism had been exposed to public ridicule on the stage, and they wished to guard that of the Eucharist from a similar profanation. They considered, too, that such mystery was conformable to the nature of this solemn Institution, and therefore concealed the priest from public view, and environed him, as the high priest of old when he entered the Holy of Holies, with the awful solitude of the sanctuary.[1]

Upon the whole, as a mere matter of taste and splendor, I prefer the Greek ritual to the Latin. It is certainly in some parts more imposing than anything we have seen in the Mass of the Roman Church. A living writer — whose opinion, however, must be taken with some allowance, on account of his overweening

[1] Eustace, *Classical Tour*, vol. ii. p. 40.

admiration of Rome — thus contrasts the two services: "Two observable characteristics of the Greek ritual, are its very dramatic nature and its humility. Its dramatic, one might almost say over-dramatic disposition may be seen particularly in the ceremonies of the Holy Week, compared with those at Rome. Its humility, in the forms of Baptism, receiving confessions, and absolving penitents. . . . . Without presuming to criticize the Liturgies of the two Churches, it may be allowable to note, that while the Greek ritual of the Eucharist is more dramatic, so to speak, than the Roman, it is scarcely so magnificent in its tone, or so rich in mystical expositions, neither does it exhibit that quickness at catching expressions of Scripture, and representing them in devotional gestures, which is so marvelous in the rubrics of the Roman Missal."[1]

The great service of the day however was in the Church of S. Maria d'Ara Cœli. This is a strange looking building on the Capitoline Hill, erected on the foundation of the old Roman temple of Jupiter Feretrius, in which the Spolia Opima were deposited. The ascent to it is by one hundred and twenty-four steps of Grecian marble taken from an ancient temple of Romulus, near the Porta Salaria. They were constructed in 1348, the expense being defrayed by the alms of the faithful after the great plague which Boccacio has so admirably described as afflicting Florence in that year. The age of the Church itself is unknown, although all agree in ascribing to it an antiquity not lower than the sixth century. Upon entering, your first impression is, that it is composed of an

[1] F. W. Faber.

assemblage of fragments. The materials have indeed been plundered indiscriminately from every ancient building within reach, and of the twenty-two large columns which separate the nave from the side aisles, no two are alike. Some are of Egyptian granite, and some of marble; some white and some black; two are Corinthian pillars elegantly fluted, and the rest are plain. The capitals, too, are all different, and as none of the pillars were originally of the same length, it was of course necessary to raise them on pedestals of various heights. The grotesque effect produced by this variety may be imagined. On one of the pillars is the inscription in antique letters — " A CUBICULO AUGUSTORUM " — which would seem to prove that the Church was built with the spoils of the palace of the Cæsars. The pavement formed of mosaic of the most rare and precious marbles, is uneven with age, and the sculptured images of knights and bishops who sleep beneath are rapidly disappearing under the tread of the thousands who pass over their resting-place. My principal interest in this building, however, arose from its connection with Gibbon, whose fascinating narrative must so often recur to the mind while dwelling in "the Eternal City." It was in this Church, as he himself tells us, "on the 15th of October, 1764, as he sat musing amidst the ruins of the Capitol, while the barefooted friars were singing Vespers, that the idea of writing the 'Decline and Fall' of the city first started to his mind."

To the Romanist, on the contrary, this Church derives its veneration from a miraculous wooden figure of the infant Saviour, called the *Santissimo Bambino*, to which they ascribe especial power in curing the sick. The legend is, that a Franciscan pilgrim carved it out of an olive-tree which grew on the Mount of Olives, and while he was sleeping over his work, St. Luke appeared and painted the image. It is a coarse daub, like divers portraits of our Lord which we have seen ascribed to St. Luke, from all of which — if we believed in their authenticity — we should draw the inference, that his talents as an artist were somewhat below those of a very ordinary sign-painter. The image is placed in a side chapel, and dressed most richly, while gems and jewelry sparkle on all parts of it. Over the infant is bending the Virgin in an elegant modern ball dress — red satin, with cord and tassel round her waist; splendid necklace, with a veil gracefully falling over her and fastened to the back of her head. Around them are pasteboard figures of the shepherds and the wise men, the oxen and the ass, while the picture is completed by canvas side-scenes, background, and clouds. The view seems to extend far into the distance, and there are the hills and palm-trees and all the features of an oriental landscape. Altogether, it is quite pretty, and the deception is as well managed as it usually is in the theatre.

On the Festival of the Epiphany this scene is all represented on a stage erected near the altar, and crowds of peasantry from the neighboring country throng the Church. In the afternoon the Bambino was brought out in solemn procession. First came the Cardinals, who offered gifts, — I suppose in imitation of the Magi, — and then the image was solemnly carried round the Church amidst kneeling thousands. The sick, and the halt, and the blind were there, "that at least the shadow of" the wooden image "passing by might overshadow some of them." Mothers held up their sick children, that they might be restored to health by a sight of the miraculous Bambino. Afterwards the procession moved to the front of the Church, where the open square on the Capitoline Hill was crowded by thousands. Here once more the image was elevated to bless the prostrate multitudes, and then for another twelvemonth it was restored to its theatrical little chapel.

In the evening we went to the Chapel of the Propaganda, which by the way is not open to ladies except on this single day. This Institution is celebrated throughout the world as the one where missionaries are educated for all heathen lands. The Armenian Bishop — a venerable looking man with a long white beard — was present at the service, which was the ordinary Vespers. The students, about eighty in number, were ranged on the two sides of the Chapel, and presented a strange mixture of all nations and colors. I counted among them, five Chinese and two Africans. Yet here they all sat side by side, without any distinction, singing together the praises of their common Lord. Surely, it must be acknowledged, that in this respect Rome carries out her own Catholic principles and declares, not only in words but by her actions, that "God hath made of one blood all nations of men for to dwell on all the face of the earth." She recognizes no distinctions of climate or country in the house of God. We had just before, as we entered the door of the Chapel, witnessed a similar evidence of this Catholic spirit. An old man, black as possible, in a clerical dress, was just getting into a carriage.

He was assisted by two priests, who with many bows and demonstrations of respect were taking leave of him. I afterwards learned, that he was an Abyssinian priest, who having spent the greater part of his life in missionary labors in his own country, had now returned to die at Rome.

The chanting at the Chapel this evening was without any pretensions to the character of fine music, yet there was something to me very inspiring in the sound. Perhaps it arose in part from the fact, that I knew what they were singing — only the pure words of inspiration, which two thousand years ago were sung on the mountains and among the valleys of Judea, and had ever since been the sacred hymns of the Christian Church. They were the regular Vesper Psalms for the evening, in the rich and picturesque language of the Vulgate, where the orientalism of Scripture is blended up with such curious felicity with the idiom of the Latin.[1] The chanting was antiphonal, the forty students ranged on one side singing the first verse, and immediately those on the other side taking up the strain and singing the second. In the middle of the Chapel stood a high lectern, and when each Psalm was ended, seven or eight students — among whom were two Chinese — left their places and gathered around it, to lead the singing of the *Gloria Patri*, in which the whole assembly on both sides joined. The organ was pealing overhead as an accompaniment, and when I heard the deep-toned sound of so many manly voices chanting the rich Latin words, and saw the upturned faces of those who stood about the lectern, I felt that it was indeed a solemn and impressive ser-

---

[1] Milman's *History of Christianity*, vol. ii. p. 334.

vice. Widely as we might differ on many points, here at least was a common ground. The words they sang were the heritage of each branch alike of the Christian Church, and if uttered with a true heart fervently, might well raise them above the cares of this lower world, to the same lofty devotion which elevated the spirit of the kingly poet, when he indited these sublime strains.

CHAPTER X.

THE TOMBS OF THE LAST STUARTS.

THE last of the Stuarts died at Rome, where the palace which they occupied in the *Piazza de S. S. Apostoli,* to this day bears the name of the *Palazzo del Pretendente.* The *Villa Muti,* too, which the Cardinal York owned, has still some relics of the family, — a portrait of Charles I., a bust of the Cardinal, a picture of the *fête* given on his promotion to the Sacred College, his favorite walking stick, having on it an ivory head of Charles I., and a bust of the Chevalier de St. George. Sir Walter Scott, when in Rome, inspected these relics with the liveliest interest. He admired the situation of the Villa, commanding a splendid view over the Campagna, but at the same time remarked, while deploring the fate of his favorite princes, that "this was a poor substitute for all the splendid palaces to which they were heirs in England and Scotland." [1]

Justly as the Stuarts were expelled from England, there is still something in the fall of a line which for ages had worn crowns and borne sceptres, that cannot but enlist our sympathy. We felt this when we were travelling in their native land — visiting the deserted palaces of Holyrood and Linlithgow, where once they held their court, or seeing the monuments of the

[1] Lockhart's *Life,* vol. vii. p. 275.

early members of their race. The chivalrous traits, indeed, which marked so many of them, particularly in the old wars of Scotland, — the gallant death of James, when he disdained to fly from the lost battle, but fell in his knightly harness on Flodden field; the bold attempt of the young Charles Edward, when he landed at Moidart with only seven attendants to recover his ancestral throne; the gentle spirit and mournful fate of the first Charles; the sufferings of Queen Mary; the romantic history of Arabella Stuart, — all these recollections seemed to crowd upon us, awaken our interest, and almost redeemed the character of the family.

It was to the Chateau of St. Germain, near Paris, that James II. retired when driven from England, and here he held the shadow of a court for twelve years, until his death. When in Paris, therefore, we felt an interest in finding his tomb, which after some inquiry we learned was in the Chapel of the *Collége des Écossais*, within the city, — an institution founded in 1325 by David, Bishop of Moray in Scotland. One morning we repaired thither, and summoning the porter, made known our wish to see the Chapel. He conducted us to it, — a small and simple apartment paved with marble, — but we looked around in vain for any monuments. None were to be seen except the inscriptions on the pavement, which told us that below were buried some old Scottish Bishops, whose armorial bearings were there carved upon their tombs, and whose names — Barclay and Beatoun — are familiar to those acquainted with the history of their native land.

Not seeing what we wished, we inquired for the

tomb of King James. The *custode* at once led us into an adjoining room which, he said, had once been part of the Chapel. Its appearance was antique from the style of the carved seats around it, and the stained glass of the pointed window. At one end was a large alcove concealed by a curtain of heavy crimson velvet. Our guide drew it aside, and before us was the massive tomb of the last Stuart king that reigned in England. It is about ten feet high, of black and white marble, executed in 1703, two years after his death. His heart is all that was interred here, the rest of his body being buried at St. Germain where he died, and where another monument to his memory has been placed by order of George IV. This one was erected by his faithful friend and the constant companion of his exile, James, Duke of Perth, governor of his son, the Pretender, who afterwards assumed the title of James III. On the top of the monument was formerly an urn of bronze gilt, containing the brain of the king. It was in that day the custom with distinguished individuals, to have the parts of their body interred in different places, and we saw the same thing in Vienna, where the Royal House of Austria are buried in one chapel, while in another are their hearts in silver and gold urns. To this College also — as is mentioned in the long Latin inscription on the monument — the king confided all his valuable manuscripts, but they unfortunately disappeared during the French Revolution.

On the pavement, in front of the king's monument, is a slab over the heart of the queen, and another over the remains of Maria Louisa, their second daughter. Around them are inscriptions in memory of James

Drummond, Duke of Perth; Mary Gordon of Huntley, Duchess of Perth; the second Duke of the same name, who died in 1720; John Caryl, Lord Dunford; the Duchess of Tyrconnel; Sir Patrick Monteath; Sir Marian O'Conoly; Dr. Andrew Hay; Dr. Lewis Innes, Confessor to James II.; and Dr. Robert Barclay. The little band who followed their exiled king in his years of banishment, and shared his fallen fortunes, are here sleeping together about his monument. They were faithful to him in life, "and in their death they were not divided."

When the visitor is wandering through St. Peter's at Rome, pausing every moment before some splendid tomb of a Pope, where the skill of Michael Angelo, or Bernini, or Canova has been lavished on the statuary, there are two monuments which will particularly arrest his attention. One is a richly decorated tomb against the wall, intended to commemorate the virtues of Maria Clementina Sobieski, wife of the Chevalier de St. George, only son of James II. At its base is a porphyry sarcophagus partially covered with alabaster drapery, in which her body is deposited. Above is a female figure, holding in her hand a medallion portrait of the queen, the size of life. It is of mosaic, but so perfect in its execution that it cannot be distinguished from a highly finished painting. In the inscription on the tomb, her titles are enumerated, and among them she is styled — "Queen of Great Britain, France, and Ireland," She was the granddaughter of King John Sobieski, who defeated the Turks at Vienna, and at the time of her marriage in 1715 was called the greatest fortune in Europe. She died at Rome in 1755.

Immediately opposite to it, against one of the broad pillars of the Church, is the celebrated monument executed by Canova to the last of this unfortunate family. Sir William Gell, who was in Rome when Scott arrived there, says that he accompanied him to St. Peter's, which was one of the first places he resolved to visit, that he might see the tomb of the last of the Stuarts. To me it was the most interesting spot in this vast building, and often as I passed through it, I felt inclined to turn from the gorgeous monuments around to this more simple tomb which recorded the termination of the long struggle of a gallant race, having on its enduring marble the proud claims which they did not abandon even in death. It is a white marble mausoleum, about fifteen feet high, on the upper part of which are sculptured the royal arms of England. Below are three portraits in *bas-relief*. Two of them are in half armor, and the third in an ecclesiastical dress. They are intended to represent the son and grandsons of James II., the last of whom died here as Cardinal York. Beneath is the inscription, — " JACOBO III. JACOBI II. MAGNÆ BRIT. REGIS FILIO, KAROLO EDVARDO, ET HENRICO, DECANO PATRVM CARDINALIVM, JACOBI III. FILIIS, REGLÆ STIRPIS STVARDLÆ POSTREMIS, ANNO MDCCCXIX." The lower part of the monument is occupied by a representation of paneled doors, closed as if never again to be opened, and on each side of them stands an angel with an inverted torch, guarding the entrance. These two female figures are beautiful, and looking mournfully down, they seem to be the guardian genii of the ill-fated family, thus watching over their last resting-place. Above the door is the quotation, —

"BEATI MORTUI QUI IN DOMINO MORIUNTUR."

The bodies of these last representatives of the Stuart race are in the crypt under the Church. While going through the vaults, I looked for their tomb in vain, and when we had passed nearly to the end, inquired of the young priest who accompanied us with his lighted taper, where it was? He said, we must return, and he would show it. We did so, and he pointed it out — a plain slab of marble, so small that we had passed it unnoticed among the many inscriptions around. It is against the wall, a few feet from the pavement, while immediately below it is a projection, about six feet long by three broad, which he touched with his hand, and told us, that within this were the bodies. Yet even in these dark passages, speaking only of death, and surrounded by the memorials of those who had long since gone down to the dust, the same lofty claims are held forth. The inscription on that simple stone announces to us, that we stand by the sepulchre of "JAMES THE THIRD, CHARLES THE THIRD, AND HENRY THE NINTH, KINGS OF ENGLAND." As the elder brother descended to the tomb, the younger assumed the barren title he had not power to enforce, and bore it in testimony of his rights, until he had done with earthly crowns forever. There is something melancholy in this inscription, when we remember how vainly, yet how gallantly they fought to regain their hereditary throne, and how many thousands were loyal to them even unto death, ascending the scaffold rather than desert the cause of the ancient line.

We felt indeed as we stood by their tomb, that a

more appropriate place for their sepulchre could not be found. They were exiled from England for their attachment to the Church of Rome, and in the noblest temple which that faith has ever reared — the most magnificent indeed which the world has ever seen — they have found their last resting-place. There their gallant hearts are mouldering, the sufferings of their exile atoning for the errors of their regal sway.

CHAPTER XI.

THE COLISEUM. — PALACE OF THE CÆSARS. — BATHS.

THE Coliseum is what formerly passed under the name of the Flavian Amphitheatre, and is now the noblest remnant of old Rome. It is, however, only a massive ruin — the mighty skeleton of what it must have been, when, thronged by the gay population of the city, its seats were occupied by nearly one hundred thousand spectators. Begun by Vespasian ten years after the destruction of Jerusalem, many thousand captive Jews were employed in its construction; and when it was finished, in the days of Titus, five thousand wild beasts were slain in the arena during the games, which lasted a hundred days, in honor of its dedication. Such was its first baptism of blood, when the fierce animal of the desert, and the still fiercer human being with whom he fought, poured out their lives together upon its sands. Here, for four hundred years, the gladiatorial shows took place, and many a wounded combatant rolled his eyes around these lofty seats, to see in despair only the signal that he was to have no mercy. To this spot, in the reign of Trajan, Ignatius was brought from Antioch to be devoured by lions, and thus, — to use his own words, — "like God's own corn, he was ground between the teeth of the wild beasts." The last martyr who died here was an eastern monk, Telemachus, who, in the reign of Honorius, travelled to Rome to protest against these barbarous exhibitions. In his noble enthusiasm he leaped into the arena to separate the combatants, and was torn to pieces by the infuriated spectators.[1] But the impression produced by this voluntary sacrifice was so profound, that the Emperor issued an edict prohibiting these bloody shows.

The Romans seem to have been a race, sanguinary beyond the ordinary rules of our nature. Even women shared in the ferocity of their mortal combats. They crowded these lofty seats around us, to watch the fortunes of the fight, when naked barbarians were arrayed against each other, in a contest from which only one must retire alive. In all their amphitheatres — here, and at Nismes, and at Pompeii — we find honorable places provided for the vestal virgins; and not only were they present, but it was their privilege to give the fatal signal, which condemned to instant death the wretch who had been unsuccessful in the fight, and to watch that the bloody mandate was thoroughly obeyed. A more fearful picture cannot be drawn than that which Prudentius gives of such a scene, —

> "Virgo — consurgit ad ictus,
> Et quoties victor ferrum jugulo inserit, illa
> Delicias ait esse, suas, pectusque jacentis
> Virgo modesta jubet, converso pollice, rumpi;
> Ni lateat pars ulla animæ vitalibus imis,
> Altius impresso dum palpitat ense secutor." [2]

So deep rooted, indeed, was this passion, that it seems to have acted like a frenzy even on those whose reason protested against it. St. Augustine tells us of a Christian young man, who, being induced by his asso-

---

[1] Theodoret, v. 26.   [2] Prudent. adv. Sym. ii. 1095.

ciates to enter the amphitheatre, for a time resolutely kept his eyes closed. At length, a tremendous shout of the spectators induced him to look out on the arena. The instant he caught the sight of blood, he seemed to imbibe the ferocious spirit of those around him; he shouted, he cheered on the combatants, he was possessed with an uncontrollable fury, and when he departed, the desire to return was too irresistible to be withstood.[1] Such was Roman character. Indeed, a greater contrast cannot be given than that which existed between the elegant theatrical shows of the Greeks, where they assembled to listen to the lofty tragedies of Æschylus or Sophocles, and the brutal exhibitions of this arena, for which the Roman populace gathered. And yet these separate scenes but illustrate the different characters of the two nations.

These bloody shows, too, were often on a gigantic scale, which we should suppose could hardly have been witnessed without insanity. We will give — in the expressive language of another — one single instance, that of the Emperor Claudius at the Lacus Fucinus. "It is one mighty theatre: the terraces of the Abruzzo are covered with eager and delighted spectators. Claudius himself, with the bloody Agrippina, the young Nero, and the infamous favorite, Narcissus, is seated at the awful show. There are slaves and criminals to the number of nineteen thousand. They are divided off into two fleets, to fight against each other on the lake. As they defile past the Emperor, they cry, 'Hail! O Emperor! The dying salute thee.' The Emperor returns the salutation in such a way, that the poor wretches believe they are pardoned, and break

---

[1] August. *Conf.* vi. 8.

forth into a frantic tumult of rejoicing, for they love life like other men, and have red blood in their bodies, and each of them a soul as immortal as thine, O Claudius. But pardon? Are all these spectators on the shelving slopes of the lake-girdling Abruzzo to be disappointed? The Emperor descends to the brink, and explains the mistake, and bids the prætorians goad the reluctant victims on board the ships, and nineteen thousand immortal beings, for whom Christ had died some twenty years before, murdered each other in a mock battle, for the pleasure of the Roman Emperor and people."[1]

It was a solemn thought, therefore, as we stood in this arena, and remembered the nature of the amusements in which the fierce multitudes of Rome rejoiced, that here for four centuries death had reaped a most abundant harvest. Leopards from the East; lions from Africa; bears from the far North; and whatever strange and rare animals the conquered provinces could anywhere furnish, were used to slaughter the helpless slaves, whose lives they considered of no value except to contribute to their sports. Here, too, was poured forth the blood of many who died to bequeath the pure faith to us; and those seats, which towered so high above us, were once filled by crowds, rejoicing with savage exultation to see how a Christian could die. Recollections, therefore, of bitter suffering crowded on us as we thought of its old magnificence, and we felt that dark must be the Penates which guarded these majestic ruins.

The latest scene of bloodshed which took place within these walls, was in the fourteenth century, and worthy of a brief notice, as giving some insight into

[1] F. W. Faber.

the manners of the times. It was in September, A. D. 1332, that the population of Rome, like their fathers ten centuries before, crowded again the old Coliseum. It had been resolved to exhibit there a bull-fight, after the Moorish and Spanish fashion, and proclamations had been sent through all Italy, inviting the young nobles to exhibit their skill and valor. The day had now arrived, and temporary seats covered these timeworn stones, while on different sides were three balconies, lined with scarlet cloth, for the three divisions of Roman ladies who were to grace the sports by their presence. The matrons from the Trastevere, beyond the Tiber, boasting of the pure blood of ancient Rome, and retaining in every feature the haughty lineaments of antiquity, were led by the fair Jacova di Rovere; while the nobility of the city were as usual divided between the rival houses of the Colonna and the Orsini. The charms of Savella Orsini — says Gibbon, to whom we are indebted for this description — are mentioned with praise, while the Colonna regretted the absence of the youngest of their house, who had sprained her ankle in the garden of Nero's tower. Contemporary annalists give the colors and devices of some twenty of the most conspicuous knights, and their names are among the most illustrious of the Papal States. Such were Malatesta, Savelli, Conti, Annabaldi, Altieri, and Corsi. None of the Orsini took the field, though three of their hereditary enemies, the Colonnas, were among the combatants. They each bore the device of their house, the single column, with inscriptions denoting the lofty greatness they claimed for their family: " Though sad, I am strong ; " " Strong as I am great ; " " If I fall, you fall with me." The latter was indeed the motto usually borne by this princely house, and was considered as addressed to the Roman people, intimating that the Colonna family was the support of the state, and if one fell, the other would be involved in the same ruin. Each champion, in succession, descended into the arena alone, with a single spear, to encounter a wild bull. The combats were dangerous and bloody, a curious renewal of the old conflicts which once took place on this same arena. In proportion, too, they were equally fatal, for eighteen of these volunteers were killed, and nine wounded. But the old chroniclers seem to think that this also had its use; for though many of the noblest families in Rome were called to mourn, yet the pomp of the funerals at the churches of St. John Lateran and St. Maria Maggiore furnished a second holyday to the people.[1]

It was on a bright sunny morning that we first went over these ruins, which awaken such a host of varied recollections. As we stood on the highest arch and looked down into the arena, and round on the wasted Campagna, all seemed as calm and peaceful as if no scene of human suffering could ever have been occurring there. Not a sound was heard, except the notes of the birds singing among the ivy which had forced itself between the stones. But these remains are in their massive character unlike anything else we have seen. The immense stones of which the building was formed, have been shattered into the most picturesque shapes, until as they project above us, they have the form of overhanging rocks. You can however plainly trace every part, — the immeasurable galleries, the seats of the Patricians and Plebeians, and the dens

[1] Gibbon's *Decline and Fall*, chap. lxxi.

below, from which, when the grating was withdrawn, the wild beasts could bound into the arena, to meet their expecting foe. As you wind up the ruined stairs, the copsewood overshadows you, and it is necessary to put aside the wild olive, the myrtle, and the fig-tree, when you thread your way through the labyrinths. The gray lichens, the variegated moss, and the wild flowers so countless in this climate, form a carpet beneath your feet, or hang in rich festoons and drapery over the ruins. The richest depth of coloring seems to pervade the whole; the sun of many ages has tinged every arch and frieze; and we have the dark stains on the mouldering ruins contrasted with the bright hues of the living vegetation. Shelley says he can scarcely believe, that when incrusted with Dorian marble and ornamented by columns of Egyptian granite, its effect could have been so sublime and impressive as in its present state.

And yet, massive as these remains are, they constitute but a small portion of the original structure. It was — as we have stated in a former chapter — utterly ruined by Robert Guiscard in the twelfth century. Having been stormed and taken, a portion of its walls was hopelessly shattered. Then for several hundred years it was used as a kind of quarry by the Romans. In the fourteenth century Urban V. offered the stones for sale, but found no purchaser except the Frangipani, who wished to use them for building their palace. Finally, the contending families agreed to leave them as common property, and in this way, the Farnese and many other palaces were erected from the materials. Yet shorn of its glory and ruined as we now see it, enough still remains to excite the wonder of the world.

> . . . . "From its mass
> Walls, palaces, half-cities, have been rear'd:
> Yet oft the enormous skeleton ye pass,
> And marvel where the spoil could have appear'd.
> Hath it indeed been plunder'd, or but clear'd?"

The wide arena is now covered with grass like a lawn, piercing the chasms of the broken arches, and thus extending far under the ruins. A few years ago a subterranean passage was discovered, communicating with the palace on the Palatine, within which it is probable that Commodus was attacked by the conspirators. Gibbon says "he was returning to his palace through a dark and narrow portico in the amphitheatre." Near at hand is the ruined *Meta Sudans*, the fountain at which the gladiators refreshed themselves after the toil and heat of their conflicts.

Although the closing of this amphitheatre was one of the noblest and most difficult triumphs of Christianity, yet as we stand within it we have sorrowful evidence, how much the spirit of that faith has changed since martyrs shed their blood upon this spot. A cross has indeed been erected in the centre, yet on it is an inscription, promising two hundred days' indulgence for each kiss which it receives: "Bacciando la S. croce si acquistano duecento giorni di indulgenza." Around the inclosure are fourteen *Stations*, that is, small shrines, each of which has painted above it some event which happened to our Lord on his way to the Cross, and the devout stop at these in succession to offer their prayers. We could see them at all times going their rounds, and then ending with a kiss to the Cross in the centre.

On one side is also a rude pulpit, from which a Capuchin was accustomed at times to preach. This service cannot be otherwise than impressive to a thoughtful mind, even while having no sympathies with the theology on which the sermon is based. The poor monk was generally no orator, yet it was a strange contrast to hear his earnest appeals echo through these old porticoes, and the doctrines of our common faith announced on that spot which once resounded only with the noise of the death-struggle, the roaring of wild beasts, and the gladiators' strife.

It is pleasant to visit these old ruins at different times through the day and night, to mark the effect produced by the change of lights and shadows. In the purple and golden hue of evening there is a mellow radiance diffused over them, which reminds us of the glowing pictures of Claude. The fading light softens down the desolation, and adds to their beauty without subtracting aught from their imposing character. Like Melrose Abbey, however, he who " would view them aright," must " visit them by the pale moonlight." This rule, indeed, Madame de Staël applies to all the remains of antiquity in this land. " The sun of Italy," she says, " should shine on festivals : but the moon is the light for ruins."

The second time we stood within these crumbling walls, it was late at night. Fortunately we came too early, and therefore had an opportunity of seeing the effect produced as the broad deep shadow which the giant building cast, was gradually retreating before the light. When we arrived, the moon was just high enough to silver one edge of the ruin, while the rest was left in darkness. All was silent around, except the step of the solitary sentinel who was pacing the arena, and the murmur which arose at times from the neighboring city. And there we waited, as the Queen of Night — so glorious in the clearness of an Italian sky — gradually mounted up, and tinged row after row of the terraces on which once the spectators sat, the contrast of her silvery hues and the deep shadows of the vaults beneath, producing an effect of which no idea can be conveyed in the cold language of prose. The dark trees waving above the broken arches stood out in bolder relief, and the rents in the shattered battlements became more apparent as the light streamed through them. There is, however, but one description which has ever done justice to the grandeur of this scene. It is that which Lord Byron has given in his " Manfred," where every allusion, and every single line indeed presents so vivid a picture to one who has been there in " the witching hour of night," that, long as the quotation is, this little sketch would be incomplete without it.

" I do remember me, that in my youth,
  When I was wandering — upon such a night
I stood within the Coliseum's wall,
'Midst the chief relics of almighty Rome;
The trees which grew along the broken arches
Waved dark in the blue midnight, and the stars
Shone through the rents of ruin ; from afar
The watch-dog bay'd beyond the Tiber; and
More near from out the Cæsars' palace came
The owl's long cry, and, interruptedly,
Of distant sentinels the fitful song
Begun and died upon the gentle wind.
Some cypresses beyond the time-worn breach
Appear'd to skirt the horizon, yet they stood
Within a bowshot. Where the Cæsars dwelt,
And dwell the tuneless birds of night, amidst
A grove which springs through level'd battlements,

> And twines its roots with the Imperial hearths,
> Ivy usurps the laurel's place of growth;
> But the gladiators' bloody circus stands,
> A noble wreck in ruinous perfection!
> While Cæsar's chambers, and the Augustan halls,
> Grovel on earth in indistinct decay.
> And thou didst shine, thou rolling moon, upon
> All this, and cast a wide and tender light,
> Which soften'd down the hoar austerity
> Of rugged desolation, and fill'd up,
> As 'twere anew, the gaps of centuries;
> Leaving that beautiful which still was so,
> And making that which was not, till the place
> Became religion, and the heart ran o'er
> With silent worship of the great of old!
> The dead, but sceptred sovereigns, who still rule
> Our spirits from their urns." . . . .

The Palace of the Cæsars, allusions to which Byron has thus mingled with his description of the Coliseum, stands not far distant. It is a mass of ruins — a mile and a half in circuit — covering the whole of the Palatine Hill. Here, century after century, the Roman Emperors lavished the wealth of a tributary world to increase the magnificence of their dwelling-place, until at last Nero surpassed them all by his *Aurea*, or Golden House. With our modern habits of estimating, we can form but little conception of its splendor. Suetonius says, — "To give an idea of the extent and magnificence of this edifice, it is sufficient to mention, that in its vestibule was placed a colossal statue of Nero one hundred and twenty feet in height. It had a triple portico, supported by a thousand columns, with a lake, like a little sea, surrounded by buildings which resembled cities. It contained fields, vineyards, pasture-ground, and groves, in which were all descriptions of animals, both wild and tame. Its interior shone with gold, gems, and mother-of-pearl. In the vaulted roofs of the dining-rooms were machines of ivory, which turned round, and from pipes scattered flowers and perfumes on the guests. The principal banqueting hall was a rotunda, so constructed that it revolved night and day, in imitation of the motion of the earth. The baths were supplied from the sea, and the sulphurous waters of Albulæ. When Nero, after dedicating this fairy palace, took up his abode there, his only observation was,— 'Now I shall begin to live like a man.' "

And what remains of all this splendor? Nothing but shapeless ruins. The battlements are leveled; the trees twine their roots through the marble floors on which once the Cæsars trod, and the whispering reeds, the tall grass, and the rank herbage wave in neglected luxuriance over the vanished pomp of the Masters of the world. We wandered over the Hill, and among the fallen columns, listening to the questionable representations of our guide, as he showed in one place the ruins of a theatre, and in another gave some shattered arches the name of a temple. The only well defined remains are those of the Baths of Livia. Tapers were lighted, and we descended into them, for they are now completely covered by the ruins and the accumulated earth above. Yet within, the frescoes and gilding are in some places as plain and fresh as ever, and beneath the dark arches are the mosaic floors, which once displayed a beauty fit for the Imperial family of Rome. Among these crumbling walls and prostrate pillars, the husbandmen now cultivate their gardens, and the bell sounds mournfully from the Monastery of Capuchin monks which has been erected on one portion of the Hill. A few tall palm-trees alone are seen within their grounds, for their rigorous discipline seems to war with the beauty of nature, and the religious house of Bonaventure is an exception to the Italian maxim, —

"Dove abitano i fratri, è grassa la terra."

Treasures of art, however, must still be concealed beneath all this rubbish, for it has raised the surface of the ground more than thirty feet above its former level. As late as the year 1720, by accident a magnificent hall was here discovered two hundred feet in length, one hundred and thirty-two in breadth, richly ornamented with statues, columns of giallo antico, and other precious marbles. Yet now this mass of crumbling desolation is a scene of confusion on which the antiquarian speculates in vain.

> "Cypress and ivy, weed and wall-flower grown
> Matted and mass'd together, hillocks heap'd
> On what were chambers, arch crush'd, columns strown
> In fragments, choked-up vaults, and frescoes steep'd
> In subterranean damps, where the owl peep'd,
> Deeming it midnight: — temples, baths, or halls?
> Pronounce who can; for all that learning reap'd
> From her research hath been, that these are walls —
> Behold the Imperial Mount! 'tis thus the mighty falls."

Among the ruins of Rome those of her Baths occupy a prominent place. A writer on antiquities thus describes them as they appeared in the days of their glory: "They were open every day to both sexes. In each of the great Baths there were sixteen hundred seats of marble, for the convenience of the bathers, and three thousand two hundred persons could bathe at the same time. There were splendid porticoes in front for promenade, arcades with shops, in which was found every kind of luxury for the bath, and halls for corporeal exercises and for the discussions of philosophy; and here the poets read their productions, and rhetoricians harangued, and sculptors and painters exhibited their works to the public. The baths were distributed into grand halls, with ceilings enormously high, and painted with admirable frescoes, supported on columns of the rarest marbles, and the basins were of oriental alabaster, porphyry, and jasper. There were in the centre, vast reservoirs for the swimmers, and crowds of slaves to attend gratuitously upon all who should come." These Baths were either entirely free, or at the utmost, the price of admission was a *quadrant*, the smallest piece of money coined, which was given to the keeper. Under the Emperors it was their policy to do everything for the amusement of the people, and when not only the necessaries of life, but also every luxury, was provided for them, and shows, races, and combats helped the dissolute population to while away the hours of the day, these magnificent structures also were erected to minister to their pleasures. Bathing was indeed an elaborate business with the Romans. They passed through a course of baths in succession, where the agency of air as well as water was applied. These were of different temperatures, hot and cold water being furnished in profusion, while between them they took gentle exercise, were anointed with oil in the sun, or in the tepid or thermal chamber, or took their food. And this process was often repeated. Many, we learn, bathed seven or eight times in the course of the day.

There are but few customs of the almost forgotten civilization of ancient Rome, of which we cannot, from some source, recover an accurate account. It is so with their magnificent *Thermæ*. Those which remain are indeed in ruins, but on the walls of that of Titus was found a fresco, containing a view of one according to the perfect arrangements of that day. Six chambers are exhibited to us in this painting, and we see the burning furnaces which heated the apartments, and in each the individuals going through the process of this much-prized luxury. But more satisfactory still is a discovery made at Pompeii, where an entire establishment was disinterred; and thus, in this miniature city of Roman splendor, we can survey these apartments, just as they were when, seventeen centuries ago, the last bathers left them. In a day which we spent rambling around this silent city of the dead, we found at noon that our guides had arranged the dinner for our party in this Hall of the Bath, and there we passed an hour, with around us the dusty fountains, the bronze pipes, and the seats for the bathers; while directly before us was the marble reservoir, with the maker's name carved on it, and the price paid him for his work. Such an hour enables us to travel back over the gulf of forgotten centuries; and when, in addition, we see the instruments of this old luxury, — the very strigils which the slaves dropped as they fled, — we feel able, in imagination, to build up once more the ruins of Rome's voluptuous baths, to wake to a second existence the gay crowds which thronged their porticoes, and to behold them as crowned with garlands, they listened to the music of the cithara, or discussed the breathing wonders of Grecian statuary which lined these halls.

We have already described the Baths of Caracalla. Those of Diocletian, on the Viminal, are very similar, and consecrated by the tradition that they were erected by the labor of forty thousand Christians. They cover an area of more than a mile in circuit, yet are now in ruins, with the exception of the Pinacotheca, or grand central hall. This — the most noble saloon of ancient Rome, which has come down to us uninjured from ancient times — was preserved by being early converted into a Christian church. For this we must thank the legend which connected its history with that of the martyrs. It was remodeled by Michael Angelo as we now see it — the Church of Santa Maria degli Angeli. Above, in the lofty vaulted roof, are the metallic rings from which the ancient lamps were suspended, and the eight massive columns of oriental granite standing around, are still in their original positions.

From these Baths but a short distance separated us from those of Titus on the Esquiline. Our course was through a street corresponding with the ancient Vicus Sceleratus, infamous in Roman history as the scene of the impiety of Tullia, who there drove her car over the dead body of her father, Servius Tullius, after he had been assassinated by her husband, Tarquin. At length, we reached a vineyard, at the end of which is the entrance to the Baths. Before us stood a row of dark arches in picturesque ruin, under which we passed, and with our guide commenced the descent. Here once stood the Villa of Mæcenas, a portion of which was incorporated into this edifice. The work of excavation is slowly going on, and future years will probably bring to light many precious remnants of antique art. In one of these halls the group of the Laocoön was found — a mere specimen, indeed, of those exquisite works, lifeless but lifelike, which classic Greece surrendered to her conquerors, and with which they filled every public building.

It is strange how admirably parts of these chambers have been preserved, and now that the earth is removed, we see them as they were seventeen centuries ago. Beneath the rubbish is often disclosed a pavement of mosaic, inlaid with the richest marbles, so that even Apuleius might here have realized what he considered the height of human felicity, —

> "Vehementer iterum ac sæpius beatos illos qui
> Super gemmas et monilia calcant!"

Above us was the arched ceiling, thirty feet high, covered with frescoes, and as our guide elevated his light on the end of a long pole, we saw the beautiful arabesque decorations so remarkable for their graceful outlines. Birds, and animals, serpents, fawns, and satyrs, are painted there, and the colors are often unchanged from their early freshness, some indeed possessing a beauty of tint in the rich, deep crimson, which modern art finds it difficult to imitate. Raphael deemed these drawings well worthy of his study, and copied and reproduced them on the walls of the Vatican. Festoons of flowers and rich tracery compose the borders, while here and there naked figures sport, and disclose that spirit of voluptuousness which was the characteristic of Rome when these halls were built. In the works of the Empire we read everywhere the proof, that her Patricians had degenerated into Sybarites, seeking only to refine vice, and pass their days in one unbroken dream of pleasure.

But what a scene must Rome have presented in the years which preceded her downfall, when she had gathered on these Seven Hills all that could be rifled from a conquered world! If her sons had lost the austerity of the Iron Age, the change had also fitted them with deeper devotion to cultivate a taste for the beautiful in Art. While they received from the Plains of the Ilissus, those graceful fables which consecrated every spot, — giving to the waters their Nymph, and to the mountain its Oread, — the faith brought with it also something of that spirit of poetry, whose true home was on the heights of Phyle, and among the groves of Cithæron and Hymettus. They learned to admire the creative power of Praxiteles and Scopas, of Phidias and Myron, writing in sculpture, on the frieze of each shrine and temple, the radiant legends of their old Mythology, or producing from the lucid marble of Pentelicus the transcendent forms of the gods they worshipped. These then became the treasures which wealth sought to collect, until at last one city contained the spoils of genius for a thousand years. How sad the change which has swept away these miracles of art! Even the peasant of the Campagna, degraded as he seems to be, realizes the fall of this Mistress of the world, and as he labors among her mouldering ruins, you may hear the words of his melancholy song, —

"Roma! Roma! Roma!
Non e piu come era prima!"

CHAPTER XII.

DRAMATIC CHARACTER OF THE CHURCH SERVICES. — SERMON BY A VICAR-GENERAL. — THE CAPUCHIN CEMETERY.

HE great trait of the Church services in Italy is their dramatic character. There seems to be a tendency to express everything by sensible images, and the evil is, that men may forget the distinction between the sign and the thing signified. Expiring Paganism in its dying struggles threw its mantle over its conqueror, and then began the imitation of heathen rites. The lustral water, the incense, and the processions of the antique faith of Greece, were too faithfully copied in the holy water, the censer, and the sacred processions of the Christian Church.

The Middle Ages increased the difficulty, from the mistaken zeal and perverted taste which then existed within the Church. It seems to have been the study of her friends, to invent new offices; to add to the ceremonies of the ritual; to render the pomp of her outward adorning more magnificent; and the dresses of her clergy more dazzling. While doctrines were gradually changing, the exterior of religion was also fast losing the simplicity of ancient times, until it became incumbered with the accumulated inventions of centuries.

Passion Week gives ample scope for the development of this dramatic taste. In many of the churches, the Gospel which contains an account of our Lord's trial, is read by different priests, who distribute among themselves the various parts of the dialogue. In some of the little country towns, the old miracle-plays — or representations of different Scripture scenes by actors — are still performed. We spent this week in Vienna, and were able as it passed, to see each step of the Crucifixion regularly represented. On the arrival of this season, the altars in the churches were stripped of their flowers, embroidered cloths, and ornaments, and all things wore an appearance of desolation. On Good Friday, the body of our Lord, as large as life, was suspended on the Cross in the different chapels, which were generally, to increase the effect, lighted only to a twilight gloom, while crowds of worshippers were kneeling before these images.

At night it was taken down, and laid out like a corpse before the altar, covered with a pall, where it remained until Easter Even was over. I do not remember a more striking scene than the Cathedral of St. Stephen presented on that occasion. It was a brilliant moonlight night when we approached it. How magnificent it looked when seen at this time, part flooded with brightness and part in the deep shadow, the rents and corroding inroads of time concealed and its fretted pinnacles and delicate tracery thrown out in bold relief against the clear sky! Its "long drawn aisles" seemed to have doubled in length, and its lofty arches and massive columns were even more imposing than in the glare of day. Through the vast building there was only a feeble lamp here and there, just sufficient to show its extent, except a distant chapel which was brilliantly lighted up. There seemed to be every possible variety. One chapel had been left in perfect darkness, and as we passed it, the moon broke forth from the clouds, and poured its rays through the tall Gothic window, lighting up the beautiful shrines, and spreading a ghastly hue over the figures on the monuments. Another had a single glimmering light at the far end, appearing like a distant star. And all around were worshippers kneeling: some in the faint light of the nave, and others just visible in the deep gloom of the arches. Here they watched in prayer through all hours of the night. Everything seemed to be skillfully arranged to produce its effect on the imagination and the senses.

On Easter Even there is a splendid procession of the Austrian Court from one chapel to another, carrying the Host to represent the body of our Lord. When Easter morning dawns, the whole scene is again changed. The gayest ornaments deck the churches, and the most cheerful music is heard in the services.

In some of the Italian churches, however, on Good Friday the representation of the Crucifixion, the "Agonie," or "Tre Ore," forms a perfect drama. Dr. Wiseman speaks of some of these services as being "worthy of ancient Tragedy." An artificial mount — in imitation of Mount Calvary — is formed as in a theatre, with pasteboard rocks and thickets, and painted trees. On the declivity are seen the Roman soldiers in armor, some mounted on pasteboard horses, while on a more elevated spot are the three crosses, to which are nailed the figures of our Lord and the two malefactors, all arranged so as to produce the best stage effect. At the time of the Crucifixion a sermon of three hours in length is delivered, the different topics of which are taken from the exclamations of our Lord upon the Cross. At last, when the priest comes to His dying cry — " It is finished " — he suddenly exclaims, — " The moment has arrived — the Saviour now expires " — and all instantly sink upon their knees. For a time there is an awful silence, while they are absorbed in prayer, until the priest again exclaims, — " They come, the holy men to bear the body of our Redeemer to the sepulchre; " and forthwith, from the side scenes issue a band of friars, clad in black, who toil up the ascent of Mount Calvary, and take down the body, amidst the groans and lamentations of the by-standers. As a preacher is always selected of wild and fervid eloquence, we may imagine the strong effect which must be produced, particularly upon the ignorant, by this service performed in a darkened church, and mingled up with every stirring appeal to the feelings.

The ordinary preaching of the Italians is deeply impassioned in its style, and I have sometimes listened to Dominicans, whose bold declamation and earnest gestures as they leaned over the pulpit, reminded me of Peter the Hermit rousing up his audience to the Crusade. They deal much in apostrophe, and you frequently hear them turn aside with the address, — " O Italy! " " O my country! " There was one sermon we heard — very different it is true in its character and style — of which I took notes, because it is a fair specimen of the kind of argument used, and because the preacher had just been appointed to a high office in the Roman Catholic Church in America.

Having seen in the "Diario di Roma," that Dr. ——, Vicar-General of ——, in the United States of America, was to preach in the Church of *S. Andrea della Valle*, we went with a party of friends, for the purpose of learning what kind of a man was to be sent out to enlighten our countrymen, and by listening to a sermon nearly one hour in length, had a very fair opportunity of forming an opinion. We found the Doctor to be rather a fine looking man, about forty-five years of age, and of a graceful delivery, although not very fluent in his style of speaking.

His text was John xv. 26, 27: "But when the Comforter is come, whom I will send unto you from the Father, even the Spirit of truth, which proceedeth from the Father, he shall testify of me: and ye also shall bear witness, because ye have been with me from the beginning."

The first part of the sermon was commonplace enough, merely a discussion of the question, Were the Apostles credible witnesses? This being finished, we reached the grand plunge — the great *non sequitur*, on which all the rest was founded. "Having thus proved the truth of religion, I have in the same way demonstrated the truth of the Catholic Church," — meaning of course, the Roman Church. Here was the fallacy which ran through the whole discourse. The object evidently was to produce a confusion in the minds of his hearers, which would lead them to look upon the Catholic Church, and the Church of Rome, as synonymous terms, and the latter as the only development of religion in the world. This Church, he said, had always been a witness for the truth, never attempting to create anything new, but only to testify to what was primitive. And of this he would give two instances.

The first was, when the Council of Nice (A. D. 325) expressed the voice of the whole Church in opposition to Arius, "who taught," said the Doctor, "that our Lord was nothing more than a mere man." This, by the way, was a mistake in ecclesiastical history, thus to impute to Arius what no one ever pretended he held, and what was only avowed by the lowest Humanitarians of a later day.

The second instance was in the sixteenth century, when Luther had begun his heresy, and *a General Council of the whole Christian world* assembled at Trent, and there recorded the condemnation of the Church against his views.

This was the Doctor's ingenious parallel; making the Council of Trent as much the voice of the whole Church as the Council of Nice, and its decrees as weighty and binding. Protestantism was then held up to scorn, as being the creed of a most miserable, contemptible minority, and the audience were assured, that the Church of Rome had all the testimony of antiquity,— to give you his language,—"looking back through a long chain of witnesses to the Apostles' days, *without the least change or shadow of variation in opinion*, not a single link being wanting," etc. Then followed a tirade against private judgment, and his hearers were left to suppose, that none who dissented from the Church of Rome had any rule of faith but their own unsettled opinions, while the unity of his own Church furnished a theme for lofty eulogium. The effect of Protestantism, he said, was shown in all the excesses from Johanna Southcote to Mormonism, while it was absolutely impossible that the weed of fanaticism could never take root in the Church of Rome. He talked, indeed, about their unity with as much assurance, as if the Port Royalists had never existed; the Jesuits and Jansenists were sworn brethren; and the Pope did not have occasion, every little while, to proscribe some new sect which springs up within their bounds.

Then came a passage on the security of their faith. "Hundreds of Protestants, at their last hour, had wished to be reconciled to the Church of Rome, while there never was — there never had been — a single Catholic who at that time wished a different faith." It would be difficult, indeed, for me to give, in this brief space, any idea of the ingenious evasions of the Vicar-General; the shrewd and cunning manner in which he left his audience to infer things which he did not dare boldly to say, and the false impressions he conveyed by only half stating a fact. Not a single reference was made to the Church of England, or a hint given of its existence; but his hearers were left to believe that the only dissent from Rome was what was witnessed in the loose, floating sects of the Continent.

He concluded by stating, that a collection would be made in aid of the missions of the Church of Rome, and some of the hooded friars, with their faces entirely covered, and only holes for their eyes, came forward to receive it. The sermon had certainly not disposed us to contribute to this object, nor did surrounding objects remove the impression. Above the High Altar was a magnificent silk canopy, which had been put up at Epiphany, and under it was what would be called, had it not been in church, a pretty puppet-show. It was a collection of figures, each about two feet high. On a lofty throne, raised several steps, sat the Virgin Mary with the infant Saviour in her arms, a magnificent crown on the head of each. By her side stood Joseph, and before her were "the three wise men," offering their gifts. They, too, were splendidly attired, rather in the costume of the Middle Ages: caps with feathers, velvet dresses with gold embroidery, and a page behind each, holding up his train. Two of the Magi were white, and one black.[1] Over them hung an immense star, cut of silver paper, two feet high, and, of course, ten times larger than the head of either of the wise men. And all this was just above the High Altar!

From the sermon we went to the Church of the Capuchins, adjoining their monastery. It was erected by Cardinal Barberini, brother of Urban VIII., and he is buried beneath the pavement, with the simple inscription, —

"Hic jacet pulvis, cinis, et nihil."

This Chapel boasts of one of Gudio's best works — the Archangel Michael trampling Lucifer under his feet. It has been called "The Catholic Apollo," from the majesty and grace with which the angel is clothed.

---

[1] They are called in Europe " the three Kings of Cologne," and we subsequently, in the Cathedral of that city, saw what are shown as their skulls. The legend is: that, when the Emperor Frederic Barbarossa stormed Milan, he obtained these bones, and presented them to the Bishop of Cologne, who had accompanied his expedition. Behind the High Altar is a magnificent shrine, within which are placed the coffins of silver-gilt, most curiously wrought. The skulls of the three kings are crowned with diadems of gold, studded with jewels, and inscribed with their names — *Gaspar, Melchior,* and *Balthazar* — written in rubies. The treasures employed about the shrine are estimated at more than 200,000 pounds sterling.

My object, however, was to visit the cemetery beneath the Church. I found a monk loitering in one of the side chapels, as if waiting to be *cicerone* to any visitors, and having made known my wish, he conducted me through the cloisters, and down a flight of steps into their old burial-place. Here are several low chapels, in which the monks are interred, the ground being composed of earth brought from Jerusalem. The largest will contain about thirty graves, and the others a somewhat smaller number. Against the walls on all sides, skulls are placed to the depth of nearly three feet, and arranged in such a way as to form niches, as if for statues. The other bones of the skeletons are around, and even above on the ceiling, as if some one in mockery had been sporting with these sad trophies of death. Legs, arms, ribs, spines, and fingers are there, formed into stars and diamonds, wreaths and festoons, altars and chandeliers, — every form, indeed, which caprice could dictate in this strange charnel-house.

In each one of these niches stands the skeleton of a monk, arrayed in his old dress. The coarse brown serge is around him, with the cowl drawn over the fleshless skull; sandals are tied on the feet; the cord is about the waist; the bones of the hands are clasped, holding a black cross, and dangling from them, also, a card inscribed with his name and the date of his death. Sometimes, instead of upright niches, they are horizontal in shape, and the skeletons are reclining as if at rest on their beds. They are first buried in the consecrated earth below, the number of graves in which is kept always filled. When, therefore, a monk dies, he is interred in the oldest grave, and the skeleton which he displaces is arrayed in the monkish dress, and fixed in one of the niches. There he remains for years, until it is time for him to give place to some one else, and then his bones are mingled with the hundreds around him, who are forming fantastic shapes on the ceiling.

It was, indeed, a ghastly display, a sort of caricature of death, to see these skulls grinning from under their hoods, — some white and glistening, some with the brown skin still undecayed and drawn like parchment over the bones. The teeth had fallen from their mouths, or else remained there black with age. And thus they are tied up, bending forward from their shallow niches, until they drop to pieces or are obliged to give place to others. The old monk spoke to me only in a low whisper, and seemed awed by the spirit of the place. He saw, indeed, his brethren around him, their dress of brown sackcloth exactly like his own, and before him, in one of these little chapels, was to be, first his grave, and then the niche from which, perhaps a century hence, his ghastly skeleton would look forth, a show to those who come after us.

On the Festival of All Souls, the scene which is witnessed here is still more striking. A solemn service is held in this Chapel of the Dead, and masses are offered for their souls. Garlands are placed on the white skulls of the skeleton monks, and bouquets of flowers in their hands. The brethren of the Order gather around the altar, formed of the bones of those who have gone before them, and the lights which flash from above are upheld by chandeliers of the same ghastly materials. The dead and the living meet together; and prayers are uttered by the aged men as they kneel at this melancholy shrine; and incense floats in clouds around these spoils of the tomb. But as they sing the hymns for the dead, with what solemn emphasis must they chant the words of the "Dies Iræ,"—

"Lacrymosa dies illa
 Qua resurget ex favilla
 Judicandus homo reus.
 Huic ergo parce Deus,
 Pie Jesu Domine!
 Dona eis requiem."

"That day of doom, that day of tears,
 When guilty man awakes in fears,
 From dust, and 'fore his Judge appears.
 O bounteous Jesus, Lord forever blest!
 Give faithful souls departed endless rest."

CHAPTER XIII.

CHRISTIAN ART. — OVERBECK.

ONE of the wonders of Rome at the present day is a German artist of the name of Overbeck, with whose reputation we had been familiar long before we left home. He is said to have brought Christian art to a higher degree of perfection than any who are now living. It is one of the pleasures indeed of this land of paintings and statues, to study the progress of art in past ages, and to mark how it has been gradually modified and changed by the progress of the religious principle.

The ancient Greeks worshipped only physical beauty, and deified the human form. They drew their inspiration from the old Mythology, and in the arts produced Apollo as the model of manly vigor, and Venus as the embodiment of female loveliness. They bequeathed this feeling to those who came after them and studied their creations of matchless grace; and thus for ages artists seemed to seek their inspiration only in "the fair humanities of old religions." Forming to themselves a standard of ideal beauty, they mused over it through long years of earnest toil, seeking to develop the conception and perpetuate it in the changeless marble. Sometimes every thought and effort were concentrated upon a single statue, which was to embody his ideas of perfection. In it the artist enshrined the noble visions he had cherished, and it constituted at once the history of his own mind and the labor of his life.

But as the Christian faith prevailed and sunk deeper into the heart of the world, a higher principle seemed to be breathed into the arts, and we can trace its progress as the mediæval ages went on. Christianity gradually spiritualized and elevated the old conceptions of beauty. The religious feeling became impressed upon the artist's mind, and the Madonna, with her chastened loveliness and holy associations, took the place of the Queen of Love. The students of art cultivated the poetry of religion. In the last century, indeed, an æsthetic school was formed on these principles, which for a long time exercised a great influence on the Rhine, but has now sunk out of notice. One of its members has beautifully set forth their views in a work entitled, " Reveries of an Art-loving Monk." The writer had once been a Protestant, but so devoted was he to these studies that he became a Romanist, because, as he said, " he could not worship the art without subscribing to the faith which gave it birth."

This is almost the history of Overbeck. At the beginning of the present century he was dismissed from the Academy at Vienna, because he did not conform himself to the artistical rules laid down by the institution. He almost entirely discarded the use of models, except for the arrangement of drapery, because he thought them unfavorable to the ideal conception of character. He trusted to his own vivid imagination to delineate correctly the images which floated before his mind. In 1809 he came to Rome, where he was shortly joined by Peter Cornelius and William Schadow, men like-minded with himself, and for a time they lived in perfect seclusion, perfecting their new principles of art.

They soon announced their fundamental doctrine, that a deep devotional feeling was the true source of an artist's inspiration. Thus, they became the apostles of a new faith which was not long wanting in disciples. They discarded the theatrical attitudes taken from the *danseurs* of the ballet, and became more true to nature, while at the same time they gave everything a religious character. But with some of their number professional enthusiasm was carried to an extent which led them back into the bosom of the Romish Church. They found indeed more affinity between the practice of the arts and her gorgeous services, than they did in the chilling, rationalistic creed in which they had been educated. Such was the case with Overbeck and Schadow, while Cornelius, we believe, remained unchanged. But these religious differences entered into their artistical feelings — diminished somewhat their fraternal intercourse — and the little brotherhood at last separated. Schadow and his pupils returned to Dusseldorf, where he was placed at the head of the Academy; Cornelius was employed by the King of Bavaria at Munich; while Overbeck preferred remaining at Rome, where everything suited his own peculiar temperament.[1]

During the years which have since passed, Over-

---

[1] *Histoire de l'Art Moderne en Allemagne.* Par le Compte A. Raczynski.

beck has continued a most bigoted Romanist, but at the same time celebrated for his austere life and saint-like character. He is indeed a perfect ascetic — one who in another age would have been canonized — living only for his faith, and using his art but to minister to its development. His very appearance tells his character. Thin, and even emaciated, there is something *spiritual* in his whole look, and it conveys the idea of one worn down by fasts and vigils. His *studio* is open but for two hours in one single day of the week, and then his rooms are filled, and he is there himself to explain the pictures. The remark had frequently been made to me, that "they were as good as sermons," and they certainly seemed to produce a calming influence on those who studied them. There was an absence of that laughing conversation which is heard in other studios, but the visitors talked in a low voice, as if affected by the very atmosphere and spirit of the place. And there stood the artist himself, with his rapt and earnest look, his gaze perhaps intently fixed on some drawing before him, his whole appearance harmonizing admirably with the scene in which he was an actor.

Overbeck devotes himself entirely to subjects of a strictly religious character, generally in illustration of some part of Scripture history. He paints but little — the only pieces he has executed being, I believe, altar-pieces for some churches. He merely draws in charcoal, and his sketches are afterwards engraved, while the originals are purchased by a society in Germany which is desirous of forming a complete collection of his works. The wonder is, the effect — the expression he can produce with such simple materials. A sheet of paper, a piece of charcoal, and bread for erasure — these are all he requires to create the beautiful forms which almost seem to "live and move and have their being" before us. He throws his whole soul into the conception, and all his deep devotion breathes forth from every figure. He one day overheard a lady, who was looking at one of his drawings, exclaim, "How beautiful! how graceful!" "Madame," said he, "it pains me to hear you say so. I was in hopes of making them more than beautiful and graceful. I wished them to be religious."

In most of his drawings, the figure of our Lord is introduced, and it is in this that the artist particularly excels. There is a degree of calm and heavenly beauty, united with a commanding dignity, which is seen in the pictures of no other artist. In this particular Raphael has not excelled him in his celebrated picture of " The Transfiguration." Overbeck, indeed, some time ago published a work, in which he asserted that no one could paint religious subjects without being himself a religious man. Correct, however, as the principle may be, his illustration of it is singularly unfortunate, for he applies it to Raphael, asserting that in his latter days, when he devoted his pencil and talent to the sensual mythology of Greece and Rome, he incapacitated himself for the loftier delineation of subjects of a sacred character. As he forcibly expresses it, " When Raphael forsook God, God forsook him." But who that has sat for hours without weariness before his " Holy Family " — the " Madonna della Seggiola "— in the Pitti Palace at Florence, but must enter his protest against such an assertion! There is an expression of indescribable beauty in the countenance of the Virgin — the mingling of deep maternal love with the lofty consciousness of being the Mother of our Lord, which forces on us the conviction that in the closing years of life he had not lost the high ideal character of his earlier Madonnas. Still more is the feeling deepened when we stand in the Hall of the Vatican, and gaze upon his last and noblest painting, which the hand of Death left unfinished, but which has remained for three centuries, the very triumph and miracle of art.

We may, however, apply Overbeck's theory to himself, for there can be no doubt but that his deep devotional feeling is the inspiration which gives life and reality to the figures he sketches. When we were at his studio, he was employed on a half-finished picture of "The Scourging of our Lord," in which the mild yet lofty endurance of the patient sufferer is finely contrasted with the demoniacal expression on the countenances of the tormentors. The face of each one is intended to represent some particular vice, such as pride, anger, envy, and it needs no key to point out which is delineated. Another drawing was, — "Our Lord sitting in the Boat, and preaching to the Multitudes on Shore." His arms are extended towards them, and His expression is the rapt look of one who alone could fully realize how much depended on their acceptance of His offers. Near it hangs "The Massacre of the Innocents." In the gallery at Bologna we have seen Guido's celebrated picture on the same subject. It has all the advantage of his splendid coloring, and the wildness of the different groups, the agony of the mothers, and the marble paleness of the infants, are most remarkable; and yet, in some respects, we prefer this sketch by Overbeck. We shudder as we look at Guido's. It is too painful in its interest. Here, on the contrary, the story is told with equal power, and yet the groups are arranged with such skill, as to show the striking points of the scene, at the same time skillfully veiling those which are too revolting to the feelings. My favorite picture, however, among them all, is one to illustrate "The Parable of the Ten Virgins." Some are trimming their lamps, while others are just starting from sleep, and in the distance is seen the approaching train of the bridegroom. Had not the artist objected to the terms, I should say that the female figures were exceedingly graceful and beautiful.

There is also one large allegorical picture, from which he has painted an altar-piece for the church at Frankfort. It represents "The Triumph of Christianity over the Arts." In the upper part of the picture is the Madonna holding the infant Christ, to represent Religion, and below her are the different schools of artists: sculptors, painters, architects, and poets. All are looking towards her, and engaged in some work which is to advance the worship of her Son. Many of them are portraits which we recognize. There stands Michael Angelo holding his plan of St. Peter's; and Raphael, whose name brings to the mind such associations of beauty; and Dante, whose genius, on its bold and fearless wing, was able to penetrate into the unseen world; and Tasso, wearing the laurel crown which so well becomes the author of "Jerusalem Delivered."

But where among them all is so perfect an illustration of the triumph of our Faith over Art, as is furnished by Overbeck himself? Every talent, and thought, and feeling, is consecrated to this cause. His object is not only to delineate the beautiful in nature, or to arrest and perpetuate by his pencil the bright visions which flit before his own inward soul, but through these instruments to inspire all around him with that love of moral beauty, which is a necessary characteristic of " the pure in heart."

CHAPTER XIV.

EXCURSION ON THE APPIAN WAY.

E have been waiting for a peculiarly fine day to make an excursion beyond the walls, and this morning, one of the most beautiful that ever dawned, was all that we could desire. Although the seventh of January, yet the sun was shining so warmly, that in our land it would have passed for June, while there was a freshness in the air, which, as Madame de Staël says, "produces something of melody on the senses."

We set out for the romantic fountain of Egeria, about three miles from the gates of the city, yet expecting, with the intermediate places of interest, to find full employment for the day. Our course led us past the Capitoline Hill, and through the Roman Forum, with its lofty, solitary pillars, gleaming in the sunlight, the Forum, —

> . . . . "Where once the mightiest spirits met
> In terrible conflict; this, while Rome was free,
> The noblest theatre on this side heaven."

We crossed the *Via Sacra*, passed under the arches of Titus and Constantine, turned from the Coliseum, and winding round the base of the Palatine Hill, and the mighty ruins of the Palace of the Cæsars, entered the Appian Way. Constructed nearly eighteen centuries ago, its solid pavement is now as firm as ever, and we rode over the same stones which in Rome's glorious day were trodden by the triumphal procession, as it slowly passed up to the Capitol. The roads which extended to all parts of the Empire were among the few works of utility constructed by the Romans, and these we can see were designed by Providence, that the world should thus devise the means by which the Church was to win it back to herself. "The legions of great Rome were for some centuries toiling with the pickaxe and spade, to construct mighty roads by which Apostles might compass the ends of the earth. Those huge arteries were the unconscious preparation which poor, blind Paganism was making for the more rapid circulation of the fresh blood that should spring up and stir that monstrous Empire, and be an element at once of health and of destruction." [1]

The old Appian Way was distinguished for the splendor of the monuments lining its sides, — similar to those now seen in the Street of the Tombs in Pompeii, — and Cicero refers to them when he says, in his "Tusculan Disputations," — "When you go out of the Porta Capena, and see the tombs of Calatinus, the Scipios, the Servilii, and the Metelli, can you consider that the buried inmates are unhappy?"

Let us endeavor then to call back seventeen centuries, and cause to pass before us the scenes of a CLASSICAL FUNERAL, as once it took place on this spot. It is the burial of one of the Metelli in the early age of the Empire, when the practice of interring the body had ceased, and that of burning been substituted in its place. The *Libertinarii* (undertakers) have performed their duty, and for some days the body, dressed in the

[1] F. W. Faber.

official robes which once it wore, has been exposed on a couch in the vestibule of the house, with its feet towards the door, and the branch of cypress waving above it. But it is now the eighth day, the time for the funeral, and the Appian Way is filled with crowds, who have poured out to see the Patrician's burial. At length there came the slow procession, the wail of voices becoming gradually more distinct, while, when it ceased, the music heard in its place sounded subdued and mournfully. First walked the Master of Ceremonies, attended by lictors dressed in black; then the musicians playing their sorrowful strains; then the mourning women, who were hired to lament the deceased, and sing the funeral song in his praise; then the slaves whom he had freed, wearing the cap of liberty; then the images of his many ancestors, and the military rewards he had gained. The corpse itself came next, on a couch of ivory, covered with purple and gold. A garland of withered flowers, enwreathed with fillets of white wool, crowned his head; in his mouth was the coin to pay the ferryman in Hades, and by his side the honey-cake to bribe the watchful Cerberus. Leaves and flowers, too, were strewn upon the bier, which was borne on the shoulders of the nearest relatives. Behind came his family in mourning, and as they walked they uttered loudly their lamentations, the females beating their breasts, and wounding their faces with their nails.

But they have at length reached the funeral pyre, as it stood altar-like in its shape, and covered with dark leaves and the cypress branches consecrated to the tomb. Loudly they chanted the Hymn for the Dead, while all arranged themselves round it, and the body was placed on its top. Then the nearest relative advanced, and with his face averted applied the torch. Perfumed oil had been poured over the wood, and the flames therefore encircled it at once, and darted up high into the air. For a long time the multitude stood around in a dread silence, while the priests flung perfumes into the fire, until the pile was consumed. Then the attendants came forward and poured red wine upon the hot, burning ashes, while the relatives gathered them with the bones into the urn. The service was now over; the priest, with the laurel branch in his hand, sprinkled those around with water of purification, and dismissed them with the word *Ilicet*. And as they departed to the city, each one often turned and bade farewell to the deceased with the mournful word *Vale*, while the parting Hymn swelled loudly forth with its touching tones: —

I.

"Farewell, O soul departed!
  Farewell, O sacred urn!
Bereaved and broken-hearted,
  To earth the mourners turn!
To the dim and dreary shore,
Thou art gone our steps before!
But thither the swift hours lead us,
And thou dost but a while precede us!
      Salve — salve!
Loved urn, and thou solemn cell,
Mute ashes! — farewell, farewell!
      Salve — salve!

II.

"Ilicet — ire licet —
Ah, vainly would we part!
Thy tomb is in the faithful heart.
About evermore we bear thee;
For who from the heart can tear thee?
Vainly we sprinkle o'er us

The drops of the cleansing stream;
And vainly bright before us
The lustral fire shall beam.
For where is the charm expelling
Thy thoughts from its sacred dwelling?
Our griefs are thy funeral feast,
And memory thy mourning priest.
   Salve — salve!

III.

" Ilicet — ire licet —
The spark from the hearth is gone
 Wherever the air shall bear it;
The elements take their own;
 The shadows receive thy spirit.
It will soothe thee to feel our grief,
 As thou glid'st by the gloomy river;
If love may in life be brief,
 In death it is fixed forever.
   Salve — salve!
In the hall which our feasts illume
The rose for an hour may bloom;
But the cypress that decks the tomb —
The cypress is green forever!
   Salve — salve! " [1]

The last lines have dispelled the vision, the shadows are gone, and there is nothing here but the barren Campagna, and the desolate tombs of Rome's forgotten sons. Yet more picturesque remains I have never seen; mighty masses of stone or brick-work utterly ruined during the wars of the Middle Ages, covered with rank vegetation, the wild vines trailing around them, or sometimes —

" With two thousand years of ivy grown
The garland of Eternity, where wave
The green leaves over all by time o'erthrown."

We first stopped at one of those to which Cicero

---

[1] This Hymn is by Sir E. L. Bulwer, and although not a translation, yet embodies so much of the spirit of the old Hymns for the Dead, that we cannot forbear giving it.

refers — the tomb of the Scipios. It is in a vineyard on the hill-side, with a single solitary cypress rising above it. Fortunately, it became covered by the soil, and was thus forgotten and unknown until the year 1780. By accident it was then discovered, and its vaults once more opened, after being closed for twenty-one centuries! The front is formed with arches and Doric columns, presenting a chaste façade. We stopped at a stone gate having over it the inscription, *Sepulchro degli Scipioni*, and the sound of wheels having brought the usual *cicerone* with a tribe of assistants from their residence in the vineyard, we mounted the broken steps which led to the tomb. Here tapers were lighted and we prepared to descend. I had expected a single chamber, but found instead a series of passages — dark and damp — extending far into the hill-side. The principal sarcophagus has been removed to the Vatican, where we had already seen it. Our guide pointed out the place from which it was taken. It bore the name of the great-grandfather of Scipio Africanus, who was Consul B. C. 297, and when opened, the skeleton was still entire, with the ring upon one of its fingers. This relic is now in the collection of the Earl of Beverley, in England. Among other inscriptions remaining here, we saw one commemorative of the Scipio who conquered in Spain, and received from thence his name of Hispanus. The noblest of them all, Scipio Africanus, is not buried here. Driven by the ingratitude of his countrymen from the city he had saved, the last part of his life was passed at Liternum, near Naples, and there are still shown the remains of his monument with a portion of the inscription, — "Ingrata patria," etc. In an excursion which we made to Baiæ, the guide took us to the top of a little hill, from which we could see in the distance the white and glistening marble, which shows where —

"Scipio sleeps by the upbraiding shore."

But what solemn funeral rites must have been here performed in this old vineyard, as one by one the members of this noble family were borne to their sepulchre, and white-robed priests gathered about this portal by which now we stood, and eloquent orators declaimed, and these hills around were covered by the thousands of Rome who had poured out to do honor to him who in Africa or Spain had led their armies to victory! Who could then have prophesied, that this would be despoiled of its noblest dust, and turned into a common show-place!

"The Scipios' tomb contains no ashes now:
The very sepulchres lie tenantless
Of their heroic dwellers."

In the same vineyard is a large Columbarium, a place where were deposited urns filled with the ashes of the slaves and freedmen. It was only discovered about four years since, and is therefore almost in its antique state. Upon descending into it, we found ourselves in an immense chamber, surrounded by little niches, each containing an urn. We removed the cover from several, which were still filled with ashes and calcined bones. Above each was a little slab containing the name. Some inscriptions I copied. "Ne tangito O mortalis. Reverere manes deos." "Hic reliciæ Pelopis. Sit tibi terra lebis." It will be perceived that the Latin here would scarcely be called classical. One slave rejoiced in the name of "Scribonia Cleopatra." Some of the freedmen were evidently men of consideration, as it is said of one, — "patri bene merenti." One, we are told, was a member of the prætorian guard; another was butler to his master; another an actor, "imitator." Sometimes it is recorded on the little monument, — "frater ejus fecit;" sometimes, — "pia mater fecit." Beneath, in a niche, still stands the little altar, with the inscription dedicating it to "Diis manibus," and above on the frescoes are the paintings, representing the Cock, and other emblems connected with Æsculapius and Mors.

From this we went to another in the same vineyard, smaller, but similar in character. The frescoes here are as fresh as if yesterday they were painted, and the bronze lamp still hangs from the ceiling, just as it was left, perhaps two thousand years ago. The ashes of these slaves yet remain, while the old heroic Scipios have been torn from their sepulchres, and their bones scattered.

Adjoining is a field, in which the Vestal Virgins, who proved unfaithful to their vows, were buried alive. After being scourged and stripped of her badges of office, the offender was attired like a corpse, and borne through the Forum with all the ceremonies of a real funeral. A vault had been prepared under ground, with a couch, and lamp, and table, with a little food, and to this the culprit was led by the Pontifex Maximus, the earth was closed over the surface, and she was left to her lingering death.

We drove on to the Church of San Sebastian, erected on the spot where tradition says that saint suffered martyrdom. The Church was open, and deserted, except by the beggars, who were sunning themselves in the porch, and it was with some trouble that we were able to find any one to be our guide. An old monk, with the cord round his waist, at length appeared, and in most choice Italian we signified our wish to descend into the Catacombs. This is one of the openings, and from here they have been traced (it is said) for twenty miles, but owing to the loss of life from persons wandering into them, most of the intricate passages have now been closed. In the sacristy of the Church, a plan of the Catacombs, as they extend for a few miles, was hanging up, which represented them as being most complicated — crossing and recrossing in every possible way. A Jesuit, belonging to the Church of Gesu, in Rome, was about to publish a new engraving, but it was not yet completed when we left the city. The passages are generally ranged, one above the other, in three stories, and this renders them more intricate from the many stairs which ascend and descend.

Each one of the party was furnished with a light, and we followed our guide down a flight of stone steps, worn by the feet of the multitudes who had trodden them for eighteen centuries past. At the bottom commenced the Catacombs, — damp, winding passages, — often not more than three feet wide, and so low that sometimes we were obliged to stoop. Then, again, they would expand into apartments arched overhead, and large enough to contain a small company. On each side were cavities, in which were placed the bodies of the dead, or niches for the urns containing their ashes, and small apertures, where lamps were found. But few sarcophagi were discovered here, for no pomp or ceremony attended the burial of the early Christians, when their friends hastily laid them in these dark vaults. They sought not the sculptured marble to inclose their remains, but were contented with the rude emblems which were carved above, merely to show that for the body resting there they expected a share in the glory of the Resurrection. Very many of the graves were those of children, and sometimes a whole family were interred together. The cavities were cut into the soft stone, just large enough for the body, with a semicircular excavation for the head, and the opening was closed with a thin slab of marble.

Most of the inscriptions have been removed to the Museum of the Vatican, where we had already seen them. They are arranged there in the same gallery with those found in Pagan tombs, and contrast with them most strongly in their constant reference to a state beyond the grave, while on the Roman monuments are no expressions but those of hopeless grief. It shows how immediate was the elevating influence of the new creed. Nothing, indeed, which is gloomy or painful finds a place among these records of the martyrs. They evidently laid the athlete of Christ to his rest without any sorrow that his fight was over, or any expression of vengeance against those who doomed him to death. They thought too much of his celestial recompense to associate with it the tortures and evils of this lower life. The words "in pace" are frequently to be deciphered, and in one case I made out, — "in pace et in †." They are covered, too, with symbolical representations. The most frequent are the well-known monogram of Christ, formed by the Greek letters X and P, — the old emblem of the fish, ΙΧΘΥΣ, the letters of which are composed of the initials of the Greek words, Ἰησοῦς Χριστὸς Θεοῦ Υἱὸς Σωτηρ, "Jesus

Christ, the Son of God, the Saviour;" the ship, to represent the Church; the anchor, an emblem of hope; the stag, to show " the hart which thirsteth after the water brooks; the hare, the timid Christian hunted by persecutors; the lion, the emblem of the tribe of Judah; the dove, indicating the simplicity, and the cock, the vigilance of the Christian; the peacock and the phœnix, emblems of the Resurrection; the vine, the olive branch, the palm, and the lamb. Some bear the signs of martyrdom, and one only, a rudely sculptured view of a man devoured by wild beasts.

These are the simple memorials by which devotion endeavored to hallow the tombs of the departed, and inscribe upon them the unfading hopes which live beyond the grave. Even the Cross itself, the primal symbol of Christianity, which for ages was used in its simplest form, seemed to convey to their minds nothing depressing or melancholy. They adorned it with crowns and flowers, as if rather a sign of all that was cheerful and inspiring.

It is instructive to remark, that in none of these monuments of the early centuries do we see any representation of the Godhead, as is now so common in the Romish churches, under the figures of an old man, a young man, and a dove. The reason has been admirably given by Milman, when he says, — " Reverential awe, diffidence in their own skill, the still dominant sense of the purely spiritual nature of the Parental Deity, or perhaps the exclusive habit of dwelling upon the Son as the direct object of religious worship, restrained early Christian art from those attempts to which we are scarcely reconciled by the sublimity and originality of Michael Angelo and Raphael. Even the symbolic representation of the Father was rare. Where it does appear, it is under the symbol of an immense hand issuing from a cloud, or a ray of light streaming from heaven, to imply, it may be presumed, the creative and all-enlightening power of the Universal Father." The earliest instance we have of the Eternal Father represented under a human form, is contained in a Latin Bible, — described by Montfaucon, — which was presented by the Canons of the Church of Tours to Charles the Bold, in the year 850. So long did it take the monkish artists of the Church to reach the present height of irreverence!

Neither do we find in the Roman Catacombs any representation of the Virgin and Child. This too was a subject unattempted in the early Church. And when at last they began thus to shadow forth their conceptions of the maternal tenderness of the mother for the Infant Saviour, she is always represented veiled. They endeavored to express the idea by the attitude alone, without attempting to portray the mingled feelings which they supposed should characterize the countenance of her, who with all the affections of human nature was chosen to be the Mother of the Lord. It was not, we believe, till the sixth century that these representations were seen; and then as the superstitious feeling increased which led to the worship of the Virgin, she was more and more surrounded with those emblems which exalted her at last to adoration as the Queen of Heaven.

The same statement is true with regard to the Crucifixion. Not a single attempt to portray it is to be seen on any of these ancient monuments. The early Church evidently viewed this mysterious subject with a reverence too deep and awful to allow its members to attempt a delineation. There is indeed no symbol of our faith, in the use of which we can trace the successive steps so clearly as in this.[1] The lofty faith of the primitive Christians dwelt so much upon the Divinity of our Lord, that they shrank in reverence from the idea of coarsely representing the mere corporeal pangs which weighed Him down in the hour of His mortal agony. Such thoughts were reserved for the days of monachism, when the gloomy monks, who were the artists of the Church, brooded in the solitude of their cells over these scenes of suffering, and when they attempted to portray them, forgetting all that was tender and sublime, furnished only that which was painful and repulsive. The followers of St. Basil, we are told, gave the last degradation to this solemn subject, and spread through Western Christendom memorials of the Passion which were only " of the earth, earthly."

These Catacombs therefore furnish a valuable chapter for Ecclesiastical History, for we derive from them most of the information we have with regard to Christian symbolism. The early martyrs, by whom they were for a long while peopled, " being dead, still speak." They tell their own simple faith and devotion by the changeless emblems which are as expressive as words. And as we trace these pictured inscriptions down

---

[1] Cardinal Bona — as quoted by Milman, to whose *History of Christianity* we have been much indebted on this subject — gives the following as the progress of the gradual change: I. The simple Cross. II. The Cross with the Lamb at the foot of it. III. Christ clothed on the Cross, with hands uplifted in prayer, but not nailed to it. IV. Christ fastened to the Cross with four nails, still living, and with open eyes. He was not represented as dead till the tenth or eleventh century.

through successive generations, they unfold to us the gradual change which crept over the feelings of the Church. It seems to present a strange contrast. The respect of its members for her who was "blessed among women" gradually deepened into adoration, while a reverence for some of the most sublime mysteries of our faith was proportionally fading from their minds. Themes which at first they regarded with so sacred an awe that they scarcely dared to comment on them in words, lost at last their divine idealism, and were coarsely shadowed forth by sensible objects. Thus it is that in her own bosom, and in places which she consecrates as most holy, Papal Rome contains the evidence of that silent change which, as centuries went by, was working in the minds of her members.

Our guide pointed out to us, as we passed along, some tombs which had never been opened, and whose inmates had been left to slumber on as seventeen centuries ago they were laid to their rest. There was one, the thin marble side of which had cracked, so that he could insert a small taper. He bade us look in, and there we saw the remains of the skeleton, lying as it was placed by its brethren in the faith in those early days of persecution and trial. In these gloomy caverns the followers of our Lord were then accustomed to meet, thus in secret to eat the bread of life, and with tears to drink the water of life. In one of these little chapels which tradition has thus consecrated, there were found still remaining, a simple earthen altar, and an antique Cross set in the rock above it. It was with no ordinary feelings that we stood on this spot and looked on these evidences of early worship. They had remained here perhaps unchanged since the days of the Apostles, and where we then were, men may have bowed in prayer who had themselves seen their Lord in the flesh. The remains were around us of those who had received the mightiest of all consecrations, that of suffering, and whose spirits were as noble as any who had their proud monuments on the Appian Way, and whose names are now as " familiar in our ears as household words." But no historian registered the deeds of the despised Nazarenes. They had no poet, and they died.

"Carent quia vate sacro."

This was to us a most interesting scene, yet one to be felt more than to be described. We were glad however to ascend the worn steps and find ourselves once more in the Church above. We noticed, indeed, that the corners we turned in these intricate passages were marked with white paint to guide us, yet a sudden current of air extinguishing our lights would make these signs useless, and from the crumbling nature of the rock there is always danger of the caving in of a gallery, or some other accident, which might involve a party in one common fate. Some years ago, we were told, a school of nearly thirty youth with their teacher entered these Catacombs on a visit, and never reappeared. Every search was made, but in vain. The scene which then was exhibited in these dark passages, and the chill which gradually crept over their young spirits as hope yielded to despair could be described only by Dante, in terms in which he has portrayed the death of Ugolino and his sons in the Tower of Famine at Pisa.[1]

[1] *Inf.* xxxiii. 21-75.

On reëntering the Church, the old monk lighted two candles in a side chapel, and with great reverence proceeded to display a host of relics, such as the blood of the martyrs, and the arrows with which St. Sebastian was pierced. The most holy relic is a stone containing impressions of our Saviour's feet. As St. Peter was fleeing from Rome to avoid martyrdom, — the legend tells us, — he met our Lord apparently going towards it. "Domine, quo vadis?" (Lord, whither goest thou?) asked the Apostle, and was answered, that his Master was going to suffer death again, since His servants deserted their post. St. Peter therefore returned and submitted to death, but on the place where his Lord stood were found these indentations in the hard stone, and a Church has been erected there, called by the name, " Domine quo vadis." Our faith however not being very strong, we soon turned from these wonders, and drove to our next stopping-place — the tomb of Cæcilia Metella. This is one of the best preserved antiquities in Rome, a massive tower seventy feet in diameter, which Lord Byron has well described in the lines —

> "There is a stern round tower of other days,
> Firm as a fortress, with its fence of stone,
> Such as an army's baffled strength delays,
> Standing with half its battlements alone."

No one indeed would take it for anything but a fortress. Built of massive granite blocks, and with walls twenty-five feet thick, it seems intended to defy the inroads of time and the strength of man. We entered the low portal, and there among the ruins which had fallen about, and the trailing ivy which hung in heavy festoons, we came to the single apartment in the centre, now open above to the sky. And yet, the sole treasure placed in this tower of strength, so guarded and enshrined, was — a woman's grave. By some it is conjectured to have been the wife of Metellus; by others, his daughter. Standing within the monument, we read the speculations of Childe Harold on this subject, which are some of the finest stanzas he has ever written. We cannot forbear copying them, although they may be familiar to many of our readers.

> "But who was she, the lady of the dead,
>   Tomb'd in a palace? Was she chaste and fair?
>   Worthy a king's — or more — a Roman's bed?
>   What race of chiefs and heroes did she bear?
>   What daughter of her beauties was the heir?
>   How lived — how loved — how died she? Was she not
>   So honor'd — and conspicuously there,
>   Where meaner relics must not dare to rot,
> Placed to commemorate a more than mortal lot!
>
> "Perchance she died in youth: it may be, bow'd
>   With woes far heavier than the ponderous tomb
>   That weigh'd upon her gentle dust; a cloud
>   Might gather o'er her beauty, and a gloom
>   In her dark eye, prophetic of the doom
>   Heaven gives its favorites — early death; yet shed
>   A sunset charm around her, and illume
>   With hectic light, the Hesperus of the dead,
> Of her consuming cheek the autumnal leaf-like red.
>
> "Perchance she died in age — surviving all,
>   Charms, kindred, children — with the silver gray
>   On her long tresses, which might yet recall,
>   It may be, still a something of the day
>   When they were braided, and her proud array
>   And lovely form were envied, praised, and eyed
>   By Rome — but whither would conjecture stray?
>   Thus much alone we know — Metella died,
> The wealthiest Roman's wife: behold his love or pride!"

But all this care has proved useless. The splendid sarcophagus of white marble has long since been removed from its little chamber so massively built up, and may be seen standing in the open court of the Farnese Palace, exposed to the action of every storm. And the tomb itself has been devoted to a purpose far different from that intended by the builder. " This," says Sismondi, " with the tombs of Adrian and Augustus, became fortresses of banditti, in the thirteenth century, and were taken by Brancellone, the Bolognese governor of Rome, who hanged the marauders from the walls."

Adjoining this " woman's grave " are the ruins of a fortress, which in the Middle Ages was a stronghold in succession of the Savelli and Gaetani families. Their armorial bearings are still to be seen upon the walls, and the round windows of the Chapel standing above the ruins give them a most picturesque appearance. In the valley beneath are the wide-spread remains of what is commonly called " the Circus of Caracalla." It is of course crumbling into decay, yet every part may still easily be traced. The great gate-way, the high raised balcony for the Emperor, the *carceres* or cells, in which the chariots stood previous to starting, the *spina*, or division through the centre, around which they swept in the eager contest, — all can be marked. The course was about half a mile around and was repeated several times, but it is evident that the victory must have depended principally upon the skill of the charioteer in turning. The wall is now broken so that we easily sprang over it, and all is fast settling down to the level of the meadow. The high vines are growing over it, the flowers are crushed beneath our feet as we walk, and no sign of life meets our view but the green lizards which sport among the ruins.

Our last place of visit was the Fountain of Egeria, a name which throughout the world is associated with all that is poetical. Twenty-five centuries have gone since Numa consecrated this spot, and many generations have passed away, yet it still continues to be a place of pilgrimage. Our guide led us by the remains of the old Temple of Bacchus, and around the base of the hill, till suddenly the grotto opened before us. It is under an antique arch on which the hill seems to rest, and at its extremity the little spring gushes out, and flows over its pebbly channel as clear as crystal, until it is lost in the green meadow which stretches away in front. Around the grotto are niches which once evidently contained statues, but they have long since gone. One only — a recumbent figure, sadly mutilated — remains above the spot from which the stream trickles out. Juvenal objected in his day to the marble ornaments and the art which had spoiled the grotto, declaring that the goddess would be much more honored if the fountain was inclosed only with its border of living green —

"Viridi si margine clauderet undas
Herba."

But time has at length wrought the change which he desired. The stones of the old chamber are clothed with moss and evergreens; the *Adiantum Capillus* waves over the fountain; while from the roof hang down long wreaths of creeping plants, till they obscure the entrance, and diffuse a twilight gloom within. And when, standing before this little shrine, we look around, we see on the one side the thick grove, dark with shade, in which Numa is said to have met the goddess, and on the other the sweeping arches of the Claudian aqueduct, with the purple hills for their background, extending far along the scene. They stretch over the wide Campagna, till they reach the spot where once stood the vanished palaces of Mæcenas and Domitian, and we lose sight of them among the distant mountains of Albano. Altogether, this is as poetical a spot as the earth can furnish, nor could one be found more lovely even among the Grecian solitudes which Theocritus so beautifully describes. The Dryad and Nymph have indeed gone forever, yet, fable or not, we cannot help feeling, as we think of the legend, —

> "Whatsoe'er thy birth,
> Thou wert a beautiful thought, and softly bodied forth."

CHAPTER XV.

THE CARDINALS. — INTERVIEW WITH CARDINAL MEZZOFANTI.

HILE the visitor is wandering among the ruins of Rome, he will sometimes be roused from his reveries by the approach of a splendid carriage, flaming with scarlet and gold, and three footmen in gorgeous liveries clustering on behind, all contrasting strangely with the time-worn relics of former ages, and the filth and wretchedness of the modern city. That is the equipage of a Cardinal. Within sits an old man, dressed also in scarlet. That is his Eminence.

For centuries the College of the Cardinals has been, in many respects, the most powerful legislative body in Europe, and the highest object of ecclesiastical ambition. The sons of the first monarchs considered the dignity a prize worthy of their aim, and the Pope could often win the sovereign himself to his views by the bribe of a Cardinal's hat for one of his family. Reginald Pole, the last of the powerful race of the Plantagenets, and one of the gentlest and holiest of men, was a Cardinal, and since his death, no ecclesiastic of that rank has ever resided at the Court of England. He was ill of the same fever as his royal cousin, Queen Mary, and in their last hours constant messages were passing between them. When she expired, foreseeing the ruin of his faith, he expressed his satisfaction at the prospect of speedy dissolution, which actually took place in a few hours. He died, it has been beautifully said, "as if by a mysterious instinct, in the very last night whose moon shone upon the rich tillage-lands and dusky woodland chases of Catholic England, still, for one night still, a portion of the Roman Obedience."[1] The last of the exiled Stuarts also died at Rome in the same office, under the title of Cardinal York.

The Cardinals are seventy in number, this being the limit fixed by Sextus V. in allusion to the "seventy disciples of our Lord." The College, however, is seldom full, as some appointments are kept in reserve to meet emergencies. They are the Princes of the Church, and are divided into three ranks: 1. Six Cardinal Bishops; 2. Fifty Cardinal Priests; 3. Fourteen Cardinal Deacons. The dignity has, however, now been thrown open to laymen, and the Governor of Rome, who is recognized so often in the streets by his violet stockings and short black silk cloak, usually receives a Cardinal's hat at the expiration of his term of office. They meet occasionally as the Consistory, sitting in the full dignity of the purple, with the Pontiff presiding in person. This, however, is a mere matter of form to receive foreign ambassadors, or to add to the splendor of the Court. Their chief prerogative is when they meet in Conclave to elect a Pope. This is a power which they gained in the eleventh century, under Nicholas II., when a Council conferred on them the exclusive right of voting at Papal elections, thus setting aside the ancient privilege of the Roman clergy and people to nominate their Bishop. Hildebrand,

[1] Rev F. W. Faber.

afterwards Gregory VII., was then Cardinal Archdeacon of Rome, the great minister of the Pope's reign, and director of all his measures, and this was one of the steps which he had proposed to increase the power of the Papacy. The voice was indeed the voice of Nicholas, but the hand was the hand of Hildebrand. For nine days after the Pontiff's death the Cardinal Chamberlain exercises supreme authority, and even has the right to coin money in his own name, and impressed with his own arms. From the shortness of time these pieces are necessarily scarce. One of them, however, issued on the death of Pius VII., came into my hands, while in Rome. It bears the arms, surmounted by a Cardinal's hat, and around them the inscription, — "SEDE VACANTE MDCCCXXIII." On the ninth day the funeral of the deceased Pope takes place, and on the ensuing day the Cardinals meet in secret Conclave to elect his successor. There they remain immured in one of the great halls of the Vatican till they can agree in the choice; the Senator of Rome, the Patriarchs and Bishops who are in the city, guarding the different entrances to the Conclave, to prevent all influence and intrigue. The qualifications of a candidate are, that he shall be fifty-five years of age, a Cardinal, and an Italian by birth. It requires a vote of two thirds, and then France, Austria, and Spain have each the power of putting a veto on one candidate. As might be expected, all the power of the government is in the hands of the Cardinals, and they divide most of its offices among themselves. Each one has also a salary, in addition to the emolument derived from his post.

At present, the Sacred College consists of fifty-five members — two named by Pius VII., seven by Leo

XII., forty-six by Gregory XVI. The Dean of the College is Cardinal Padini, eighty-seven years of age. Scwartzenburg is the youngest of the Cardinals, being scarcely thirty-six. Sixty-two Cardinals have died since the accession of Gregory XVI.

The person I most wished to see in Rome — I may almost say in Europe — was Cardinal Mezzofanti, for his name is known through the world as one of the literary prodigies of the age. The son of an humble tradesman, he commenced his early career as a librarian. His birthplace, as he mentioned to me himself, was Bologna. When an obscure priest in the north of Italy, he was called upon to confess some criminals who were to suffer death the next day. They proved to be foreigners condemned for piracy, and he found himself utterly unable to hold any intercourse with them. Overwhelmed with grief at this unlooked for impediment, he retired to his home, spent the night in studying their language, and the next morning confessed them " in their own tongue wherein they were born." Such at least is the common story told here, and his friends ascribe his success to miraculous assistance, which was afforded him as a reward for his zeal in the discharge of his holy office.

From that time his talent was rapidly developed. His knowledge of languages seems to be almost intuitive, for he acquires them without the least apparent difficulty. At the age of thirty-six, he is said to have read twenty, and to have conversed fluently in eighteen languages. At the present time he speaks forty-two, or, as he sometimes sportively says, " forty-two, and Bolognese " — considering his native language so curious a dialect of the Italian, that he might count it as one.

He at one time filled the chair of Professor of Greek and Oriental Literature in the University of his native city, and his fame even then was widely spread through Europe. When the revolt broke out in 1831, and Bologna for a time threw off the Papal rule, Mezzofanti exerted himself so earnestly in behalf of the Pope, that he was soon afterwards called to Rome, and rewarded with an appointment under Maï. When that distinguished scholar was made a Cardinal, Mezzofanti was raised to the same dignity. Perhaps the most lively account of him is that given by Lord Byron, in his " Detached Thoughts." " I do not recollect," says he, " a single foreign literary character that I wished to see twice, except, perhaps, Mezzofanti, who was a prodigy of language, a Briareus of the parts of speech, a walking library, who ought to have lived at the time of the Tower of Babel, as universal interpreter; a real miracle, and without pretension, too. I tried him in all the languages, of which I knew only an oath or adjuration of the gods against postilions, savages, pirates, boatmen, sailors, pilots, gondoliers, muleteers, camel-drivers, vetturini, postmasters, horses, and houses, and everything in post! and he puzzled me in my own idiom."

And yet, with all these high qualifications, there is a modesty about Cardinal Mezzofanti, which shrinks from anything like praise. When complimented on the subject of his acquirements, he sometimes answers, " Do not mention it: I am only a dictionary badly bound." A Russian princess, a short time ago, having occasion to send him a note, he replied at once in her own language, and in terms so perfectly correct and idiomatic, that she could not help responding, complimenting him on the manner in which he wrote Russian. He immediately answered it, stating "that he was sorry he could not return the compliment as to the manner in which *she* wrote Russian."

I had a letter of introduction to him, and the very last morning I was in Rome, feeling that I should not be satisfied to depart without seeing him, I determined to present it. Upon calling at his palace, I found several servants in the anteroom, to one of whom I gave my letter and card. He entered with them, and in a moment the Cardinal's secretary came out to conduct me to him. After passing through a long suite of rooms, I was ushered into one where I found his Eminence, who, advancing cordially, invited me to walk into his library. He is a small, lively looking man, apparently over seventy. He speaks English with a slight foreign accent, yet remarkably correct. Indeed, I never before met with a foreigner who could talk for ten minutes without using some word with a shade of meaning not exactly right; yet in the long conversation I had with the Cardinal, I detected nothing like this. He did not use a single expression or word in any way which was not strictly and idiomatically correct.[1] He converses too without the slightest hesitation, never being at the least loss for the proper phrase.

In talking about him some time before to an ecclesiastic, I quoted Lady Blessington's remark, "that she did not believe he had made much progress in the liter-

---

[1] An American gentleman who has known him for many years, told me he called on him when he was Censor of the Press at Bologna, in company with an English naval captain, some of whose books, being on the prohibited list, had been seized at the Custom-house. The captain was in a towering rage, and Mezzofanti, in the course of his explanations, made use of the expression, — " I *enter into* your feelings." Nine foreigners out of ten, in attempting to convey this idea, would have been just as likely to say, — " I *walk into* your feelings."

ature of those forty-two languages, but was rather like a man who spent his time in manufacturing keys to palaces, which he had not time to enter," — and I inquired whether this was true. " Try him," said he, laughing; and having now the opportunity, I endeavored to do so. I led him, therefore, to talk of Lord Byron and his works, and then of English literature generally. He gave me, in the course of his conversation, quite a discussion on the question, Which was the golden period of the English language? and of course fixed on the days of Addison. He drew a comparison between the characteristics of the French, Italian, and Spanish languages, spoke of Lockhart's translations from the Spanish, and incidentally referred to various other English writers. He then went on to speak of American literature, and paid high compliments to the pure style of some of our best writers. He expressed the opinion that with many it had been evidently formed by a careful study of the old authors — those " wells of English undefiled " — and that in the last fifty years we had imported fewer foreign words than had been done in England. He spoke very warmly of the works of Mr. Fenimore Cooper, whose name, by the way, is better known on the Continent than that of any other American writer.

In referring to our Indian languages, here marked that the only one with which he was well acquainted was the Algonquin, although he knew something of the Chippewa and the Delaware, and asked whether I understood Algonquin? I instantly disowned any knowledge of the literature of that respectable tribe of savages, for I was afraid the next thing would be a proposal that we should continue the conversation in their mellifluous tongue. He learned it from an Algonquin missionary, who returned to Rome, and lived just long enough to enable the Cardinal to begin the study. He had read the works of Mr. Duponceau of Philadelphia on the subject of Indian languages, and spoke very highly of them.

And yet, all this conversation by no means satisfied me as to the depth of the Cardinal's literary acquirements. There was nothing said which gave evidence of more than a superficial acquaintance with English literature—the kind of knowledge which passes current in society, and which is necessarily picked up by one who meets so often with cultivated people of that country. His acquirements in words are certainly wonderful, but I could not help asking myself their use. I have never yet heard of their being of any practical benefit to the world, during the long life of their possessor. He has never displayed anything philosophical in his character of mind, none of that power of combination which enables Schlegel to excel in all questions of philology, and gives him a talent for discriminating and a power of handling the resources of a language, which have never been surpassed. With Mezzofanti, on the contrary, everything seems to be in detail, and therefore he turns it to no valuable purpose.

After having made a visit which far exceeded what the bounds of etiquette would allow, I felt obliged to rise, with the apology, "that I had already intruded too long upon the time of his Eminence;" but he assured me, "This was not the case — and that he only regretted, as I was about to leave Rome immediately, our first interview was necessarily our last." He inquired the ages of my children, and said, "In five or six years they will be old enough to visit Italy, and then

I trust you will return to Rome, but "—and his voice changed—" you will not find me here: I am too old to hope for it." When I left the library, he insisted on accompanying me through the long suite of rooms to the last, in which was his secretary—and gave me his parting blessing, with the wish, "that I might have a pleasant journey to Naples." When half-way across the apartment, I heard his voice, and turning round, saw him still standing in the threshold, stretching out his hands to me, and adding to his last sentence—" and a pleasant voyage home afterwards."

In the narrow compass of this chapter, I can give but a few of the points on which he touched in our long conversation—matters of faith relating to his Church—information about the Propaganda, Cardinals Weld and Acton, and Bishop Wiseman—inquiries about the attention to Greek and Latin in our colleges—and questions about the progress of his Church in America. Still less can I give any idea on paper, of the simplicity and kindness of manner which so much charmed me, in one whose reputation is unequaled in the world, and who seems so little affected by the princely dignity of Cardinal with which he has been invested. We parted, never probably to see each other again in this world, yet long shall I remember the old Cardinal's friendly smile; and I trust we may meet again in that better land where all differences are forgotten, and our Father welcomes as His children all those who loved Him in sincerity and truth, while toiling onward through the shadows of this lower life.

CHAPTER XVI.

THE PROTESTANT BURIAL-GROUND.

THERE are few spots in Rome which the stranger will naturally visit with so much interest as the Protestant Burial-ground. At a distance from his own home, he knows not but that the hand of death may here arrest him, and should this be the case, within these walls he must find his resting-place. But wherever he might wander through the wide world, he could not find a more lovely spot in which to lie down for his long, last sleep.

We rode out to it on one of those bright and balmy days, which in an Italian atmosphere remind us of the first warm days of our own spring. Just by the Porta San Paolo rises a lofty pyramid, one hundred and twenty feet in height, built of slabs of white Carrara marble, but now perfectly black with age. It is the noble sepulchre of Caius Cestius, erected in accordance with the directions of his will in the age of Augustus. It is of solid masonry, except the little chamber within, which once contained his sarcophagus. There was nothing about it which the hand of violence could rifle; nothing to tempt cupidity; no statues or carvings which could be removed to the museums; and therefore it has been permitted to remain uninjured. Its very form — adopted by the ancients in imitation of the flames that rose from the funeral pyres — was well calculated to resist the influence of the weather. In the days of Aurelian it was built into the city walls, to prevent its being used as a fortress by any attacking enemy, and this aided in securing its preservation. Except, therefore, in the change of color, and in the ivy which has trailed around it, and forced its roots into the crevices of the stones, it is but little altered from what it appeared eighteen centuries ago. Beneath it is the burial-ground, on the slope of the hill looking towards "the Eternal City," and in the direction of the East, so that the sun's first rays rest upon it, and there they spread their warmth, till the dreariness of winter is unknown on this hallowed spot. There are a hundred graves scattered among the trees, and the huge pyramid towers over them, as if in mockery of the humble monuments on which it looks down.

In the very atmosphere of Rome there is something which induces pensiveness. It is a characteristic, indeed, of these southern climes. The calmness of the air is unbroken by the lightest zephyr; the blades of grass are motionless; the leaves rustle not, and there seems to be a deep sleep resting on everything. You are insensibly led to musing, and we felt this influence when we stood in silence among these graves. At a distance we saw those grand and solemn ruins which centuries had bequeathed to us, while around were the monuments of those who were all gathered from other lands, not one of whom but was mingling his dust with the soil of a country which was not his. We read the inscriptions, and they appealed to us in our language, through its medium claiming with us a nearer brotherhood than with the strangers who dwelt around.

And even the tomb of Cestius, that old majestic pile, has something also in common with the sleepers there. "It is itself," says Rogers, "a stranger. It has stood there till the language spoken about it has changed; and the shepherd born at its foot can read its inscription no longer."

There are two inclosures for this cemetery. We entered the first, and were struck at once with its air of romantic beauty. It is formed in terraces which mount up, one above the other, to the tomb of the old Roman, and the massive walls and battlements of the ancient city. The walks were lined with flowers, which in this "divinest climate" — as Shelley called it — spring up of themselves, and odoriferous shrubs which fill the air with their rich perfume. It seems as if the grave was robbed of half its gloominess, when we know that the balmy airs of spring will be thus ever breathed about us, and its rich drapery cover our sepulchres. Very many of these tombs are those of Germans, and among them one particularly beautiful, of an artist, having carved upon it, in *bas-relief*, his brush and palette wreathed with poppies. We were surprised to see how few of the English were buried here, when so many come abroad for health, and often end their days in this city. Most of those who are interred in this spot for a time, are finally removed to their own country, for there is no nation among whom there still lingers so much of that old desire to mingle their dust with that of the friends they have known and loved, and which made the ancient patriarch bequeath to his son the direction, — "I will lie with my fathers; bury me in their burying-place." Among all the forms, indeed, of oriental benediction, there is none more expressive than the wish, — "May you die among your kindred!"

On the highest terrace we found the grave of an American, Edward Abeel, of New York. Half-way up the gentle declivity are the monuments of several more of our countrymen: Mr. John Hone, and William Henry Elliot, both of New York, and young Deveaux, of Charleston, South Carolina. On the tomb of the latter, who was one of the most promising artists we had in Italy, was a striking *bas-relief* portrait, executed by his friend and countryman, Brown, in whose studio I had also seen a most admirable bust. The fate of this young man was a melancholy one, sacrificed as he was to the jealous police regulations of the country. Travelling in Upper Italy, he reached Bologna, where some late disturbances had made the authorities peculiarly vigilant. There being some trifling informality about his passport, it was thrown back to him, and he was ordered at once to quit the city. The day was closing, but he was obliged to hire the first vehicle he could procure, and leaving his baggage behind him, ride all night. He skirted the Apennines, and avoiding the larger towns, managed to pass through the country, and at length in some way get into Rome. The first night, however, a storm came on, — the wagon was an open one, — and being without any change of clothes, he was obliged to remain in that state for several days. The consequence was, a cold, which fastened on his lungs, and, after lingering some months, he died at Rome in April last. During his illness every possible attempt was made to attach him to the Church of Rome. The Rev. Pierce Conelley, once a clergyman of the Episcopal Church in the United

States, but who some years ago abjured the true Catholic faith, was unceasing in his attentions. An English lady also, another proselyte, was exceedingly busy in her efforts. Among other schemes which she proposed in her mistaken benevolence was, that *Il Santissimo Bambino* — the little image in the Church of Ara Cœli, which we have described in a former chapter — should be brought to his sick room, and laid upon the bed. She certified that, in the case of a friend in the last stage of consumption, this process had produced an entire restoration to health. But poor Deveaux had not faith enough. He could not forget the truer teachings of his youth, and the lessons he had learned in his distant home. His nurse put a consecrated medal under his pillow, but he had so little trust in the promised cure it was to produce, that he presented it to a friend who happened to visit him.

There were better instructions, however, at hand, and he was not destined to die without having his last hours cheered by the pure truths of the Gospel. Providentially, he had become acquainted with a clergyman of our Church from his own land,[1] who became deeply interested in his situation, visited him often, and before his death administered to him the Holy Communion.

The most beautiful monument in the cemetery is that erected to the memory of Miss Bathurst, whose melancholy end produced so strong a sensation some years ago. Her father, a short time before, while engaged in some diplomatic mission in Austria, had suddenly disappeared, and his fate was never known. The daughter, a beautiful and accomplished girl, was riding

[1] Rev. Henry L. Storrs, Rector of St. John's Church, Yonkers, Westchester County, New York.

on the banks of the Tiber with her uncle, Lord Aylmer, and the Duke de Lavel Montmorenci, when attempting to turn her horse, he backed into the river, and she was swept away by the current. The groom, who alone could swim, had just been sent back on some errand, and her friends were forced to see her sink without the power of rescuing her. Several months elapsed before her body could be recovered, and laid to its rest in this sweet spot. On her tomb is sculptured a beautiful representation (executed by Westmacott) of an angel receiving her from the waves.

As we passed along, we had looked in vain for the grave of Shelley, and were at last obliged to ask the *custode*. He led us to the very top of the terrace, and there, close under the old wall, is a flat slab, which marks the resting-place of this gifted yet unfortunate poet. It bears the inscription,— " Percy Bysshe Shelley, Cor Cordium, Natus IV. Aug. MDCCXCII., obiit viii. Jul. MDCCCXXII.

> " Nothing of him that doth fade
> But doth suffer a sea change
> Into something rich and strange."

His tombstone lies low upon the ground; the wild-flowers cluster around, and the tall grass waves above it, so that we had to put them one side to read the epitaph. We stood by it for a few moments, and thought of his strange eventful history, his brilliant talents, his high-souled, lofty honor, all ruined and rendered useless by that fearful perversion of principle, which left him without chart or compass to guide him on life's stormy sea. Then came back to remembrance — though years have passed since we read it — the strange account which Trelawney has given of the burning of poor Shelley's remains in the Gulf of Spezzia, when he and Lord Byron reared the funeral pile, which, as far as circumstances would allow, was conformed to the customs of antiquity. Frankincense and wine were poured upon the wood, and for leagues around the extraordinary beauty of the flame was noticed, as it shot high into the air, illuminating the night. And when it had gone down, the friends who watched found that all had been reduced to ashes but the heart alone, on which the fire seemed to have no power. We looked around, and at a distance towered high the massive ruins of the Baths of Caracalla, among which he was accustomed to wander when writing his " Prometheus Unbound," a work so lofty in its tone, so penetrated with the spirit of the old Grecian tragedies, that, widely different as we know it to be in plot, it still seems almost to compensate us for the lost drama of Æschylus, the name of which it has borrowed.

Are there such things as presentiments, when the spirit reaches forward into the shadowy future, and the affections in anticipation gather around scenes in which one day they are to have a deeper interest? It seems to have been the case with Shelley, as he loved to linger about this spot, and so often recorded his admiration of what was to be his final resting-place. When he first visited Rome, he spoke of it as "the most beautiful and solemn cemetery he ever beheld;" and adds, " To see the sun shining on its bright grass, fresh, when we first saw it, with the autumnal dews, and hear the whispering of the winds among the leaves of the trees which have overgrown the tomb of Cestius, and the soil which is stirring in the sun-warm earth, and to mark the tombs, mostly of women and young people who were buried there, one might, if one were to die, desire the sleep they seem to sleep." About a year before his own death, the place had acquired an additional interest in his eyes, for there his friend Keats rested, "after life's fitful fever." In his lament over him, Shelley says, —

> "Go thou to Rome, — at once the Paradise,
> The grave, the city, and the wilderness;
> And where its wrecks like shatter'd mountains rise,
> And flowering weeds, and fragrant copses, dress
> The bones of Desolation's nakedness,
> Pass, till the Spirit of the spot shall lead
> Thy footsteps to a slope of green access,
> Where, like an infant's smile over the dead,
> A light of laughing flowers along the grass is spread.
>
> "And gray walls moulder round, on which dull Time
> Feeds, like slow fire upon a hoary brand;
> And one keen pyramid with wedge sublime,
> Pavilioning the dust of him who plann'd
> This refuge for his memory, doth stand
> Like flame transform'd to marble; and beneath,
> A field is spread, on which a newer band
> Have pitch'd in Heaven's smile their camp of death,
> Welcoming him we lose with scarce extinguish'd breath.
>
> "Here pause: these graves are all too young as yet
> To have outgrown the sorrows which consign'd
> Its charge to each."

And then, as if the shadows of the grave he was approaching already rested on his spirit, he adds, —

> "From the world's bitter wind
> Seek shelter in the shadow of the tomb.
> What Adonais is, why fear we to become?
> . . . . Die,
> If thou wouldst be with that which thou dost seek!
> Follow where all is fled — Rome's azure sky,
> Flowers, ruins, statues, music, words are weak
> The glory they transfuse with fitting truth to speak.
>
> "Why linger, why turn back, why shrink, my heart?
> Thy hopes are gone before: from all things here

> They have departed; *thou shouldst now depart!*
> A light is pass'd from the revolving year,
> And man, and woman; and what still is dear
> Attracts to crush, repels to make thee wither.
> The soft sky smiles — the low wind whispers near;
> 'Tis Adonais calls! oh, hasten hither,
> No more let Life divide what Death can join together."

Near this declivity is another inclosure, not as beautifully situated as the first, but only a few yards distant. The grave of Keats is near the entrance. His monument is of white marble, bearing a lyre in *basso relievo*, and under it this inscription, —

> This grave
> contains all that was mortal
> of a
> YOUNG ENGLISH POET,
> who,
> on his death-bed
> in the bitterness of his heart
> at the malicious power of his enemies,
> desired
> these words to be engraven on his tombstone —
> HERE LIES ONE
> WHOSE NAME WAS WRIT IN WATER.
> Feb. 24th, 1821.

Poor Keats! his history is the most melancholy one written in the annals of literature. The early promise was most brilliant; but he was poor and friendless, and as his opinions differed from those of the "Quarterly," on the publication of his "Endymion," the editor, Gifford, attacked him with all the savage bitterness in his power, pouring out his malice on the unoffending victim, because he knew the object of his cruelty could not retaliate. Having naturally a feeble constitution, and a mind keenly sensitive, the blow seemed to crush him, and he told a friend, with tears, that "his heart was breaking." He was persuaded to try the mild air of Italy, but he went there only to die. Some time before that event took place, he perceived its approach, and remarked that he "felt the flowers growing over him." We feel, when we think of his story, that Shelley's address to Gifford, in the preface to "Adonais," is not one whit too severe, — "Miserable man! you, one of the meanest, have wantonly defaced one of the noblest specimens of the workmanship of God. Nor shall it be your excuse, that, murderer as you are, you have spoken daggers, but used none."

But Keats will never be forgotten while the English language exists. He was, indeed, like Koerner, of Germany, cut off too early to show any maturity of power: but "Endymion," and "Lamia," and "Isabella," are rich in gems of thought, and display on every page the wealth of genius. Shelley's splendid dirge would alone be sufficient to preserve his memory, and the estimate he formed of his brother poet may be gathered from those noble stanzas, in which, in imitation of a sublime scene in the prophet Isaiah, he represents the gifted of other days rising to greet the spirit of the youthful bard, —

> "The inheritors of unfulfill'd renown
> Rose from their thrones built beyond mortal thought,
> Far in the Unapparent. Chatterton
> Rose pale, his solemn agony had not
> Yet faded from him; Sydney, as he fought
> And as he fell, and as he lived and loved,
> Sublimely mild, a spirit without spot,
> Arose; and Lucan, by his death approved:
> Oblivion, as they rose, shrank like a thing reproved.
>
> "And many more, whose names on earth are dark,
> But whose transmitted effluence cannot die
> So long as fire outlives the parent spark,
> Rose, robed in dazzling immortality.
> 'Thou art become as one of us,' they cry,

> 'It was for thee yon kingless sphere has long
> Swung blind in unascended majesty,
> Silent alone amid a heaven of song:
> Assume thy winged throne, thou Vesper of our throng!'"

Near the grave of Keats is that of Dr. Bell, whose "Observations on the Fine Arts in Italy" have long been a text-book for all who visit that country; and also the monument of the Rev. Augustus Wm. Hare, of Oxford, whose volume of sermons, published since his death, has rendered his name well known to Churchmen in America as well as in England. He seems to have ended his life in the place where it was begun, having been born — the inscription tells us — in Rome in 1792, and having died there in 1834. There is but one American buried here — Mr. Daniel Remsen, of New York.

We lingered in this lovely place until the increasing dampness, showing that the dews of evening were falling, warned us to return home. The sun had begun to sink in the west, and the massive tomb of Cestius threw its broad shadow over the burying-ground, as we turned away from it. How many hearts in distant lands are sorrowing for those who are so quietly sleeping here! Beautiful spot! which never knows the chill of winter, and where Nature herself is ever wreathing with living flowers the graves of those whose homes and friends are far away, well may the heart yearn towards thee, and the living feel, that thus they should like to rest!

CHAPTER XVII.

THE PALACES OF ROME.

THE palaces of Rome may well be illustrated by the same comparison which Faber uses with regard to those of Genoa: " old pages of history torn from some illuminated manuscript of the Middle Ages, and whereon the illuminations are well-nigh faded or effaced, by time and violence." Historically many of them are interesting, bearing the names of the noblest families of mediæval days, by whose descendants they are still occupied. Others remind us only of the nepotism of the Popes, whose first care sometimes was to ennoble their nephews, and then their short reigns were spent in building up the power of these newly risen houses, at the expense of the Church and country. And when in addition to this, we find some of them, like the Farnese, erecting their palaces by despoiling the Coliseum and other monuments of ancient Rome, we cannot look without indignation on the sacrilege of these upstart princes.

The only palaces, if we except the modern ones of the Torlonia family, which are kept up with any degree of splendor, are those of the Doria and Borghese. For the general appearance of the rest, one description will answer. You find a vast pile of buildings, often running round the four sides of a square, with the quadrangle in the centre surrounded by a marble colonnade. Entering the large arched gateway, some old servitors are lounging about, bearing in their appearance evidences of their master's dilapidated fortunes. One of them takes you in charge and commences the ordinary routine of sight-seeing. You first enter an immense hall, often hung round with the largest and worst pictures of the palace, and on one side a throne with a high velvet canopy, covered with the armorial bearings of the family. From this elevated seat, until feudal privileges were abolished, the prince was accustomed to administer justice. You follow your guide on, up marble staircases, and over mosaic floors, till you come to long suites of rooms, the walls covered with paintings while here and there antique statues are dispersed about, and richly inlaid cabinets stand against the sides. Through these you wander, gazing on the works of art, until you have gone round the square, and find yourself in the hall from which you set out.

It would be useless to attempt describing many of these collections, for while a catalogue of paintings might recall to my mind the beautiful forms on which I have gazed hour after hour, it could awaken no corresponding feeling in the mind of the reader. Some of them are celebrated for one or two remarkable pictures, while the rest of the collection is made up of inferior ones and old family portraits. Such is the *Palazzo Rospigliosi*, where in the cassino of the garden is the far-famed "Aurora" by Guido, so many copies of which have been brought to our own country. It is a large fresco on the ceiling. Around the chariot of the Sun are seen female figures advancing most gracefully hand in hand, to typify the Hours. They are decked in gay and flowing drapery, — "pictis incinctæ vestibus Horæ,"— while before them is Aurora, scattering flowers. It is called Guido's most brilliant performance, and certainly nothing could exceed the glory he has spread around the chariot of the God of Day, combining in one matchless performance all the beautiful features in which the poets have arrayed the Morning. In the *Villa Lodovisi*, which is without the city walls, occupying a part of Sallust's gardens, is the rival picture, the "Aurora" of Guercino. The goddess is in her car drawn by fiery horses, while the shades of Night appear to be vanishing at her approach. Tithon, whose couch she had just quitted, is seen half-awake, while the Morning Star, as a winged Genius bearing a torch, is following her course. The Hours, unlike those of Guido, are represented as infants, fluttering before her and extinguishing the stars — an idea perhaps borrowed from Statius, who describes Aurora as chasing the stars before her with her whip, —

"Moto leviter fugat astra flagello."

In the other compartments are Daybreak, represented as a youth with a torch in one hand and flowers in the other; Evening, a young female sleeping; and Night, personified as an aged woman poring over a book. The first rays of light seem just penetrating into her gloomy abode, scaring her companions, the owl and the bat, who are shrinking from the unwelcome intrusion.

In the *Palazzo Spada*, the great attraction is the colossal statue of Pompey, nine feet high. For three centuries it has been asserted to be the one "at whose base great Cæsar fell," and notwithstanding the discussion of critics, has retained its name and authority. It was certainly found buried on the spot where we are told Augustus had it placed, before the Theatre of Pompey. The statue holds a globe in its hand, an emblem of power, which seems hardly in republican taste, and rather brings it down to the days of the Empire. The answer to this is, that it was only a well-merited compliment to him who found Asia Minor the boundary, and left it the centre of the Roman Empire. Could we believe this view, it would certainly be with no ordinary interest that we stand at its pedestal. We should call back eighteen centuries as we gaze upon the lineaments of him, who was second to Rome's great Master, in fortune only, remembering that tragedy in the Senate House, when in the retributions of Nemesis, that rival was prostrated at the base of this stern looking statue, bathing it with his blood.

Gibbon describes the manner in which this relic of antiquity was found in digging the foundations of a house. When first discovered, the head was under one building and the body under another. The two owners therefore quarreled, and were on the point of dividing the statue, — thus rivaling the judgment of Solomon, — when Julius III. interposed, and gave them five hundred crowns which they thankfully received, as being susceptible of a more easy partition. This antique figure has since then made one appearance in public. When the French held Rome, they determined to have Voltaire's tragedy of Brutus performed in the Coliseum, and to give it greater effect decided that their Cæsar, like the original Dictator, should fall at the base of this statue. It was accordingly transported to the place of exhibition, although in so doing they were obliged temporarily to deprive it of the right arm,

One of the largest collections of paintings is found in the *Palazzo Borghese*. Among them is the " Cumæan Sibyl " of Domenichino, so familiar through copies dispersed everywhere, though no copy can give the beauty of the original. Nameless and by an unknown artist, this picture would anywhere arrest attention. We look upon it however with a new association of interest, since Bulwer has adopted it as the portrait of the high-souled Nina di Raselli, and in his own fascinating language, thus added the description, — " Why this is called the Cumæan Sibyl I know not, save that it has something strange and unearthly in the dark beauty of the eyes. I beseech thee, mistake not this sibyl for another, for Roman galleries abound in sibyls. The sibyl I speak of is dark, and the face has an eastern cast: the robe and turban, gorgeous though they be, grow dim before the rich but transparent roses of the cheek; the hair would be black, save for that golden glow which mellows it to a hue and lustre never seen but in the South, and even in the South most rare; the features, not Grecian, are yet faultless; the mouth, the brow, the ripe and exquisite contour, all are human and voluptuous; the expression, the aspect, is something more; the form is perhaps too full for the ideal of loveliness, for the proportions of sculpture, for the delicacy of Athenian models; but the luxuriant fault has a majesty. Gaze long upon that picture: it charms, yet commands the eye."

There is another portrait in this gallery on which too we may gaze with interest, for it gives us the lineaments of one who in his day was the troubler of Italy, shrinking from no means to gain his end, using the dagger and the poison with perfect recklessness to remove a rival, and without compunction throwing aside his priestly office and Cardinal's rank to become the leader of armies, when a temporal principality was within his reach. It is the picture of a young man, but with no flush of youth upon his countenance. The face is pale and sallow, the lips compressed, and the look keenly intellectual. You would decide that every line and feature revealed the character of an accomplished, yet unprincipled intriguer. The judgment would be right, for that is Raphael's portrait of Cæsar Borgia.

Look at one more picture, which is founded on a legend of the Church of Rome. It is "St. Anthony preaching to the Fishes," by Paul Veronese. The sermon which he delivered on that occasion can be purchased in any of the bookstores in this city. It commences with the salutation, "Cari et amati pesci" (dearly beloved fish), and at its conclusion, the legend tells us, the fish bowed to him, " Congesti di profonda umiltà e con reverente sembiante di religione" (with profound humility, and a grave and religious countenance). The artist seems to have endeavored to exhibit this happy close of the Saint's lecture, and the upturned eyes of the fish are certainly very edifying. After the discourse was over, and this flattering testimonial in its behalf had been received, the Saint gave them his blessing, and the congregation dispersed.

The Borghese family is one of the most wealthy of the Roman nobility, and distinguished also for its public liberality. Just beyond the city is the *Villa Borghese*, occupying a portion of the Pincian Hill, and, with its gardens and pleasure grounds, covering a circuit of more than three miles in extent. And yet its walks are open to all who choose to enter, prince or peasant; and there they may wander about or ride, with a perfect wilderness of statues around them, while at every turn graceful temples arrest the attention, and the eye is refreshed by the sight of water, spread out into lakes, or flung high into the air by sparkling fountains. Here and there are Latin inscriptions declaring the wish of the noble owner that all should unite in the enjoyment which these splendid gardens offer. One of them states, that "all these things are prepared for strangers rather than for the master."

The last Prince Borghese married Napoleon's beautiful sister Pauline. Of the reality of her beauty indeed the present generation have a good opportunity of judging, for her statue, almost in a state of nudity, was executed by Canova, and is esteemed one of his most finished works. She is taken in the character of Venus, reclining gracefully on a couch, and holding in one hand the apple which Paris had just awarded her in the contest of beauty with the other goddesses. The present Prince married a lady as widely different in character from the Princess Pauline as is possible. She was a daughter of the Earl of Shrewsbury, and died about two years ago, leaving behind her a character for sanctity, which seems to have been gained by a life of earnest devotion and ceaseless charity seldom witnessed in her elevated rank. She would steal away from the magnificence of their villa, where everything was around her to win the affections to earth, and in the dress of one of the Sisterhood of Charity, go through the city seeking everywhere distress and misery to which she might minister. I read her funeral sermon while in Rome, and if half is true which is there related, or which I heard mentioned in conversation as illustrating her spirit of self-denial, she deserves to be canonized more than nine tenths of those who now figure in the Romish calendar.

Her sister, the Lady Catherine Talbot, likewise married one of the first noblemen in Italy — the Prince Doria. Their palace, we have already said, is one of the most splendid in Rome, and kept in a degree of style and elegance befitting such a place. More than one thousand pictures are arranged in its long galleries, where the magnificence of everything around is in admirable harmony. The great charm of this collection consists in its Claudes. As we walk on, we are arrested every little while by one of those bright glowing pictures, generally a sunset, whose radiance is thrown over the whole landscape, until it forms a scene of fairy enchantment on which poets love to muse, and which Claude alone could embody and spread upon the canvas.

We never however passed the *Palazzo Doria* in the Corso, without thinking that its owner was out of place. The Dorias seem to belong to Genoa, where the name of Andrea Doria will always remain the noblest on the page of her history. His immense wealth enabled him to support a fleet of twenty-two galleys, and with this he turned the scale and freed his country from the yoke of France. He declined the offer of the ducal coronet for life, and, had he wished, there is no doubt but that he might have acquired the absolute sovereignty. But a few weeks before, we had been through his palace in Genoa. On its front is a long Latin inscription, in which the stately old Admiral, "Il Principe," — to use the title which Charles V. granted him, — informs us that he erected this residence for himself and his successors, "Œdes sibi et successoribus instauravit, MDXXVIII." Around the palace are extensive gardens which descend to the shore of the Mediterranean, and thus their walls are washed by the waves of that sea on which he won immortal glory. You wander on through walks of cypress and orange, while statues and fountains and vases placed around, all seem in perfect harmony with the beauty of the grounds. The palace can lay no claim to the magnificence of that in Rome, but its historical associations invest it with far greater interest. The absence of the family, however, has suffered it to fall somewhat into decay, and unless care is taken, a few years more will efface entirely the splendid frescoes with which Perino decorated it in the days of the Great Admiral.

As a whole, however, no palace interested us so much as the *Colonna*. There is something, to be sure, in the association of the name, for through all the Middle Ages it was the noblest family in Rome. Their lineage runs back to some remote source on the banks of the Rhine, where the wildest legends mingle with the truth. It was even maintained, in support of their old Roman origin, that they were descended from a cousin of Nero, who escaped from the city, and founded Mentz in Germany; and Gibbon tells us, that "the sovereigns of Germany were not ashamed of a real or fabulous affinity with a noble race, which in the revolutions of seven hundred years has been often illustrated by merit, and always by fortune." They are supposed to have descended from the ancient

Counts of Tusculum, but the first historical mention of them is in the middle of the eleventh century, when the Countess Emelia of Palestrina married a baron described as *De Columna*. Thus Palestrina, which is about twelve miles from Colonna, passed into their hands, and for centuries after it was their mountain fastness, and celebrated in all their struggles with the Popes.

To the student of ecclesiastical history this place is particularly associated with the contest of the family with Boniface VIII. He was one of the Gaetani family, and the two Cardinals Giacamo and Pietro Colonna, having vainly opposed his election, retired with their kinsman Sciarra to this castle, and there openly disclaimed his authority. He at once excommunicated them, offered plenary indulgence to all who would take up arms against the family, and was thus enabled, after a gallant resistance, to take their stronghold. Their power broken, the Cardinals agreed to come to Anagni, where the Pope was residing, and make their submission. Then was witnessed one of those acts of treachery, not unusual in the Papal history. Boniface was advised to "promise much and perform little," and he fully acted up to the counsel; for which Dante in his "Inferno" has condemned him to immortal infamy. He nominally granted them pardon, but at the same time took measures to have Palestrina razed to the ground, and the whole Colonna family hunted out of Italy.

But the hour of retribution came. Sciarra Colonna, after a series of most romantic adventures, returned to Rome just as the King of France, Philippe le Bel, had dispatched William de Nogaret to seize the Pope, and with this party he allied himself. It was in 1303 that Boniface was residing at Anagni, some fifty miles from Rome, and believing all his enemies crushed, he had prepared a Bull, in which he maintained "that, as Vicar of Jesus Christ, he had the power to govern kings with a rod of iron, and to dash them in pieces like a potter's vessel." The eighth of September, the anniversary of the Nativity of the Virgin, was the time selected for its publication, but the very day preceding, his dream of dominion was most rudely broken. Shouts were heard along the streets of Anagni, — " Long life to the King of France! Death to Boniface!" and looking from his palace window, the Pope beheld a band of three hundred horsemen headed by his old enemy, just surrounding the Pontifical residence.

Boniface was now in his eighty-seventh year, but age had not broken the courage of one of whom it was written, "Regnabit ut Leo," — he shall reign as a lion, — and he prepared with firmness to meet his foes. He clothed himself in his official robes, placed the crown of Constantine on his head, and with the keys and cross in his hands, seated himself in the Pontifical Chair. Sciarra Colonna rushed first into his presence, but struck by the dignified composure of his enemy, he went no further than verbal insults. Nogaret followed, but feeling less reverence, he dragged the Pope forth, and committed him to close imprisonment. Three days afterwards the people rose, expelled the intruders, and rescued Boniface, but they could not soothe his wounded spirit, and he shortly died from the violence of his passions and the disgrace which he felt had been inflicted on him.

His successor, Benedict XI., absolved the Colonnas from excommunication, and they shortly after began to rebuild Palestrina, which in 1311 was ready to receive Henry of Luxembourg, Emperor of Germany, when he came to Rome to be crowned. Louis of Bavaria resided there at his coronation in 1328; and twice Stephen Colonna repulsed Rienzi from its walls, when he was vainly attempting to seize it.

It is this Stephen Colonna who stands preëminent among the heroes of the Middle Ages, and whose name, in the mind of every Italian scholar, is so intimately associated with that of Petrarch. It is worth while learning Italian to read the letters which the poet addressed to him, styling him "a phœnix sprung from the ashes of the ancient Romans." Nor was this praise undeserved. In every change of fortune, and even in exile, Stephen Colonna sustained his dignity. When driven from his country, and an attendant asked him, "Where is now your fortress?" he laid his hand on his heart, and answered, "Here." Amidst the feuds of Rome, or at the Court of Avignon, he commanded no feeling but that of reverence.

But these historical recollections have led us from our subject. At Avignon we had seen the deserted Colonna palace standing directly opposite to that of the Popes, and which was occupied by some of the family during the residence there of the Papal Court — "the Babylonish captivity," as Petrarch calls it; but it cannot compare in splendor with this one at Rome. The latter was commenced in 1417 by Pope Martin V. (Oddone Colonna). Here also afterwards lived Cardinal Borromeo and Pope Julius II.; and in the fifteenth century, when Andrew Paleologus, the Emperor of the East, visited Rome, it was here that he made his home. The palace seems to preserve its distinctive character as the peculiar residence of the family, and in all parts of it we learn something of their past history, until the whole building becomes, as it were, one record of their deeds. Everywhere we see their armorial bearings — the column, surmounted by the crown — the latter emblem being added by Louis of Bavaria at his coronation, out of gratitude to the family for their assistance; while on the walls are portraits of Cardinals and Popes, and the leaders of armies, — men whose names were celebrated in their day, — all claiming descent from the Colonna.

These are mostly arranged in the great gallery, more than two hundred feet in length, the noblest hall in Rome, and not surpassed by any in Europe. Its ceiling is painted in fresco with a representation of the battle of Lepanto, where the Roman galleys were led by a prince of this family. It was on Sunday, the seventh of October, A. D. 1571, that the Crescent and the Cross were thus arrayed against each other; and it added to the courage of the Christian soldiers to know, that on that day all their brethren through Christendom were offering up prayers for the success of the arms they wielded. It is an additional circumstance of interest, tha the galleys of Genoa were led by John Andrew Doria, a descendant of the great admiral. After a conflict of four hours victory declared for the Cross. Upwards of fifteen thousand Turks fell in the battle, sixty-two ships were sunk and a hundred and twenty taken, while more than twelve thousand Christian slaves found in the Ottoman vessels were set at liberty. The arrival of the news in Rome, we are told, revived the memory of her ancient glory, and it was determined to bestow upon Prince Colonna the honor of a modern triumph. He was received with all possible splendor by the Senator and Magistrates of the city, and, like the old Consuls, escorted with pomp and acclamations to the Capitol. His portrait hangs upon the wall, showing in all his bearing, the chivalrous soldier.

Yet near it is one which interests us more. It is the picture of Vittoria Colonna, the sweet poetess, whose sonnets will live as long as the language in which they are written, and who well deserved the title her countrymen bestowed upon her, — "The most beautiful and glorious lady." She was the wife of the Marquis of Pescara, and when efforts were made to turn him from his fidelity to the Spanish cause, she wrote to him these noble admonitions, — "Remember your virtue, which raises you above fortune and above kings. By that alone, and not by the splendor of titles, is glory acquired, that glory which it will be your happiness and pride to transmit unspotted to your posterity." Her husband was killed at the battle of Pavia, and thenceforth she retired from the world. Most beautiful in mind and person, she had no lack of suitors, but she remained constant to the memory of the lost, and when she celebrates his praises, the deep and true tenderness of her lines shows the earnestness of her affection. But she was also a priestess of religion, and consecrated her lyre to the mysteries and graces of our faith, leaning indeed so much to the purer doctrines which then began to spread, heralding the Reformation, that she often drew upon herself reproach and satire. But her purity of song was so well acknowledged, that even in life she gained the title of Divine, which was granted to Dante and Ariosto only after death. Her fame indeed spread widely, so that Ariosto dedicated to her a number of his immortal verses.

But she has another claim to our interest. It was to her that Michael Angelo Buonarotti devoted his muse, when turning from Sculpture and Painting he sought the inspiration of their sister Poetry. He worshipped her with that Platonic love which at this period had begun to imbue the minds of Italian poets, redeeming the passion from all that was earthly, showing it purified by the loftiest virtue, and raising its object almost to the confines of Divinity. His love, therefore, was not like that of Dante for his Beatrice, or of Petrarch for his Laura, for they shared too deeply in the feelings of mere mortals. But while every line of Buonarotti glows with tenderness, we perceive that it is something sacred, partaking of the love which he might have had for an object purely ideal, the sort of abstract devotion with which he would have worshipped the beautiful in art. And did she, who had refused the hand of princes, return this affection? There is no evidence that she did. She admired him as an almost inspired artist, and often wrote to him with warm regard, yet no tinge of earthly passion appears in any of the lines of Vittoria Colonna. Her life glided quietly away in the convent near Rome in which she resided, yet without taking the vows, and there she died in old age, a few years before her impassioned admirer.

With all these associations, is it to be wondered that we gazed long upon her picture? How sweet and calm appears her countenance seen thus among the warlike princes of her race; as strange as the contrast furnished by the soft and melodious verses she could weave, while they were engaged in wild forays and deeds of blood! As we stand before it, we forget the last three centuries, and remember only that age so glorious for Italy, when at once she exchanged the darkness which had shrouded her, for all that was noble in the arts or elevated in poetry.

The most beautiful woman we have seen in Italy is a princess of the Colonna family. It was in the lofty halls of one of these old feudal palaces, when the radiance of an hundred lamps flashing back from the gilded ceilings and marble columns, presented a scene of elegance, for the display of which no place is better adapted than the palace of a Roman prince. The saloons were filled with the noblest of these sunny climes, whose names recalled associations which stretched back to the mediæval times. Rich music fell on the ear; jewels flashed before the eye; and the beauty of England was seen by the side of the more impassioned loveliness of Southern Europe. Around the Princess Doria, a circle of her countrymen had gathered, claiming her to themselves, as a descendant of the old heroic Talbots. But among all present, "the observed of all observers," was this member of the princely house of Colonna, of whom we have spoken. As the light flashed from the diamond tiara on her head, she seemed worthy to be a queen, even in this land where beauty is an inheritance and where the classical features of the lowest peasantry are often those from which Raphael might have drawn his inspiration.

But the fortunes of this noble house seem now to be waning, for the age of chivalry is gone, and that of utilitarianism has taken its place.

> "And noble name, and cultured land,
> Palace and park, and vassal band,
> Are powerless to the notes of hand
> Of Rothschild, or the Barings."

The present prince is seldom in Rome. Having married a lady of Naples, he generally resides in that city. In the last century the family even sold to the Ludovisi the estate of Colonna, thus alienating a place from which they derive their name; and in the seventeenth century they parted with Palestrina, their old feudal stronghold. It was purchased by Carlo Barberini, brother to Urban VIII., for the sum of seven hundred and seventy-five thousand dollars. And to show how much interest is often felt by these Roman nobles in historical recollections, it is related that the last Prince Barberini, whose family had not seen Palestrina for three generations, being asked, why he did not visit so interesting a spot, a short day's journey from his palace in Rome, replied, "Why, my father never visited it; besides, it is too long a journey for my own horses, and not worth the expense of posting." [1]

We will refer to but one more of these palaces; that of the *Barberini*. The family was formerly one of the most powerful in Rome, being built up by Pope Urban

---

[1] Lady Morgan, twenty years ago, related a story equally good of the Borghese family. Their library had not been opened for many years before the revolution. Some time after that event, and the young prince had married into the Bonaparte family, a visit to it was proposed as a frolic after dinner. After a long search for keys, the party proceeded thither with lights, when, on opening the door, the singular spectacle presented itself of the whole room in a blaze. This sudden conflagration was caused by the cobwebs which covered the walls taking fire the moment the candles were brought in. The flame ran rapidly round, and was extinguished as rapidly. Stores of gold, silver, and ivory work of the most beautiful description were found in the *Guarda-roba* of the palace, where they had been long forgotten.

VIII. (Mateo Barberini), whose reign was noted for its nepotism. Their crest — the bee — is seen on buildings in every part of the city, and is sculptured even in the interior of St. Peter's, and on the canopy over the High Altar, which was also erected by the same Pope.

The library is celebrated for its manuscripts, containing all the correspondence of Urban VIII. Some of them are of great historical value; such as the official reports on the state of the Church of Rome in England during the reign of Charles I. They must contain much matter for a history of the Stuart family, which would throw light upon many hitherto disputed points. Mabillon, who in 1686 came into Italy with a commission from the King of France to collect manuscripts, had an opportunity of examining those in the Barberini library, and gives a pleasant account of some original papers he found there.[1] They contain a negotiation between the Spaniards and Urban VIII. It seems there was a saint held in great reverence in some parts of Spain, of the name of Viar. The more to encourage his worship, they petitioned the Pope to grant some special indulgences to his altars. He naturally, in reply, inquired into the proofs of his sanctity, when they produced a monumental stone which had been dug up, and on which the whole claim rested, having on it the letters, S. VIAR. Unfortunately, however, the antiquarians of the day immediately perceived it to be a fragment of some old Roman inscription, in memory of one who had been " PræfectuS. VIARum," or " Overseer of the Highways."

This palace once contained a fine gallery of paint-

[1] Mabil. *Iter. Ital.*, p 144.

ings, but as the fortune of the family was reduced, many of them were scattered, and now form the principal attraction of other collections in the city. And yet there is one remaining in the gallery, which renders it in some respects the favorite collection in Rome. It is the portrait of Beatrice Cenci. The *custode* carried us through the different rooms, and pointed out one picture after another, but we hastily turned from them all in our impatience to see the gem of the collection. At length he drew aside a curtain, and there we saw the original with which copies had so long made us familiar. They have been multiplied all over the world, and the engravings too have been widely circulated, but not one that we had ever seen conveyed an idea of that touching expression which gives such a charm to the portrait by Guido.

The history of Beatrice Cenci is one of those strange tales which seem more like the wildest fiction than anything which could have happened in real life. Shelley has made it the foundation of his tragedy of "The Cenci," where the darker features are hinted at, while in the development of the plot, historical truth seems as far as possible to have been observed. Her father was of a noble Roman family, and in the sixteenth century one of the most powerful barons of Italy. He was leagued with all the restless evil spirits in the land, and indeed one of those demons in human form who seem to leave us in doubt whether or not he can be of the same nature with his fellow-men. In the tragedy, he thus describes his own fiend-like tastes and pursuits in language which history tells us is but too strictly true : —

> "When I was young, I thought of nothing else
> But pleasure; and I fed on honey-sweets;
> Men, by St. Thomas! cannot live like bees,
> And I grew tired; yet, till I kill'd a foe,
> And heard his groans, and heard his children's groans,
> Knew I not what delight was else on earth,
> Which now delights me little. I the rather
> Look on such pangs as terror ill conceals:
> The dry fix'd eyeball; the pale quivering lip,
> Which tells me that the spirit weeps within
> Tears bitterer than the bloody sweat of Christ.
> I rarely kill the body, which preserves,
> Like a strong prison, the soul within my power,
> Wherein I feed it with the breath of fear
> For hourly pain."

Although his wealth was almost countless, yet his children were kept in poverty. Two of his sons sent into Spain, died in want, and his daughter, with her stepmother, were treated with the most shocking brutality. Yet none dared to interfere, for Count Cenci was an enemy who struck without giving any warning, and whose blow was never in vain. Shelley represents Cardinal Camillo remonstrating with him on his daughter's "strange and uncomplaining wrongs," when he receives this characteristic answer, —

> "Cardinal,
> One thing I pray you, recollect henceforth,
> And so we shall converse with less restraint.
> A man you knew, spoke of my wife and daughter:
> He was accustom'd to frequent my house;
> So the next day *his* wife and daughter came
> And ask'd if I had seen him; and I smil'd:
> I think they never saw him any more."

But the secret of his immunity was his enormous wealth. Whatever deed of wickedness was detected, he could always purchase his pardon from the Pope. A grant was made of one of his fiefs to a nephew of the Pontiff, and all was hushed up. Count Cenci had therefore reason to say, —

> "No doubt Pope Clement,
> And his most charitable nephews, pray
> That the Apostle Peter and the saints
> Will grant for their sakes that I long enjoy
> Strength, wealth, and pride, and lust, and length of days
> Wherein to act the deeds which are the stewards
> Of their revenue."

At length his iniquity reached its climax, and he attempted an outrage upon the person of his daughter, Beatrice. Shortly afterwards he was found strangled in his bed, at the Castle of Petrella, among the Apulian Apennines. Whether or not Beatrice was guilty of plotting his death cannot be determined, yet it is evident she was at this time suffering from an almost total alienation of reason. She was arrested, with her stepmother and brother, and put to torture, but nothing could be extorted from her. Shelley states, that the murderers employed by her confessed when put to the rack; but another version of the story is, that seeing her younger brother, Bernardo, exposed to torture, she assumed the guilt of the deed to herself, for the sake of saving him. The true account it is difficult to procure, as it exists only in the records of the Court, and the government does not permit it to be made public.

Every effort was made to save Beatrice, but the Pope would not commute her sentence of death, for the treasury needed replenishing, and he wished to confiscate the Cenci estates. The night before her execution, she made for herself a robe of white sackcloth, with a loose, winding head-dress of the same material, and it was finished but an hour before she left her prison. Guido, says the family tradition, saw her mount the scaffold, and, struck with her exquisite beauty, painted her portrait from memory. The picture originally belonged to the Colonna family, and still has the column and crown painted in one corner. With so romantic a history attached to it, no one can wonder that this is the favorite picture in Rome. We gaze upon it, and Beatrice seems before us, showing a face of childlike loveliness, utterly unlike that of one who could ever have been an actor in such a terrible tragedy. The head is turned on one side, as if she was leaving you, yet looking back. From the folds of the white drapery, her golden hair escapes and falls about her neck. The large, full eyes look mournfully from the canvas, and the delicate features are all swollen with weeping. The whole expression is one deeply pathetic — the countenance of a gentle being who had been stricken with despair, yet from whose every lineament there beams forth an exquisite loveliness. "Beatrice Cenci," says Shelley, "appears to have been one of those rare persons in whom energy and gentleness dwell together, without destroying one another: her nature was simple and profound. The crimes and miseries, in which she was an actor and a sufferer, are as the mask, and the mantle, in which circumstances clothed her for her impersonation on the scene of the world."

Since this tragedy, the old palace of the Cenci, in the city, has stood desolate and uninhabited, as if stricken by a curse. The family, we believe, ended at that time; its sole survivor, the young Bernardo, disappeared, and was generally supposed to have been placed in a monastery. We wandered over the courts of the palace, and look through its deep, dark dungeons, with the interest with which this strange story has invested it. It is now in the most obscure quarter of Rome — an immense, gloomy, and deserted pile of massive architecture, without doors, or windows, or any sign of human habitation, yet showing, by its antique friezes of fine workmanship, the magnificence which it once possessed. There seems to brood over it a spirit of desolate and ruined grandeur. Adjoining it is the little Chapel of S. Thommaso a' Cenci, erected by the notorious Count Francisco Cenci, of whom we have been speaking, and endowed to offer up masses for the peace of his soul. What a strange contradiction of traits! Yet thus religion is often exhibited in this land. Shelley truly says, that in an Italian, " it is interwoven with the whole fabric of life. It is adoration, faith, submission, penitence, blind admiration; not a rule for moral conduct. It has no necessary connection with any one virtue. The most atrocious villain may be rigidly devout, and, without any shock to established faith, confess himself to be so. Religion pervades intensely the whole frame of society, and is, according to the temper of the mind which it inhabits, a passion, a persuasion, an excuse, a refuge: never a check."

To believe in the innocence of Beatrice, is part of the creed of an Italian. Her story is one of those romantic traditions which sink deeply into the popular mind. Every beggar on the steps of the *Scala di Spagna* is perfectly familiar with it. He knows her portrait as well as he does the pictures of the Madonna, and no possible evidence could turn him from the conviction that she was a victim unjustly sacrificed. Every Roman acts most religiously on the parting advice she is represented as giving to the young Bernardo, —

> "One thing more, my child:
> For thine own sake be constant to the love
> Thou bearest us; and to the faith that I,
> Though wrapt in a strange cloud of crime and shame,
> Lived ever holy and unstain'd. And though
> Ill tongues shall wound me, and our common name
> Be as a mark stamp'd on thine innocent brow
> For men to point at as they pass, do thou
> Forbear, and never think a thought unkind
> Of those who perhaps love thee in their graves."

CHAPTER XVIII.

EXCURSION TO TIVOLI.

THE neighborhood of Rome abounds with scenes to which the visitor can make delightful excursions. We have been to-day to Tivoli, to which every one goes, and we therefore followed the example of the rest of the world. The sun was just rising as we passed through the gate of San Lorenzo, and near the old Church of the same name. It stands close without the walls, and is one of the most ancient in the world. We may still see within it, the upper row of columns for the female gallery, preserved unaltered from an early age. Our road led for nearly the whole distance over the desolate Campagna, which we traversed by the Via Tiburtina, in some parts passing over the ancient pavement, formed by large blocks of lava.[1] Here and there was a tomb, or the remains of some shattered monument — the only tokens existing of the thousands who once inhabited this waste region, now given up to sterility and miasma.

A few miles brought us to a canal which drains the sulphureous lake of Salfatara. The water which flows through it is of a milky color, and long before we reached it, the sulphureous fumes and gas gave notice

[1] It has been discovered by excavating, that this ancient road has been paved three times, the pavements being found one above the other.

of its vicinity. The lake was once a mile in circuit, but has been gradually diminishing until but little of it is visible. It is filled with floating islands, composed of small masses of reeds and other substances matted together, and which are carried to and fro by the wind, like those of the Vadimon Lake of which Pliny has given such a minute account.[1] These bituminous masses gradually add to the solid concretions on the margin of the lake, and probably in the course of a short time the remaining surface will be hid. For a considerable space around, the ground sounds hollow under foot, showing that we are only treading on the crust which covers the lake.

A short distance further and we crossed the Anio by the Ponte Lucana, a bridge well known to visitors in Rome by the picture of Poussin in the Doria Palace. Near it stands the lofty tomb of Plautius Silvanus, who accompanied Claudius on his expedition into Britain. Like all these massive monuments, it was during the Middle Ages converted into a fortress, and the battlements by which it was crowned still remain. It is a most picturesque ruin, and a favorite subject with the landscape painters of all countries. From this spot we left the main road, and by a narrow and vile lane rode to Hadrian's Villa. It is a strange mass of ruins, far more extensive even than the Palace of the Cæsars, and giving proof of that spirit of luxury which was the absorbing feeling in the latter days of Rome. It was originally constructed on a plan surpassing everything else that even Imperial magnificence had attempted, and covering a space of from eight to ten miles in circuit. Into this one spot the Emperor in-

---

[1] Ep. vii. 20.

tended to gather an imitation of all that he had seen in his travels, which most interested him. Here were a Lyceum, an Academy, a Pœcile in imitation of that at Athens, a Vale of Tempe, a Serapeon of Canopus like the one at Alexandria, a stream called the Euripus, a Library, Barracks for the Guards, a Tartarus, Elysian Fields, and temples dedicated to a perfect Pantheon of gods. He had —

> " Collected
> All things that strike, ennoble — from the depths
> Of Egypt, from the classic fields of Greece,
> Her groves, her temples — all things that inspire
> Wonder, delight."

We found the usual *cicerone*, and spent some hours in wandering about among the massive ruins. To attempt to describe them would be useless. They are found in every possible form and shape, scattered over this vast space. Sometimes lofty arches towered over our heads, wreathed with ivy, and crowned by shrubs and bushes waving in the breeze, and then we came to the ruins of a theatre, where the circular seats were still visible, sixteen centuries after the audience had been turned to dust. A long range of broken arches in a most picturesque form, show where once the Prætorian guards were quartered, and the massive remains of baths give some idea of the magnificence of this portion of the palace. Sometimes our guide led us under ground through galleries and crypts, on the ceilings of which are still seen the remains of fresco paintings; and then clambering over fallen columns we came to the edge of a hill, and in a deserted meadow below we saw all that was left of Hadrian's Vale of Tempe. What a perfect paradise must it have been in its day, when human ingenuity had here exhausted all its skill! Let the imagination rebuild once more these fallen piles; rear these crumbling arches; transform, as of old, into a fairy scene these groves and gardens; and we can scarcely believe that there ever has existed such a reality in this every-day world. It would rather seem some artist's glorious dream, or what the Italians in common expression call, "un pezzo di cielo caduto in terra," — a little bit of heaven fallen upon the earth.

But Time here has not been the only spoiler. For centuries the degenerate Romans used these ruins as they would a quarry, and plundered them for porphyry and marble columns to adorn their palaces and churches. Their excavations indeed brought many gems of art to light, for here were found the Venus de Medici, the celebrated Vase which we saw in Warwick Castle in England, and many others of those beautiful works which now enrich the museums of Europe. But the work of desolation is at length complete. Lofty trees have sprung up in every part, twining their roots among the massive stones, and thick vines have grown over the fluted columns, so that you have to tear them aside to see the sculptures on their capitals. Not a sound was heard except when the bee hummed about us as he flitted among the wild flowers to gather his honey. All was as quiet as the first Sabbath after the Creation. The traces of man's luxury were rapidly disappearing, and Nature was again claiming this beautiful spot for her own.

At this villa Hadrian resided when he was seized with his last and fatal illness. Here he had everything gathered around him to make life happy, and every luxury at hand which the world could furnish. The gems of art filled his palaces, and from the portico in front he had a distant view of Rome with its many towers gleaming in the sunlight — the magnificent Metropolis of the Earth, of which he was the absolute master. How hard then must it have been for him to see the gates of Eternity opening before him, "not knowing the things that should befall him there!" Yet amid all his pomps and pleasures, he seems to have made as great preparations for his death as for his life, and the mightiest monument in Rome is the one he reared to receive his remains. But there, as elsewhere, Time has made sad changes and utterly defeated the builder's object. The Imperial tomb of Hadrian was soon perverted to be a fortress for the living; its sculptured ornaments were gradually defaced by the hand of violence; Belisarius hurled on the invading Goths the beautiful statues which adorned the interior; and now it stands naked and frowning, as the Papal Castle of St. Angelo. Even the marble sarcophagus which once held his body has been seized by modern spoilers, and now holds the ashes of Pope Innocent II.

A few miles further and we leave the Campagna, commencing the ascent of the hills by a road which winds through olive groves until it reaches Tivoli. Bold rocks jutting out into the road; the old olive-trees, with their gnarled and twisted stems; simple shrines before which the *contradina* are kneeling in their picturesque costumes; and above, the old and hoary ruins of two thousand years — these are the features of the landscape. The peasantry seemed to be enjoying themselves — some, basking lazily in the sunshine, inhaling an atmosphere, which to breathe is luxury; and some, as in the days of Virgil, reclining *sub tegmine fagi*, but we fear that in this accidental circumstance alone like the hero of the First Bucolic.

There are few places about which linger so many classical associations as Tivoli. Five centuries before the founding of Rome, here stood the ancient Tibur, and when the colonists of Romulus had gathered on the Seven Hills, they found it a powerful rival not to be reduced until after years of warfare. Then it became a mere suburb of Rome, the delightful retreat of its patricians, and the prison of its captives. Hither they sent Syphax, King of Numidia, and here he ended his days, being thus saved the mortification of gracing the triumph of Scipio Africanus. As Livy tells us, — "Syphax was withdrawn rather from the gaze of the multitude, than from the glory of the conqueror, by dying a little before the triumph, at Tibur."[1] In the Vatican, however, is a monumental inscription found in this place, bearing the name of the captive king, which expressly states that he was led in the triumph. How the fiery African fretted away his life, we know not, though Polybius tells us that he died in prison, and Claudian that he swallowed poison, —

"Haurire venena
Compulimus dirum Syphacem."

Two centuries more brought the days of Roman luxury, when the same beauty of scenery which now attracts so many visitors, made it the favorite residence of poets, philosophers, and statesmen, and the ruins of their villas are still scattered about through the lovely valleys and on the hill-sides. Then, its praises began

[1] Lib. i. c. 13.

to be sung in the harmonious measures of verse, and thus by Roman poets the name of Tivoli was first invested with those sweet associations, which still cling to it wherever it is heard. Virgil bestowed on it the epithet, "Superbum Tibur," and to this day these words are borne as the motto on the city arms. Catullus, who was a wealthy patrician as well as a poet, had here his villa, in whose praises he delighted to dwell; Propertius pays his tribute to the beauty of these hills and valleys; and the words "lucus Tiburni" often occur in the sweetest lyrics of Horace. His verses, he tells us, were often composed when wandering among its shady groves, —

> "Circa nemus, uvidique
> Tiburis ripas operosa parvus
> Carmina fingo."

That he had a villa here, we do not believe, nor is any credit to be attached to the scattered ruins which here go by his name."[1] The very terms he uses proves the fact. When expressing the earnest wish that he might spend his declining years among its retreats, his language is —

> "Sit meæ sedes utinam senectæ."

But the "sit utinam" shows that it was rather a hope fondly cherished, than anything which he had realized. He lived in a day, however, when the Roman Patricians delighted to patronize genius, and here at the table of his friend Mæcenas and the other lordly patrons whom he celebrates in his verses, the poet was undoubtedly often found, a visitor in Tibur, though not a resident. Some miles distant, in a little valley formed by the ridges of Mount Lucretilis, is the probable site of Hor-

[1] Eustace, ii. 70.

ace's modest Sabine farm. There, the features of the landscape so graphically portrayed in his lines, remain unchanged, and we recognize them at once. Even " the pine waving over the villa," and " the ilex spreading around the rocks," as they shade the ruined wall and broken mosaic pavement, still mark the fidelity of his descriptions.

Nearly three centuries later, and a captive princess came to Tibur, to transfer to its hills the regal luxury of the East. It was Zenobia, Queen of Palmyra, to whom Aurelian gave his palace in this place, and whose daughter he elevated to his throne as Empress of Rome. How must the haughty spirit of the eastern queen have chafed within her, when thus forced to live within sight of Imperial Rome, where a captive she had walked to grace the triumph of her conqueror! The memory of that day, when exposed to the rude gaze of a Roman populace, she formed a part of the same pageant with gladiators, and wild beasts from the East, and captives from Gaul, and the rich and gorgeous treasures of her own palace borne as spoils of war, must have recurred with crushing weight to the mind of one who had hitherto been served only with the abject servility of oriental ceremony. And when there was mingled with this, the recollections of her proud Palmyra, — that glorious city of the desert, — we may well believe, that among the millions who owed allegiance to Aurelian, there was no one more wretched than the mother of his queen. But all her magnificence has passed away, and no traces of her existence here remain, except the ruins of the Baths she erected on the Anio, and which still retain the name " Bagni di Regina."

With the Middle Ages, the luxury and splendor of Tivoli — for in the eighth century it had taken this name — passed away, and it became the centre of strife and warfare. Its convenient distance from Rome rendered it a place of importance, and for centuries it was deeply concerned in all the struggles between the Emperors and Popes — the Guelphs and Ghibellines. Whenever a faction was expelled from the city, its adherents passed over the Campagna, made here their first halting-place, and fortifying themselves, waited the opportunity to return. It seemed as if for Tivoli the Iron Age had been renewed. In succession it became a stronghold of the powerful houses of the Colonna and the Orsini. Here, too, for a time, were the head-quarters of Rienzi, and on the Square of San Lorenzo he once publicly harangued the people with that wild eloquence, which so often enabled him to sway the minds of men, and from a peasant to become the Tribune of Rome.

A miserable, dirty town, filled with some fifteen thousand inhabitants, as ferocious and lawless as ages of strife and misrule could make them, is all that remains of this classical and once powerful place. The contrast between the old Roman elegance and the dinner they furnished us at the inn *La Regina*, was as great as that which we afterwards found at Capua, the vilest, dirtiest place in all Italy, but which we only remembered as the city whose luxury enervated the army of Hannibal. We passed through the town, picking up a guide on our way, and commenced a survey of the Falls. These are certainly exceedingly beautiful. There is a wide, deep valley, the circuit of which is about three miles, and on one side, half-way up the mountain, the town has been built. Beneath it, far below its foundations, the rocks are perforated by caverns, out of which and all around the circle of the romantic glen, the cascades come dashing forth, flinging their spray into the air, and when the sun shines, arched by the most beautiful rainbows. There are more than twenty of these wild mountain torrents seen from different points, as you ride round the terrace which forms the sides of the valley. It is about an hundred feet to the bottom, and the water rushes down, leaping from rock to rock, and beautifully contrasting its sheet of silvery foam with the brilliant verdure of the valley behind. The streams seem to race forth and hurry on as if they were eager to meet below, where they unite in the quiet river, and glide peacefully away together. Every step varies and changes the prospect. At one time the foaming water disappears entirely among the chasms in the rocks, or darts away behind the trees and drooping vines, or sinks into some retired grotto, and then once more suddenly dashes forth, and flings itself over a precipice in one dazzling sheet of foam, which is again lost to sight in the dark gulf beneath. Wilder scenes I have seen in my own land, yet never one uniting so much of the grandeur of nature with the soft and beautiful. The contrast is so striking, between the brilliant sunlight above, imparting an emerald tint to the vines and shrubs on which it rests, and the deep gloom of the gulf beneath.

And all the way up the glen for miles is a succession of the same scenes of beauty. At times, we come to a spot of calm and peaceful loveliness, which almost seems to have escaped the curse, and reminds us of the glory of Eden before the earth had grown aged, and ceased to reflect back the serenity of Heaven. Then is heard again the murmur of the little stream as it falls over the rocks, and then, a little further on, not a sound breaks the stillness, as we reach some retired valley, where the water spreads out into a succession of little mirrors, in whose bosom we see the deep blue of the sky above, —

"Bright lakes, those glistening eyes of solitude." [1]

Upon a lofty crag, on the very edge of the wild circular valley, and overlooking the picturesque scene we have described, stands the little Temple of the Tiburtine Sibyl. It is a light and fairy thing, not more than twenty feet in diameter, circular, like that of Vesta at Rome, and surrounded by elegant Corinthian columns. What rites were performed there we know not, or what deity was worshipped in this picturesque little fane, yet a more romantic spot could not have been selected, or a more beautiful shrine built for any faith. Visible from every point of the landscape, it might well have been dedicated to the nymph of these gushing fountains. It seemed in perfect character with the scene, — harmonizing well with the deep foliage around it, and the lonely torrent on which it looked down, — resting there in its antique beauty, the relic of an age of taste and elegance, which even succeeding barbarism had not the heart to destroy.

A little further on is the ruined Villa of Mæcenas, where the patron of Virgil and Horace passed the months of summer heat, free from the cares of statesmanship. It looks out over the Campagna, and in the

[1] *The Gipsies*, by A. P. Stanley.

distance he might have seen the Imperial City, with the golden towers of the Capitol soaring high above it. Through three of the massive arches which still remain, the torrent has found its way, and goes dashing on until it is lost in the valley beneath. We returned to the town, and followed our guide as he unlocked a gate, and conducted us down a steep and rocky path, which led to the bottom of the glen. Here, among the vines, wet with spray, stalactites hang about glittering like gems, and the water has worn its way into the soft rock, forming in every direction strangely shaped grottoes, where the moss has grown, covering them like a rich carpet. The largest is called the Cavern of Neptune, though it would much more appropriately bear the name of some water nymph.

From these Alban hills — which we cross on the road from Naples — the traveller should always have his first view of Rome, if he would avoid disappointment. On every other side but little of the city is seen until you are almost under its walls. Here, on the contrary, the Campagna spreads out before us in all its dreariness, and from the Mediterranean on the one side, to the Apennines on the other, we have one wide prospect of desolation, broken only here and there by a few scattered ruins, while in the centre of this mighty plain rises the city, its domes, and cupolas, and columns, seen at a single glance from the distance of nearly twenty miles. There is something, indeed, awful in this desolate grandeur contrasting so strongly with the glorious landscape, on which Hannibal and Pyrrhus gazed from this very spot.

It was among these hills, too, that Claude painted many of his landscapes. His house still stands on the Pincian Mount, near the Convent of Santa Trinita, so that even from the window of his studio he looked over Rome, and day after day watched the changing lights, and the rich glow, which he has transferred so faithfully to his canvas. We wonder not, indeed, that he lingered among such scenes! In our own land we have scenery which Salvator Rosa would have delighted to paint, yet of its grand features we may become weary. There is little to enlist the heart and the affections. We have no PAST. But we can never tire of the calm loveliness of an Italian landscape. It is not nature alone. It is mingled everywhere with those graceful forms, which three thousand years ago art assumed, and which have still survived, only more beautiful from age.

The sun was going down in cloudless beauty when we commenced our descent of the hills. Its beams lighted up the distant dome of St. Peter's, and shed their mellow radiance over the dreary Campagna. The whole scene was bathed in a flood of that golden light which Raphael has painted in his "Transfiguration," imparting even an air of cheerfulness to the dark cypresses and pines, which overshadowed the old tombs on the plain below. Then came the gradual change. The rich purple which crested the hills melted from our sight, as one by one the stars came out. The golden tints faded from the landscape, lingered awhile longer in the western sky, and then were exchanged for that deep blue which characterizes the brief Italian night. With the windows closed to escape the deadly malaria which was rising around, we drove rapidly on, and by eight o'clock were once more within the gates of the city.

CHAPTER XIX.

THE CHURCHES OF ROME.

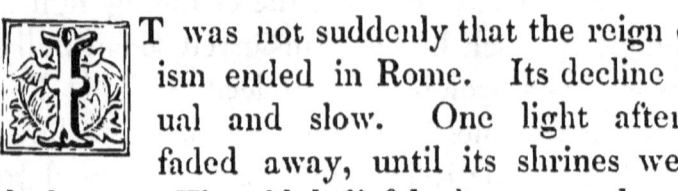T was not suddenly that the reign of Paganism ended in Rome. Its decline was gradual and slow. One light after another faded away, until its shrines were left in darkness. The old belief had to pass through many stages before its power was ended, and it was numbered with those forgotten forms of faith which have had their day. It first ceased to be a popular religion and lost its hold upon the hearts of the multitude; then, it passed into a system of philosophy for the learned; and ere it expired, had still further degenerated into a mere allegory to employ the ingenuity of its disciples. Long, however, it lingered, even after Christianity had become dominant, and none dared to confess openly their allegiance to its rival. It was not until A. D. 410, that we can look for its last expiring throes. When in that year, for the first time the Imperial City was occupied by the invaders, a shock was felt throughout the world, and men wildly turned to any cause which might account for her fall. Many, in their despair, ascribed this disastrous consummation to the new religion, and to win back the gods they supposed had forsaken them, offered for the last time sacrifices at their long-deserted shrines.

But as step by step Paganism retreated, Christianity followed hard upon its footsteps. When the fires had gone out on its altars, and no more worshippers crowded its temples, the new faith at once succeeded to them as spoils won in the conflict she was waging; and it is to this cause — as in the case of the Pantheon — we may probably ascribe the preservation of some of these relics of antiquity. They were generally, however, too contracted; the interior, or *penetralia*, being only intended to receive the images of the gods, and not adapted, therefore, to the meeting of assemblies which had now become numerous.

The Christians naturally turned then to the *Basilicas*, or Halls of Justice, some of which, as the population of the city decreased, or perhaps as the government grew more absolute, became useless. And most admirably did they answer the purpose of Christian worship. The large area and the long aisles seemed built to accommodate a numerous audience, while the semicircular retreat (*apsis*) at the end, elevated on its flight of steps, needed but little change to prepare it for the Bishop and his Presbyters. Several of these were therefore granted by the Christian Emperors to the Church, and consecrated for the performance of their services. But yet this new consecration of heathen temples seemed often insufficient to expel the Paganism which lingered about their walls, or to change the associations with which a half-Christianized people regarded the spot. And in some cases we trace these feelings existing even to this day. Under the brow of the Palatine Hill is a circular building, once the Temple of Romulus, to which the women of ancient Rome were accustomed to carry their children when ill, that the priests might pray for their recovery. It is now the Church of St. Theodore, and you may at any time see the women of modern Rome carrying thither their children on the same occasions.

You have been with us, gentle reader, in a ramble through the palaces of Rome, where historical associations crowd upon the mind, and miracles of art meet the eye on every side : shall we make also a pilgrimage to some of her churches? Few indeed will there be time to visit, — half a dozen perhaps, selected from some two hundred, — yet you will find them no less interesting than the feudal residences of her nobility. The traces of antiquity are there also, for you can stand within the walls where they worshipped, who for fourteen centuries have been hymning praises in the Paradise of God. There, too, painting and sculpture have placed their noblest works, for you are among a people, the spirit of whose faith it is, to dedicate the best they have to their Lord. No Gothic architecture indeed is seen, with its painted windows and "dim religious light:" for this, you must resort to Milan and study its magnificent Cathedral. And yet, when you wander through one of the churches in Rome, you feel that Genius has written on every side the traces of its presence. "Incense-breathing" chapels are about you — and delicate carvings wrought out from the marble as if it could be moulded up at will — and all so rich and quaint and clerkly, that you scarcely feel the want of that solemn architecture, which in Northern Europe seems alone to be ecclesiastical.

The mere literary man turns with the deepest interest to the Church of *St. Onofrio*, for the adjoining monastery of the hermits of St. Jerome is consecrated as the place where the author of "Gerusalemme Liberata" breathed his last. Strange and sorrowful had been his pilgrimage through life! At one time flattered at the most brilliant courts; then wandering through the land which was ringing with his genius, yet wayworn, unknown, and in poverty; then a prisoner in the dungeons of Ferrara, — he had come at last to Rome, where it seemed as if he was to receive a reward for all his trials. He was soon to be solemnly crowned with laurel at the Capitol, yet ere the day for the ceremony arrived, there were symptoms that the springs of life were giving way, and he was conveyed to the monastery of St. Onofrio.

In this garden looking over Rome, and blending, in the mind of one who gazes from its terraces, a sense of the present beauty of nature with a remembrance of the ancient glory of the city, Tasso was accustomed to sit. The poor monks will point out to you the very spot. It was there where a noble oak once cast its shade, but three years ago an autumn storm uprooted it. In those cloisters is the room in which he died: and as you enter the Church, turn to your left, and you will see a plain marble slab, with the simple inscription, —

"TORQUATI TASSO OSSA."

And thus sleeps the first epic poet of Italy — a brilliant spirit, which, with the customary reward of genius, passed through life in sorrow and pain. Yet no poetic visions filled his mind, as in feebleness he paced the walks and cloisters of this old monastery. He had done with human praise forever, and was girding up his spirit for the realities of the world to come. "I have come to this monastery of St. Onofrio," he wrote to his best friend, a few days before his death, "not only because the air is commended by physicians, as more salubrious than in any other part of Rome, but that I may, as it were, commence in this high place, and in the conversation of these devout fathers, my conversation in heaven. Pray God for me; and be assured that as I have loved and honored you in this present life, so in that other and more real life will I do for you all that belongs to charity unfeigned and true, and to the Divine Mercy I recommend both you and myself."

We were wandering one morning about the Esquiline, when we found ourselves near the Church of *San Clemente*, probably the least changed from ancient times of any in Rome. The quarter of the city in which it stands is nearly deserted. Vacant squares — grass-grown streets — and mouldering ruins, show how the wave of population has receded from the spot. Wishing a *cicerone*, we entered the Dominican monastery adjoining the Church, but all there was as silent as it was without. We traversed the long stone passages without meeting any of the monks, and at last determined to explore the Church ourselves. The interior transports us back at once to the early centuries of our faith. There, on an elevated platform, and divided from the rest of the Church by two gates, are the *apsis* or tribune, the ancient altar, and the episcopal seat. In front is the marble inclosure, having on the sides the *ambones* or marble pulpits from which the Epistle and Gospel were read. The aisles terminate in two recesses, anciently called *Exedræ* or *Cellæ*, and then appropriated to private devotion in prayer and meditation. They are now converted into chapels. This is probably the only Church which preserves the form of the old Basilicas. It is mentioned as ancient by authors of the fourth century, and though often repaired and decorated, has never been deprived of its primitive shape and fashion.

Let us pass on a short distance and we come to the Church of *S. Pietro in Vincoli*. Its name and the chain sculptured over the portal give an explanation of its object. It is intended to preserve the chain with which St. Peter was bound when a prisoner in Jerusalem, and on the first of August this holy relic is shown publicly to the people.

Much more interesting, however, to the visitor is Michael Angelo's celebrated statue of Moses, which is considered by many to rival the grandest productions of the Grecian chisel. It is colossal in its size, and represents him with that sternness upon his countenance which we may imagine was imprinted there when he rebuked the idolatry of his people. It was intended as one of forty statues which were to ornament the tomb of Julius II. The monument, however, was never executed, only five of the statues being finished at the time of Michael Angelo's death. Of these, three are in this Church; one is in Paris; and the fifth in the Boboli Gardens in Florence. The Pope himself was buried in the Vatican.

There is a peculiarity about this figure, which, majestic as it is, has often exposed it to ridicule. On each side of the head of Moses, a small horn is just budding forth. "One critic," says Forsyth, "compares his head to a goat's;" and we often see the same peculiarity in paintings of the Middle Ages. What does it mean? I have never seen any explanation given, but the following struck me as being a natural solution. In the original Hebrew the same word, קרנים, is used both for *horns* and *rays of light*, and it was of course easy to confound them. When therefore it is said in Exodus xxxiv. 29, that as Moses came down from the Mount, "he wist not that the skin of his face shone," the Vulgate — the version of the Church of Rome — renders it, "Et ignorabat quod cornuta esset facies sua;" "and he did not know that his face was horned." It was this phrase, then, which probably led to the mistake, and accounts for the manner in which both painters and sculptors were accustomed to represent the Jewish Lawgiver. In our own version, indeed, precisely the same mistake is made with this word in another passage. In Habakkuk it says, "He had *horns* coming out of his hand." It should, of course, be *rays of light*.

We pass on to the magnificent Basilica of *S. Maria Maggiore*, the noblest Church in Rome dedicated to the Virgin, and hence its name. It stands in an open square, and the exterior is richly ornamented, while the nave in the interior is nearly three hundred feet in length. The elaborately carved roof is richly gilded, and derives an additional interest from the fact, that the gold used was the first ever brought to Europe from Peru. It was presented to Alexander VI. by Ferdinand and Isabella of Spain. Now and then the great services of the Church are performed in this splendid Basilica; as on Christmas Eve, when the Cradle of our Lord is carried in procession; and on the festivals of the Assumption and the Nativity of the Virgin, when the Pope himself performs High Mass at its altar.

Just behind it, however, is a little Church not often visited, but which once in the year is the scene of some strange ceremonies. It is dedicated to St. Anthony, the patron of the brute creation, and every January, when his Festival comes round, there is a service for their especial benefit. The first time I witnessed it, I was involuntarily a participant to some extent in the ceremony. We were riding with a lady, when crossing the open square a priest in his surplice was seen standing on the steps of this little Church, while one carriage after another was driving up to it, stopping before him for a few minutes, and then passing on to make room for others.

"What," she inquired of the courier, "are they doing there?"

"Blessing the horses, Madame."

"Then tell the coachman to drive up, and we will have ours blessed."

So accordingly up he drove. The servants reverently took off their hats, and the priest commenced reading a prayer from his book. When he had finished, he took a brush from the hand of an attendant, dipped it in a bucket of holy water at his feet, and sprinkled the horses, repeating the words, —

"Per intercessionem Beati Antonii Abatis, hæc animalia liberenter, a malis, in nomine Patris, et Filii, et Spiritus Sancti. Amen." (Through the intercession of the blessed Abbot Anthony, may these animals be delivered from evil, in the name of the Father, and of the Son, and of the Holy Ghost. Amen).

A small fee was handed to the priest, and we continued our ride. For several days this service is constantly going on. The following Sunday, however, was the great day. Then, the Square was crowded with animals, and thousands of people were there as spectators. The magnificent carriages of the Pope, each drawn by six horses, and the scarcely less splendid equipages of the Cardinals and the Roman princes came up, to go through the ceremony. Long rows of post-horses arrived from different parts of the city, and the mules of the peasantry from the country, decked out in ribbons and flowers, while their masters were in all their best array. A friend told me, that on one of these days he saw a young man drag up to the church door a miserable looking little dog, which he held by a string while the service was read, and the poor cur received his share of holy water.

What is the precise meaning of this ceremony? Or, what particular benefit are the animals expected to derive from this service, which seems like an inferior kind of baptism? These are questions to which it is difficult to procure definite answers. In "Geraldine," however, a book published in defense of the Church of Rome, and recommended by Bishop Kenrick, as "a work of great interest, directed to remove prejudice, and present the light of truth," is a defense of this service, from which we make the following quotation, —

"'But what good did all the blessing and sprinkling do the cattle, and their owners,' said Miss Leonard, 'when they left the good monk, just as vicious and distempered as when they came to him?'"

"'That is indeed begging the question,' said Geraldine; '*I do not believe that the cattle were so much so after the blessing as before.*'" [1]

[1] Vol. iii. p. 40.

In another work of fiction, also, we lately found a rather more complete summing up of the benefits, as given by an Italian peasant, — " Is it not a good horse which we have? then it has also had this year St. Antonio's blessing; my fellow decked him out with bunches of silken ribbons, opened the Bible before him, and sprinkled him with holy water; and no devil, or evil eye, can have any influence on him this year." [1]

From the Basilica of S. Maria Maggiore, a broad, deserted avenue leads to that of *St. John Lateran*. This section of the city, indeed, seems scarcely inhabited, an air of desolation pervades it, and the malaria reigns on every side. And yet, a few centuries ago the Lateran Palace was esteemed the most salubrious residence in Rome. Now it stands deserted, and as we look around, we see open fields and vineyards among the decaying houses, and silent moss-grown squares.

This magnificent Basilica was commenced by Constantine in the fourth century, he assisting with his own hands to dig the foundation. He had previously conferred upon the Church the adjoining Lateran Palace, — so called from Plautius Lateranus, who was put to death by Nero for being engaged in the conspiracy of Piso, — the beginning of those gifts to the Bishop of Rome, which drew forth the comments of Dante, when he thus lamented the system it originated, —

> "Ah, Constantine! to how much ill gave birth,
> Not thy conversion, but that plenteous dower,
> Which the first wealthy Father gained from thee." [2]

For a thousand years this palace was the residence

---

[1] *The Improvisatore*, vol. i. p. 296.   [2] *Il Inferno*, xix. 18.

of the Popes — the scene of all the licentiousness and fierce feuds of the Middle Ages, which finally wearied out men's minds, and prepared them to welcome the changes of the Reformation. The ceremony of taking possession of the palace is still the first form used after the election of the new Pope, although it has long ceased to be the Pontifical residence. In 1693 Innocent XII. turned it into an hospital for the poor, and in the last year a portion has been set apart for a museum, to receive those works of art for which no room can be found in the Vatican.

The Church itself has always been regarded as the first of Christian churches, and bears over its portal the proud inscription, — "SACROSANCTA LATERANENSIS ECCLESIA, OMNIUM URBIS ET ORBIS ECCLESIARUM MATER ET CAPUT." Its Chapter still takes precedence over that of St. Peter's, and thus, for fifteen centuries, it has retained its privileges.

The exterior of the building is of a ponderous yet sumptuous architecture. It is, however, of that kind, overloaded with ornament, which seems to leave no definite impression on the mind. It has been truly remarked, that no one can look for half an hour at the simple Grecian temples at Pæstum, without being able to make a rough sketch of them, while few of those even who have spent a winter at Rome, could give on paper any idea of the front of S. Maria Maggiore or St. John Lateran. The interior has a most imposing effect from the multitude of pillars which are seen, nearly three hundred being employed. There are five aisles, divided by four rows of piers. Its decorations, too, are rich in the extreme, corresponding with the rank, antiquity, and magnitude of the Basilica.

The bronze tomb of Martin V., of the princely house of Colonna; the Corsini Chapel, covered with the richest marbles, and *bas-reliefs*, and gems; and the Gothic tabernacle above the High Altar, constructed in the fourteenth century, to receive the heads of St. Peter and St. Paul, which happened then to be discovered among the ruins of the old Basilica, are unsurpassed in magnificence by anything in Rome.

The devout Romanist visits this Church with reverence, on account of its multitude of precious relics. They are varied in their character, and certainly wonderful in their claims. There are divers pillars, some of which are from Pilate's house, and one belonged to the Temple at Jerusalem. It bears marks of the earthquake which took place at the Crucifixion, having been at that time split in two. Here is a piece of the table on which our Lord and His disciples leaned when they ate the Last Supper; and on that slab of marble the Roman soldiers cast lots, when they divided the garments of Christ. You cannot doubt the legend, for the stone itself bears the inscription, — "Et super vestem meam miserunt sortem." The one, however, which the priest evidently shows with the highest degree of satisfaction, is a marble altar, the very sight of which settles a theological difficulty, and should be sufficient to convert a heretic. A miracle, they tell us, was wrought upon it to prove the doctrine of transubstantiation. A priest, who had suffered some impious doubts on this point to enter his mind, was once standing before it consecrating the elements, when as soon as the prayer had been pronounced, and the change taken place, the holy wafer fell from his hand, and sunk through the marble, leaving the marks of blood as it went. The hole through which it passed, and the stain it made, are both before you! This miracle took place at Bolsena, and in the Vatican is a fresco, by Raphael, intended to illustrate it. On one side of the altar stands the priest, for whose benefit the wonder had taken place, regarding the wafer with astonishment and reverence, while behind him are the choir boys, and people pressing forward, with awe and curiosity on their countenances. On the other side, Julius II. is kneeling in prayer, attended by his Cardinals and Swiss guards.

But the student of ecclesiastical history has better reasons to enlist his interest in this ancient Church. Five General Councils, from the twelfth to the sixteenth century, met within its walls. In one of them, which was held A. D. 1215, were present, the Patriarchs of Constantinople and Jerusalem, four hundred Bishops, and Ambassadors of France, England, Hungary, Aragon, Sicily, and Cyprus. Here, too, for many centuries the Popes were always elected, and thus from these walls proceeded that influence which was to be felt throughout the Christian world.

These were the recollections which crowded our minds as we stood within this silent Church, where no sound was heard but the scarcely audible voice of a priest celebrating the Mass in a distant chapel. And particularly we thought of the strange scene which took place when these arches rang with the name of Hildebrand, as he was thus suddenly summoned to the Pontifical throne. It was on a morning of April, 1073, that before this High Altar stood the bier of Pope Alexander II., while the whole building was densely crowded with those who had come to witness the funeral services.

The solemn requiem was wailing forth, and all were uniting in its petitions to commend the soul of the departed Pontiff to its Judge, when suddenly the softened strain was overwhelmed by a shout. None could tell by whom it was commenced, for it seemed to burst at once from every part of the edifice. The mighty crowd which had gathered there appeared to have but one voice. The cry was, "Hildebrand." "Hildebrand shall be Pope." "St. Peter chooses our Archdeacon Hildebrand." In vain did the subject of this uproar rush from the funeral procession to the pulpit, and, by impassioned gestures, implore silence. Ten thousand voices echoed the cry, — it swelled louder and louder, — nor did it cease till a Cardinal came forward and announced, that "we, the Cardinal Bishops, do, with one voice, elect Hildebrand to be henceforth your spiritual pastor and our own." Eagerly was he hurried to the Pontifical throne; arrayed hastily in the scarlet robe and tiara; the Cardinals paid their obeisance, and the still louder shouts of the people hailed him as Gregory VII. Thus on this spot was consummated an election which was to result in crushing the feudal despotism of the age, wresting all sacerdotal power from the hands of the Emperor, and triumphantly asserting the loftiest claims of the Hierarchy, until the Roman Pontiff became the ruler of the civilized world. Nearly eight centuries have since gone by, but the spirit of Gregory is living still in the Church of Rome. It bears in its whole organization the impress of his gigantic character. In every department, — in its very frame and groundwork, — we can trace the influence of that tumultuous hour which then passed within these walls.

We left the Church, and stood for some time on its steps looking at the deserted avenues and squares around it. Directly in front towers up an obelisk, the loftiest in Rome. It rises in the air nearly one hundred and fifty feet, a single shaft of red granite, covered with hieroglyphics. Rameses erected it in Thebes, and Pliny tells us that he lived during the Trojan war. A hundred and twenty thousand men had been employed in cutting it from its native quarry, and there for ages it stood, under the burning sun of Egypt, and among its massive temples. Strange and mysterious rites were performed around it; new creeds grew up; revolutions rolled on; dynasties passed away; and as the centuries went by, it beheld one kingdom after another crumble into ruins at its base. At length, the people who reared it ceased to be a nation, — their antique faith vanished from the earth, — and the land around became once more a desert. Then came an iron race from the distant West, and after years of toil it was removed to gratify the pride of a Roman Emperor. Fourteen centuries have since passed, and we behold it now as fresh and unchanged as when it stood in the heart of Egypt, and the priests of Isis looked upon it towering above their Sacred Groves. It still bears upon its sides the chronicles of forgotten ages, but modern wisdom cannot decipher their strange characters. What a history could that old obelisk relate, and to what a mysterious and shadowy antiquity does it carry back the mind!

On one side of the Basilica stands the Baptistery, a small octagonal building which is said to have been erected by the Emperor Constantine, and though frequently repaired, yet it has always been done in accordance with its original design. This account of its erection may be true, for it is the unvarying testimony of tradition. Within it is a large porphyry vase which is always shown as the one in which Constantine received the rite of Baptism. And yet, it is a fact proved by the authority of all Greek and Latin writers, that the first Christian Emperor was not initiated into the Church until sinking beneath his last mortal sickness, and then, the service was performed in a distant land. Theodoret says, " The Emperor was taken ill at Nicomedia, a city of Bithynia. Being thus led to reflect on the uncertainty of life, he received the holy rite of Baptism, which he had intended to have deferred until he could be baptized in the river Jordan." [1] And Socrates confirms it with his authority : — " In the following year the Emperor Constantine was attacked with a dangerous malady ; he therefore left Constantinople, and made a voyage to Helenopolis, to try the effect of its medicinal hot springs. Perceiving, however, that his illness increased, he deferred the use of the baths; and removing from Helenopolis to Nicomedia, he took up his residence in the suburbs, and there received Christian Baptism." [2] This fact, indeed, has always been one of the mysteries of ecclesiastical history. More than twenty-five years had passed since he avowed himself a Christian, before he took the very first step in the profession of our faith. Was it from superstition, because he believed that Baptism washed away all sins of the past, and therefore it was well to defer it as late as possible? Or, was it because he did not wish to alienate entirely his heathen subjects, lest in

[1] Theod., *Eccles. Hist.* lib. i. chap. 32.
[2] Soc., *Eccles. Hist.* lib. i. chap. 39.

some unexpected emergency their allegiance should fail; while at the same time the Christians who surrounded him, relieved from persecution, were willing to receive their Imperial convert on almost any terms, and therefore forbore too much to press this point, trusting that greater light would lead him naturally to adopt it? As a fact, however, this delay of Baptism seems to be certain, and throws discredit, therefore, on the claims of the prophyry vase.

But the use to which it was appropriated on the night of August 1st, A. D. 1347, has much more surely connected it with history. Then, the Tribune Rienzi watched through the midnight hours beside his armor, as was the custom of those who on the morrow were to receive the knightly order of the Santo Spirito, and from some strange association in his mind, — so colored by the wild mysticism which Arnold of Brescia had inculcated two centuries earlier, — he ordered his bath to be prepared in this vase which was looked upon as consecrated. But the Papal Court had no sympathy with such visionary superstition, and when the Tribune fell and was imprisoned in the dungeons of Avignon, this act of sacrilege was one of the strongest charges against him.

On the other side of the Basilica is a noble portico constructed by Sixtus V. and intended to cover the *Scala Santa* or Holy Staircase. This consists of twenty-eight broad marble steps, which tradition tells us are the indentical steps once belonging to Pilate's house, and by which our Lord descended when he left the Judgment Seat. The marvel of course is, that they could have escaped the destruction of Jerusalem, and all the vicissitudes which for centuries befell the

Christians. I find, however, upon consulting a Roman Catholic work, the legend is, that during the forty years the judgments which fell on Jerusalem were suspended, the Christians were on the watch to secure all the relics of their Master, and returning from Pella, after the siege, when terror and confusion reigned, they concealed and carried away the precious steps. No one is now permitted to ascend them but on their knees, and an Indulgence of about two hundred and fifty years is promised to each one who accomplishes the feat, at the same time, " devoutly meditating on the Passion." At whatever part of the day you are there, you see numbers going through the painful service. Men and women — people of rank and beggars — old persons and children — are toiling up, often quite exhausted before they reach the top. When they have gained the highest step, they stoop down and kiss a brass cross inserted in the marble, and the penance is over. At one time, indeed, there seemed to be danger that the marble itself would be worn out by the knees of the countless pilgrims who availed themselves of the offers of Indulgence. By order of Clement XII., therefore, the steps were covered with planks of wood, which have been obliged to be renewed three times.

Luther tells us of an incident in his own life which occurred on this spot. When the poor Saxon monk was in Rome, while his mind was in its transition state, — disgusted with the superstitions around him, and yet not knowing to what else to turn, — he determined to gain the Indulgence promised for ascending this staircase. While he was slowly climbing up, he seemed to hear a voice speaking from the depth of his heart, " The just shall live by faith." He started in terror from the steps up which he had been crawling, and struck with shame at his degradation, fled from this scene of his folly.

The little Chapel at the top contains a large number of relics, and is therefore so sacred that no woman is allowed to enter it. An inscription indeed states, that " there is no place more holy in all the world." Among these relics are some of the barley-loaves and fishes, part of the purple robe, and of the reed with which Christ was smitten. The most remarkable, however, is a very sacred painting, claiming to be a correct likeness of our Lord at the age of twelve years. According to this portrait he was precisely five feet eight inches high at that age. It was begun by St. Luke, but leaving it for a time, on his return he found it miraculously finished.

On each side of the Holy Staircase is a lateral one, by which pilgrims can descend, and as these steps have not the same sanctity, they may be ascended also in the ordinary way.

There is one other Church which deserves a brief notice. We rode out one afternoon to the Basilica of *San Paolo fuori le mure*, on the road to Ostia, about two miles beyond the Porta San Paolo. Formerly, we are told, a portico, supported by marble pillars. and covered with gilt copper, extended the whole of this distance from the gate to the Church, but no traces of it can now be seen. Tradition informs us, that the original edifice was erected by Constantine on this spot, where repose the remains of the Apostle Paul. In the fourth century, a still more magnificent one was built by the Emperor Theodosius in its place, and thenceforth it became a spot to which every pilgrim to the Holy City turned his steps. Ancient writers, indeed, seem hardly able to find words with which to describe its splendor. They tell us of its five aisles; its lofty nave, two hundred and sixty feet long, and a hundred and forty wide; its pillars, a hundred and thirty-eight in number, and of such rare marbles, and exquisite workmanship, that they were believed to have been transported from an Athenian temple described by Pausanius. Some were of porphyry, and others of that beautiful marble called *pavonazzo* — white, tinged with delicate purple. On the top of these pillars was the celebrated series of portraits of the Popes, from St. Peter to Pius VII. Their true history seems to be, that they were commenced by Leo I. in the fifth century, who had his predecessors also painted. Before his time they are, of course, therefore imaginary, but afterwards, with some exceptions, they might have been genuine.

But all this has long since passed away. About twenty years ago the Church took fire, and the flames raged with such violence that the whole was entirely consumed, and even the splendid columns completely calcined or split into fragments. The rebuilding, however, was immediately commenced, on a scale which will be second only to St. Peter's, and large sums are constantly contributed by princes and sovereigns in all quarters of the world. The High Altar and transept have alone been finished, and many years will elapse before the nave is completed. Even as we saw it, however, its magnificence is great, and the marble pillars are the most splendid we have ever seen.

But, except as a mere monument, the Church will

be utterly useless, for no one can live in this neighborhood of pestilence. It stands in one of the most deadly portions of the Campagna, — the adjoining monastery of Benedictine monks has been for years almost deserted, — and the road which leads to it from the city seems entirely unfrequented. Even the priests, who minister at the altars, can remain but for a short time in winter. As soon as the spring approaches, they are obliged to fly from the deadly malaria. For whose benefit, then, has this sumptuous pile been erected, and from whence are to come the worshippers? May we not also ask the question, "To what purpose is this waste?"

From thence the road leads on about three miles through low, marshy grounds, until we reach the spot on which St. Paul is said to have been beheaded. It is related that such was the manner of his death, his right as a Roman citizen having freed him from the more ignominious punishment of the Cross. Here stand close together three churches, which date from the early times of Christianity. In one of them, *S. Paolo alle tre Fontane*, are three fountains, which are said to have sprung up where the head of the Apostle struck and bounded three times. Though close together, the water is entirely different. In the first it is brackish, and of a milky color; in the second it is less so, and in the third entirely pure. Here, too, are the same evidences of the malaria. There are but three priests to perform service, who in winter are relieved every week, and in summer merely go out to say Mass. And yet, with all these precautions, two had died during the season. They looked languid and miserable, and said that rich, generous living was prescribed for them, but one effect of the malaria was to take away all appetite.

Such are a few of the Roman churches. With our ideas we can scarcely imagine the effect often produced. We leave the bright glare of an Italian sun, and when we enter, find, instead, a subdued and softened light; the immense building perhaps stretches out with five aisles, and a perfect forest of Corinthian columns, the shafts of different colored and precious marbles. The ceiling is carved and gilt, while the pavement beneath is formed of mosaics. No pews obstruct the view, but we look through the whole immense length, and here and there, lessened by the distance, see some priest gliding noiselessly along, or some worshipper kneeling at a pillar's base, with his face turned to the altar. There seems a strange stillness in the very atmosphere — an impressive solemnity pervading the interior of the vast sanctuary.

But whence came the means to erect these costly buildings? They were the free-will offerings which thousands made to their Lord — the donations of men who cared more for the glory of His house than for the splendor of their own residences. It is the fashion to call all this the fruit of superstition, but is it not thus too often that avarice and worldliness excuse their stinted avarice? Whatever other motives may have mingled in their minds, they who have thus sacrificed their worldly wealth showed a realizing sense of the life to come, and a belief that there is such a thing as "laying up treasures in heaven."

CHAPTER XX.

EXHIBITION AT THE PROPAGANDA. — FUNERALS. — VESPERS AT THE CONVENT OF SANTA TRINITA.

NEAR our lodgings is the College of the *Propaganda*, and we seldom pass it without seeing a Cardinal's carriage at the door. It was founded by Gregory XV., in 1622, and has since been justly regarded by the Church of Rome as her right arm of strength — the school in which are trained her missionaries for every foreign land. The building is vast, supplied with a magnificent library, and with a press by which books are printed in almost every known language. It is particularly rich in oriental characters, and has produced many works celebrated for their typographical beauty. The number of students — as I mentioned when speaking of the Epiphany services — is about eighty. It is of course a cherished and favored institution.

When in Naples we saw a branch of it, devoted entirely to the instruction of young Chinese youths. It was an extensive establishment, but bearing marks of decay, and evidently not kept up as it once had been. The saloon into which we were first shown was painted with representations in fresco of the martyrdom of some of the Jesuit missionaries in China. It was once a handsome apartment, but now had a dingy, unfurnished appearance. The priest who was at its head treated us with great politeness, sending for all his pupils to introduce to us, and at his request they showed us the articles and utensils they had brought from their native land, read aloud to us from a Chinese book, and gave us our names written in the characters of their own language. The number at one time was large, but for some years has been gradually diminishing, and now only amounts to eight. One of these young men had been in the Institution thirteen years, and one had just arrived. After some years' training they generally go to Rome for a short time, and then return as missionaries to their own country.

The Examination has recently taken place at the Institution in Rome, and was followed by an Exhibition very much like those of our College Commencements. It consisted of Essays, Poems, and Colloques by the students, among whom were two from the United States. The Catholic character of the Institution is shown by the fact, that these compositions were in *fifty-nine different languages and dialects.* Cardinal Mezzofanti has since given me a *programme* of the exercises, and I will copy the list of languages in which they were delivered, to show the wide reach taken by the missionary operations of this Church: —

I. Ebbraico Letterale.
II. Samaritano.
III. Etiopico.
IV. Caldeo Letterale.
V. Siriaco.
VI. Sabeo.
VII. Copto.
VIII. Greco Letterale.
IX. Armeno Letterale.
X. Ode Saffica Latina.
XI. Arabo.
XII. Kurdo.
XIII. Persiano.
XIV. Indostano.
XV. Turco.
XVI. Maltese.
XVII. Giorgiano.
XVIII. Norwegiano.
XIX. Dialogo Cinese Letterale, (by two students from Siam.)

XX. Esametri Latini.
XXI. Sanscrito.
XXII. Concanico,
(by a student from Goa.)
XXIII. Singalese,
(by a student from Ceylon.)
XXIV. Amarico.
XXV. Angolano.
XXVI. Caldeo Volgare.
XXVII. Ebraico Rabbinico.
XXVIII. Armeno Odierno.
XXIX. Greco Odierno.
XXX. Sonetto Italiano.
XXXI. Svedese.
XXXII. Dialogo Peguano,
(by two students from Pegu.)
XXXIII. Inno Italiano.
XXXIV. Illirico.
XXXV. Albanese.
XXXVI. Polacco.
XXXVII. Sloveno.
XXXVIII. Bulgaro.
XXXIX. Tedesco antico.
XL. Tedesco Letterale.
XLI. Swizzero.
XLII. Lingua della Rezia.
XLIII. Olandese.
XLIV. Danese.
XLV. Inglese,
(by Sig. Elder of Baltimore.)
XLVI. Scozzese.
XLVII. Celtico.
XLVIII. Irlandese.
XLIX. Chilese.
L. Spagnuolo.
LI. Portoghese.
LII. Catalano
LIII. Francese.
LIV. Terzine, [ington.)
(by Sig. Cummings of Wash-
LV. Siciliano.
LVI. Nizzardo.
LVII. Epigramma Latino.
LVIII. Dialogo Cinese Odierno,
(by three Chinese students.)
LIX. Lingua Originaria della Nu-
ova Olanda.
(by the Missionary Apostolic
and Vicar-General of New
Holland.)

I copy this as a curiosity. We often hear of the many languages spoken by the students in this College from all parts of the world, and here is an exhibition of what is really done. When shall our own Church be thus prepared to go forth with the pure Gospel to " all nations, and kindreds, and people, and tongues!"

There are probably few communities in the world which can equal that of Rome in charitable associations. They are called *Confraternities*, and are formed by the voluntary union of individuals, often of high rank, who in the midst of all the wretchedness around them, devote a portion of their time to its relief. Many of these are never seen by the mere traveller, or their existence even suspected, for their sphere of labor is private, yet it would be difficult to estimate the amount of happiness they must diffuse.

One fraternity, for example, is intended to seek out humble but respectable families who would not be likely to apply for alms, and in some delicate way to relieve their necessities. The members of another visit the hospitals, learn the situation of the patients, and often personally attend to them. Others visit the jails, and furnish comfort and support to prisoners who are without friends or means. Others by voluntary donations pay debts which the poor have unavoidably contracted, and thus relieve their minds from trouble. Others seek the sick through the abodes of wretchedness in the city, supply them with food, medicine, and professional assistance, and attend them through their illness. Others come in when the last hour is over, defray the expenses of the burial, attend to the performance of the religious rites, and themselves bear the body to the grave.[1]

Such are their self-denying labors for the relief of suffering humanity. The wretched need no other claim upon them, except that they share in a common nature. No "Anniversary" is required to awaken their flagging zeal; no "Report" is sent out on the wings of the press, to trumpet forth their doings to the world; no "List of subscribers" publishes their charities through the land. The members indeed scarcely know each other, for their visits are made in the dress of the fraternity, so that none can recognize the individuals. But year after year they

[1] Eustace, *Class. Tour*, iii. p. 263.

labor on — uncheered by the voice of human praise — their good deeds known only to their Father who seeth in secret.

Those who attend to funerals, we have frequently seen when engaged in the performance of this duty. They form that "Ancient Brotherhood" — as Rogers calls it — which extends over all Italy. Men of the highest rank — laymen as well as priests — belong to it, and when summoned to this charitable work they go forth shrouded in white dresses, with high pointed cowls on their heads, veiling their faces, and leaving only holes for the eyes. There is something peculiarly ghastly in their whole appearance, so that when they walk behind the dead, "they seem," says Corinne, "like the ghosts of those they follow."

There is much solemnity in funerals abroad, where the Church steps in at once, and takes possession of the deceased as under its protection, under the sanction of its religious authority; and if it makes an exhibition, it is with authority, and this proclamation has holiness in it. All that is not ecclesiastical is kept out of sight. There is nothing intermediate between the deceased and the Church. The undertaker interferes not, intrudes not here to spoil all. Death, it is true, reigns for the hour, but Religion triumphs. The Church certifies the triumph, and the resurrection."[1]

We have often had these feelings while in Rome, for there is nothing more striking there than their funeral processions. They always take place at night, when the darkness seems in unison with the service, and we have never met them passing through the streets, without being arrested by the solemnity of the

---

[1] Prof. Wilson's *Miscellanies*, iii. p. 79.

scene. The corpse is generally borne upon an open bier; the head exposed, ghastly and white as marble; the feet, too, uncovered; and the light pall thrown over the body, showing plainly its shape and outline. The hands are clasped upon the breast, as if the departed had died in prayer, and the attitude had been left unchanged.

Everything in the service is intended to be significant of the hour when the dead shall rise again from the dust. The priests bear lights, to signify that immediately before the general Resurrection " the stars shall fall from heaven;" and the Cross, to denote that then " the sign of the Son of Man shall be seen." The mournful notes in which they sing the Penitential Psalms, declare that in that hour " all kindreds of the earth shall wail because of Him;" while the bells, which are heard ceaselessly ringing, call upon all to pray for the peace of the departed soul. The bier is borne by these hooded brothers, while other members of the fraternity carry tall waxen tapers, which flicker in the evening wind and throw their light upon the corpse, deepening the shadows, and bringing out everything in bold relief. And as the solemn procession sweeps by, they chant in melancholy tones the funeral anthem: —

> " Quantus tremor est futurus,
> Quando Judex est venturus
> Cuncta stricte discussurus!
>
> " Turba mirum spargens sonum
> Per sepulchra regionum,
> Coget omnes ante thronum.

> "Quid sum miser tunc dicturus?
> Quem patronum rogaturus,
> Cum vix justus sit securus?"[1]

There is something indescribably touching in the whole service, as we see the glancing lights at a distance, or hear their old monastic chants floating through the long dark streets. Sometimes the voices would have about them a sorrowful wail, as if lamenting the lot of poor humanity, and crying over him they were bearing along, "Alas, for thee, my brother!" Then would come a louder strain, swelling out like the surges of a far-off sea, partaking even of a sound of triumph, as if they celebrated the victory which one day the dead should have over the grave. And then, once more, it would sink into a mournful note, and faintly you would catch the words of the solemn dirge they were hymning, as the wind bore to you the plaintive prayer, —

> "Miserere Domine!"

There can be no life more difficult than that which passes within a convent. Its members enter, and are at once cut off from all intercourse with the outward

---

[1] "How shall poor mortals quake with fears,
When their impartial Judge appears,
Who all their causes strictly hears!

"His trumpet sends a dreadful tone;
The noise through all the graves is blown,
And calls the dead before His throne.

"What plea can I, in sin, pretend?
What patron move to stand my friend,
When scarce the just themselves defend?"

world, except what they can have within the limits of the high-walled garden around them. The objects of deepest earthly interest they know, are the trees and flowers whose growth they watch, and the birds which pay them a passing visit. No changes come to them, except those wrought by the gradual approach of age, as with stealthy step it almost imperceptibly draws nigh. No field of outward labor occupies their thoughts, but everything is centred in themselves. And thus they go on through long years of solitary watching, and mortification, and weariness, and perpetual prayer, unvisited by any of those joys which gather around the path of social life, until at last, they quietly lie down to their long sleep in the humble cemetery of the convent.

But if any have a pleasant lot, it must be the Sisters of the Convent of Santa Trinita. It is situated on the Pincian Hill, looking over the whole of Rome which rises beneath it, with its pinnacles, and domes, and towers. What a dreamy existence must its inmates pass, while everything on which the eye rests invites to meditation! The deep blue of an Italian sky is over their heads, the luxuriance of nature is around them, while at their feet are scattered the noblest monuments of ages that are gone. We had frequently been told that the most touching music to be heard in Rome was that of their Vesper service, but that some persons having lately misbehaved during its performance, an order had been issued to exclude all Protestants. For this of course we could not blame them. No one has a right to go into a foreign church merely to gratify his curiosity, and then by levity interrupt the worship. However he may differ from them, he should regard their feelings for the sanctity of the place and the service. But the conduct of foreigners in Rome is generally in this particular very exceptionable. They seem to regard the most solemn rites and ceremonies of the Church of Rome as merely intended for their amusement, and act accordingly. There certainly is nothing religious in their conduct, and the most we can say of it is that it may be somewhat classical, for they take in a degree the place of the Chorus in the ancient Greek Tragedy, by continually making their comments aloud, and giving their opinion on whatever is going forward.

Some of our friends had lately attempted to gain admittance to this service, but without success. We determined, however, to make the trial, and one afternoon walked up to the Convent. The chapel was closed, so we proceeded to a side door and boldly rang the bell. In a moment, a nun in her close white cap appeared at the little grating, and after reconnoitring us, inquired our business. We stated, that we came to attend Vespers; whereupon we were informed that we could not be admitted, and the grating closed. We lingered about on the Pincian Hill, until a short time after seeing some persons ascend the steps who we supposed to be members of the Roman Catholic Church, we joined them and mingled with their party. Fortunately a different nun came to the grating, through which a brief conversation took place, when the door opened, and we all quietly walked in together.

The upper part of the chapel was separated from the rest by a high grating, within which was the altar, while at the other end was a lofty organ gallery communicating with the Convent. In a few moments a priest with four or five attendants entered, and knelt before the Altar. Then a side door within the grating opened, and some forty scholars, their heads covered with white veils, came in, and after gracefully kneeling for a moment before the crucifix, ranged themselves on each side. In the high choir gallery we could just see the white caps of the nuns appearing above the railing.

At length the service began. The organ played a few fitful notes, when a single female voice was heard from among the nuns chanting in the most plaintive manner. It seemed indeed to wail out as if a funeral dirge. Others presently joined in, and the sounds sweetly filled the chapel. They ceased, and instantly were heard the manly voices of the priest and his attendants, as kneeling like statues, with their faces towards the altar, they sang the response. Then came again those soft and melancholy tones from the organ gallery, and thus they alternated through the whole Evening Psalms. It was the only time in the service of the Church that we had heard male and female voices together, and the contrast was striking. I know not why it was too that the voices of these nuns sounded so plaintively, but they seemed in harmony with the service, heard in the waning twilight; and the whole effect was deeply devotional. The tones at times seemed to be almost unearthly, as if they had been purified from the frailty of this lower world — the outpourings of a spirit utterly divorced from all the cares of this wearing life, —

"Musical, but sadly sweet."

Madame de Staël says, "Those who have not heard Italian singing can form no idea of music. The human voice is soft and sweet as the flowers and skies. This charm was made but for such a clime: each reflect the other. The Italians have ever devotedly loved music. Dante, in his 'Purgatory,' meets the best singer of his day, and asks him for one of his delicious airs. The entranced spirits forget themselves as they hear it, until their guardian recalls them to the truth." And this view of Italian enthusiasm is correct. In other lands they may bring music to the highest point of perfect execution, but here they seem intensely to feel it. The sweet sounds to which they listen enter into their very souls. And when, in addition, the sentiments embodied lead our thoughts on to the solemn realities of the future, the strains fall upon the ear with a touching power of which words can give no adequate idea.

But to return to the Convent Vespers. Besides ourselves, there were only about forty persons present, all of whom were undoubtedly members of the Church of Rome, except one English gentleman, who probably gained admission very much as we did. Their deeply devotional manner, as they knelt upon the marble pavement, contributed much to the solemnity of the scene. They were evidently not mere spectators, but worshippers. As the service proceeded, the twilight deepened, the incense spread through the dark arches above us like a thin white cloud, and the only lights being the candles about the Altar, the rest of the chapel was gradually involved in gloom. There was an absence of all that parade and show which generally mark the services of the Church of Rome, and altogether it was the most impressive one which we attended in Italy. For months afterwards we were haunted by the solemn melody of these tremulous, plaintive tones. They reminded us of those " spiritual creatures," whose songs, when " in full harmonic number joined," our first parents heard in the bowers of Paradise, " from the steep of echoing hill or thicket " —

> " Celestial voices
> Sole, or responsive each to other's note,
> Singing their great Creator ! "

CHAPTER XXI.

THE ROMAN PEOPLE. — THE CIVIL GOVERNMENT OF THE PAPAL COURT.

'T is the fashion to abuse the Italians. Travellers pass through the country, meeting only the custom-house officers, the postilions, and the hangers-on at inns, and decide authoritatively on the worthlessness of the people. It is, of course, evident, that they see the worst portion, and can learn nothing of those traits of national character which lie below the surface. The first view is certainly not prepossessing. The traveller finds wretchedness on every side of him, and therefore records at once a condemnation against the whole country, which a little more time induces him to revoke. Such was the case with Shelley. Nothing can be more widely different than the opinion which he expresses of the people on first entering Italy, and that which we find in his letters only six weeks afterwards.

And this is particularly the case in the Papal States. Your first greeting is from a crowd of beggars. In Tuscany nothing of the kind is seen, and it proves therefore that the evil is the result of wretched government. During a residence of several weeks in Florence, we were scarcely ever asked for charity, and on our way through the country saw only an active, industrious population. The instant, however, that we once more crossed the frontiers, and entered the territories of the Church, on our way to Bologna, the old scene was renewed, and the carriage surrounded by swarms, entreating relief in the name of the Madonna, and all the saints in the Calendar.

In Rome itself we meet with apparently the most wretched population in all Italy. There is no trade or commerce, and it seems as if half the people supported themselves by begging. Wherever you go, they gather around, and you have constantly dinned into your ears, " *Carità, forestieri* " (charity, strangers). They particularly collect on the steps of the *Scala di Spagna*, because strangers generally reside in that vicinity, and there they lie in wait, wishing you " good morning," and for a *bajoccho*, adding to it a profusion of prayers for your welfare. In addition to the difficulty of finding any employment, this delicious climate probably indisposes them to active exertion. Their maxim is, " *Dolce far niente* " (it is sweet to do nothing), and they make life one long *siesta*. It glides away in a graceful listlessness, — a dreamy, sleepy indolence, — until illness, or the feebleness of age, warns them that they will soon have done with it forever. Then, some Brotherhood nurses them in their last agonies, and buries them when dead. This state of things, it is true, cannot be pleasant to a stranger, for it brings constantly before him, misery, real or feigned, in every form, until there is danger lest his heart may at last become hardened against every exhibition.

Robberies, too, are frequent. Almost the only light in the narrow streets is that which comes from the faintly twinkling lamps hung before the pictures of the Madonna. There is ample opportunity, therefore, for the assassin to do his work, and, concealed in a dark alley or doorway, he waits to spring on the passer-by. With him the old demand — "Your money or your life" — means something. The former must be immediately forthcoming, or the latter is gone; for the stiletto is sharp, and the arm that wields it skillful. Passengers, therefore, at night walk carefully in the middle of the street, looking around them with the cautious air of men, who feel that they are in an enemy's country. As it is, every week we have the tale of some murders committed. No newspaper, indeed, records them, for it is the policy of government to hush up such proofs of its weakness, yet still they are whispered about as items of the daily news. In this respect Rome is a miserable contrast to Vienna, where, so admirable are the police arrangements, that a female might at midnight walk alone, from one end of the city to the other, without being insulted.

These are things most obvious to a traveller, and which interfere most with his comfort, but they are not to be charged on the great body of the people. They are, indeed, hasty and fiery in disposition, but by no means cruel or sanguinary, and their crimes are very often the result of some sudden and almost irresistible impulse. The man of whom you hear as having, in a moment of passion, taken life, perhaps gives himself up to agonies of mind infinitely worse than the scaffold, and then passes his remaining days in a monastery, to atone, by bitter repentance, for his sin. Such are the extremes of Italian character.

Most travellers prefer the Neapolitans to the Romans. They are charmed with the light-hearted, merry air of the poor lazzaroni, or amused with the strange contrast in their traits. With scarcely any clothing, and no home nearer than the grave,— through the day lounging in the sun of their delightful climate, and at night sleeping in the grotto of Posilippo, or any other shelter that is at hand — steeped to the lips in poverty, and with no prospect before them but to die in a hospital, and be buried like a dog in the *Campo Santo*, — you would, of course, expect to find them reduced to the lowest state of brutal degradation. And yet, go out on the Mole of a beautiful day, and you will see a circle of these homeless wretches gathered around some reader, whom they have hired for a few *grana* to recite to them the "Orlando Furioso" of Ariosto, or the lofty strains of Tasso. All this, of course, fascinates a casual observer, but I prefer the Romans. They have less frivolity; more depth and solidity; more of the haughtiness and reserve of the Spaniard — in short, more character than the Neapolitans. At the same time, they excel the French in sincerity, and the Germans in refinement. The knowledge of the arts, which they imbibe from their childhood with the very air they breathe gives them a grace of mind, and a degree of civilization, which would surprise one able to look below the surface. The forms of expression, too, used by the lower orders have often an air of poetry about them, which contrasts strikingly with the uncouth speech, and glaring vulgarisms of the same classes in Northern Europe. It is, indeed, customary with us to ridicule them for their superstitions, yet, with the faith in which they were instructed, would it not be a miracle if it were otherwise? And, besides this, should not the land which has witnessed Salem witchcraft and Mormonism — without mentioning countless other developments of fierce fanaticism — remember the line —

"Mutato nomine, de te fabula narratur?"

Those who know them best commend them for being kind-hearted and generous. Charitable we know they are, and the manner in which they minister to the wants of those poorer than themselves, might teach a useful lesson to many who pride themselves on their refinement and purer faith. We refer here to the common people, for as a class they are far superior to their nobles. This, indeed, is the case through all Southern Europe, and even in Spain, where the claims of descent are still so much respected. There the Andalusian peasant is a much nobler being than his lord.

How far the stream of Roman blood has remained unmixed with that of the barbarians, who in succession became masters of the city, we cannot of course tell. In one district of Rome, on the further side of the Tiber, live a peculiar race, who probably, more than any others, retain the traits which are left of the ancient inhabitants. They are the *Trasteverini*, boasting themselves the sole, unmingled descendants of the old masters of the world. You can detect them anywhere by their noble figures and haughty bearing, as if they had the consciousness of being of a superior race. "In the tall forms, and bold profiles, of the Trasteverini women, the matrons of Rome might still discern their true successors, fresh mothers of new Gracchi; and in the fiery eye of many a male, in that wild Janiculum suburb, or among the fierce Montigiani, there linger, yet unquenched, the lightnings before which client kings and suppliant ambassadors, were wont to quail."[1] They are most careful to prevent any intermarriage with those around them; no worldly temptation, indeed, seems strong enough to induce them to contract an alliance out of their own clan. Their dress is peculiar: the men having a jacket of black velvet thrown over their shoulders, a crimson sash round their waist, and large silver buckles on their shoes; while the women, particularly on *fête* days, are gayly attired in velvet bodices, laced with gold, scarlet aprons, and their hair braided in silken nets, with large silver bodkins. Even their section of the city seems to be less changed than the rest. Their churches are old temples, but little altered; the bridges which connect them with the city occupy the same sites as those which were built two thousand years ago; and among them, they still point to one which has taken the place of that Horatius Cocles so gallantly defended. The inhabitants seem to have all the lofty spirit of those they claim as ancestors, but there is no worthy object to which to direct it.

Such then are the modern Romans, and we have given this sketch because we believe that degraded as we often see them, they possess within themselves the elements of better things. A wretched government has made them what they are. Crushing all enterprise, and discouraging any studies which may give evidence of an inquiring mind, what does it leave to its subjects but a life of hopeless inactivity? They have nothing to do — nothing for which to strive, — nothing which it is possible for them to achieve.

The time when Rome enjoyed its greatest prosperity was undoubtedly during the brief rule of the French.

[1] F. W. Faber.

When they constituted it "the Department of the Tiber," almost their first act was, the formation of an Institute of twenty-four Professors. The abuses in the administration of justice were at once removed; asylums for assassins abolished; murderers torn even from the altar to receive their punishment; and for the first time in many centuries, life began to be safe within the walls of the Eternal City. The fiery spirit of the Trasteverini impelled them to some outrage, and immediately a strong force crossed the Tiber, marched into their section, seized the ringleaders, and shot twenty-two when surrounded by their own clansmen. From that time there was the most perfect peace in the Trastevere. The feudalities of the nobles too were abolished, and the power of life and death on their estates taken from them. Prince Doria, it is said, at that time, surrendered ninety fiefs, and Borghese as many. A pressure — the crushing weight of centuries of religious despotism — seemed to be removed from Rome, and a new life began to be breathed into its people.

Nor did the antiquities escape their care. The Column of Trajan, part of the Forum, and the Baths of Titus, were excavated under their direction; and more was accomplished in a few months than had previously been done in a score of years. We have already mentioned — in describing the Vatican — that one of Napoleon's great schemes was, to carry out the plan of Raphael and have a thorough exploration of all the ruins, the execution of which was only prevented by his fall.

The Church too was cleared of the incumbrances by which it had been crippled for so long a time. This was effected by the sale of public lands, and when Pius VII. returned, he found that debts to the amount of millions had been liquidated, and in place of bankruptcy he had an overflowing treasury.

Such was the state of things when the French rule ended. The old government resumed its sway, and at once Rome glided back to the sixteenth century. If the wave of a magician's wand could in an instant transform England into what it was in the days of the Tudors, it would not be a greater change. Industry and energy only rendered their possessor liable to suspicion, and were of course seen no longer.[1] The countless ecclesiastics who filled the streets under the old *régime* once more reappeared, and Rome became again what we see it now — the city of priests and beggars.

From that time the people were again crushed down by the most grievous of all tyrannies, — that which enchains the soul and the intellect, as well as the body. The most jealous *surveillance* is kept up, strangers are narrowly watched, the strictest care is taken to exclude all heretical works, and even scientific researches are discouraged. Politics of course never form a subject of conversation among the people, for they have no right even to have opinions on these

---

[1] One result of this naturally was, the immediate formation of a new Papal debt. In 1831 it had increased to six hundred millions of Italian lire — more than twelve hundred thousand dollars, — and it has since been steadily growing. In 1832 such was the exhausted state of the public Treasury, that a foreign loan was negotiated, one was imposed on the principal cities, the funds of some of the charitable institutions in Bologna were seized, and the land-tax was increased a third; other loans were effected in succeeding years. No variety of expedient has been left untried, and yet the financial position of the government daily becomes more critical.

points. The object seems to be to keep them in ignorance of what is passing in the rest of the world. Every little while the officers of the Police make a descent on Molandini's small circulating Library,—which, by the way, is used almost entirely by foreigners, — and seize every volume which they consider exceptionable. Not a Prayer-book for the British Chapel can be kept for sale in the city, but all are obliged to be smuggled in the baggage of travellers. While we were there, there was a notice one morning at the Reading-room, that the last few numbers of the "London Times" could not be placed on the files. They contained something which the Government did not like, and had been seized by the Police. None therefore could be delivered from the Post-office, and the English had to go without the latest news from home. There is a little paper published several times a week, not much larger than a sheet of foolscap, but it is principally filled with notices of the Papal Court, festivals and fast days, services, sermons, and ecclesiastics. Any item of foreign news is generally with reference to the movements of some Royal family; that "the Emperor of Austria has taken up his residence for the summer at the Palace of Schönbrunn," or something equally important. And this is the intellectual liberty allowed by the Papal Government. Can we expect anything therefore from the people? Our only wonder is, that every spark of generous or lofty emotions is not long since trampled out, and finding them as they are, we do not feel prepared to assent to Dante's charge, when he describes them as—

"the people which of all the world
Degenerates most." [1]

[1] *Il Paradiso*, Cant. xvi. l. 56.

Mazzini, one of their own exiles, thus describes his native land: "In Italy nothing speaks. Silence is the common law. The people are silent by reason of terror, the masters are silent from policy. Conspiracies, strife, persecution, vengeance, all exist, but make no noise; they excite neither applause nor complaint: one might fancy the very steps of the scaffold were spread with velvet, so little noise do heads make when they fall."

Occasionally indeed there is an outbreak, but the Austrian troops march in, and their bayonets soon restore the cause of despotism. Yet beneath its surface the spirit of the old Carbonari still "lives, and moves, and has its being." That deep feeling of which the stern enthusiast, Arnold of Brescia, the plebeian Rienzi, and the patrician Stefano Porcaro, were in succession the developments, and which in later days burns in every page of Alfieri, is only biding its time to come forth in action. We met with individuals dispersed here and there who were writhing under the foreign yoke, and when they found we were foreigners, threw aside the customary caution and gave utterance to their indignant thoughts. The society of "Young Italy" still exists in depths to which even an Austrian police cannot penetrate, striking its roots everywhere and reaching each rank of society. Its objects are, the expulsion of the Imperial troops and the liberation of Italy; its union under one government, with Rome for the capital; and the reduction of the Pope to his spiritual duties as a Christian Bishop. Its members are often men, who, like "the last of the Tribunes," look beyond the feudal forms of the Middle Ages, and feed the kindling fires of their minds by recollections of ancient Classic Rome. The very beauty of their land, rich in so many haunting memories, presents to them its ceaseless appeal. As they wander among its antique monuments, the *admonitus locorum* awakens every noble impulse, and speaks to their souls like a clarion's voice.

And we trust that one day the time will come, when from the plains of the soft Campania, the hoary relics of Imperial Rome, the sea-girt palaces of Venice, and the olive-groves of fair Milan, shall burst one wild shout, the voice of a people rising in its might — the herald of returning freedom. And then, when their magnificent designs are accomplished, and the name of Italy is once more written among the nations of the world, another Sismondi will be needed to continue her history, assuming for his work indeed a happier name than that which the last adopted, when he was forced to inscribe upon his title-page — "Italian Republics; or, the origin, progress, and *fall of Italian freedom.*"

CHAPTER XXII.

THE PAPAL CHURCH.

THE theory on which the Roman Government is founded is a noble one, — that of rendering everything subsidiary to religion. The whole object and aim of the civil authorities is, the advancement of their faith. And, since they are clothed with despotic power to accomplish this end, we should suppose they would wield an overpowering influence for the spiritual benefit of their people. Why is it then that ignorance and degradation, are so much the characteristics of the Roman populace, except that their Church does not well and worthily use the power with which it has been intrusted?

We would attempt, however, with diffidence, the expression of an opinion on the religious state of Rome. It is most difficult, in a foreign land, to decide on the spiritual significancy with which the people invest their many ceremonies, or the degree of moral influence which these rites exert over them. Everything is, of course, more prominently brought before us, than humble, unostentatious devotion. Of the possessors of this spirit, the world knows not. Christ's true followers are often his "hidden ones." Generally, indeed, we learn nothing of a system but its glaring abuses, and from these we form our estimate. We look, for instance, upon a monastery, but remember not how many fervent prayers ascend from its altars, or how many hearts, in its gloomy cells, may be disciplining themselves by bitter penitence for the world to come. We think only of the corruptions of the system, — and they are, of course, too great to allow us ever to wish for its restoration, — yet may there not be many a spirit struggling through them, and, in spite of every difficulty, painfully winning its way on to purity and peace? The latter is the suggestion of charity, which we too often forget.

It is in this spirit, indeed, that those without her fold are too much accustomed to estimate everything which relates to the Church of Rome. They look at her course through the Middle Ages, and denounce it all as one long period of evil and darkness. And yet, at that time, the Church — changed as she may have been from her early purity — was the only antagonist of the ignorance and vice, which characterized the feudal system. It was a conflict of mental with physical power, and by the victory she gained, the world was rescued from a debasing despotism, the triumph of which would have plunged our race into hopeless slavery. If the Church substituted another tyranny in its place, it was a better one. It was something which acted on the moral impulses of man, and endeavored in its own way to guide him on to sanctity. No one, indeed, can read the writers of the "Ages" which we call "Dark," without feeling that beneath the surface was a depth of devotion, and a degree of intellectual light, for which they have never received due credit.[1] An isolated pas-

---

[1] To any one who wishes to see the oft-repeated stories of the ignorance of "the *Dark* Ages" most ably refuted, we would recommend Maitland's *Dark Ages*.

sage, or a brief allusion, discover, perhaps, a thorough acquaintance with a truth, which we have been accustomed to consider utterly forgotten, until rediscovered at the time of the Reformation. Look at one single example of this in the poems of a Spanish cavalier, Don George Manrique, who was killed in the year 1479. Where, in the present day, can we find a clearer statement of one of the great doctrines of our faith, than is given in the following verse? —

> "O Thou, that for our sins didst take
> A human form, and humbly make
>   Thy home on earth;
> Thou, that to Thy divinity
> A human nature didst ally
>   By mortal birth, —
> And in that form didst suffer here
> Torment, and agony, and fear,
>   So patiently;
> By Thy redeeming grace alone,
> And not for merits of my own,
>   O pardon me!" [1]

And yet, this was written years before Luther was born; and it was a popular ballad in Spain, sung in the castles of her nobles, and in her peasant homes through many a retired valley, nearly half a century before the Reformation began. We mention this merely to show how erroneous is popular judgment on such subjects, and the necessity there is for estimating with caution the degree of intellectual or spiritual light possessed by masses of men with whom our acquaintance, is necessarily very limited.

There are, however, many practices of the Church of Rome, which are here constantly before our eyes, so utterly at variance with every principle of true Catholic faith, that the most enlarged charity cannot forbid

[1] Longfellow's translation.

our thorough condemnation. Some of these — the relics and statue in St. Peter's, the face in the Mamertine prisons, the inscription on the Cross of the Coliseum, the services of St. Anthony's Day, and the Santa Scala — we have already mentioned in previous chapters. In the few following pages, therefore, we shall endeavor to speak of others which are most obvious.

In this city the Church is always before us. Its holy days are enforced by law, when the shops are obliged to be closed, and all business is suspended. The magnificent carriages of the Cardinals constantly dash by; processions each day pass our windows, with their lighted tapers, chanting the service as they carry the Host, and all kneel on the pavement while they remain in hearing. Wherever we walk, we find throngs of ecclesiastics of every kind. The pilgrim is here, with his "sandal-shoon and scollop-shell;" the lordly-looking priest, with his ample cloak and shovel hat, and long lines of friars,—

"White, black, and gray, with all their trumpery."

In the city of Rome their number is estimated at one in twenty-five of the population, while in the whole Papal dominions there are said to be (including nuns) nearly fifty-five thousand, — certainly ten times the number necessary for the spiritual wants of the people. The support for all this army is, of course, drawn from the impoverished inhabitants.

Of relics it is almost superfluous to write, for every church has its abundant share of bones, and ashes, and blood, of the Saints. In the Church of San Lorenzo we were shown the gridiron on which St. Lawrence suffered martyrdom, some of his teeth, and vials of his blood. In the Church of St. Praxides are marble panels, on which are engraved a list of the relics they have preserved. It is too long for insertion here, but we make from it the following selection: A tooth of St. Peter; a tooth of St. Paul; a part of the blessed Virgin Mary's chemise; part of the girdle of our Lord; part of the rod of Moses; part of the earth on which our Lord prayed before his Passion; part of the sponge with which they gave our Lord to drink, and of the reed on which it was placed; part of the sepulchre of the Virgin Mary; a picture of our Lord, which St. Peter gave to Prudens, the father of St. Praxides; part of the towel with which our Lord wiped his disciples' feet; part of the swaddling-clothes in which our Lord was wrapped at his Nativity; part of his seamless garment; three thorns from his crown, and four fragments of the true Cross. We have copied about one quarter: these, however, are sufficient to show the objects of reverence which are exhibited in every church to the credulity of the faithful.

One of the most fatal of their doctrines is that of Indulgences. It seems to be expressed so broadly and unequivocally, that there can be but one way of understanding it. Over the door of almost every church is the inscription —" INDULGENTIA PLENARIA QUOTIDIANA PERPETUA PRO VIVIS ET DEFUNCTIS." In the Church erected above the Mamertine prisons is a long Italian inscription, of which we translate the following portion: " From a prison it was consecrated a Church in honor of the said holy Apostles, by Saint Sylvester, Pope, at the prayer of the Emperor Constantine the Great, and he gave it the name of *S. Pietro in Carcere*, and granted every day to each one who visited it, one thousand two hundred years of indulgence, doubled on Sundays and commanded Festivals, and moreover every day the remission of the third part of sins. Gregory XIII. granted there plenary indulgence on the first day of August, from the first Vespers until sunset. Finally, Pius VI., in 1776, granted there every day the perpetual plenary indulgence for the living and the dead." I one day asked an ecclesiastic, what these things meant? He went into a very elaborate attempt to explain them away, at the end of which I was no wiser than before. Either I was very dull, or he darkened the matter by a multitude of words. But these inscriptions are constantly seen on every side, and how must the common and uneducated classes interpret them? Why, of course, exactly according to the literal meaning of the words.

The doctrine of Purgatory is brought before them with equal distinctness. The inscription at the Mamertine prisons, a portion of which we have given above, concludes with this sentence, " The altar of this Church of *S. Pietro in Carcere* is privileged every day forever with the liberation of one soul from Purgatory, for every mass which shall be celebrated at the same." And in almost all the Churches are inscriptions like the following, which we one morning copied from over the altar in that of *S. Maria della Pace* — " Ogni messa celebrata in quest altare, libera un anima dal purgatorio." Saying masses is indeed sometimes the only support of unbeneficed priests. They are in readiness to perform this duty for any who wish it, and thus contrive to gain a precarious living. The price for a mass is from three to four pauls, that is, from thirty to forty cents. This disgraceful traffic in sacred things shows that Rome has not improved, since Dante referred to it as the place —

> " Where gainful merchandise is made of Christ
> Throughout the livelong day." [1]

The Rev. Dr. Jarvis, in a work — "No Union with Rome" — published a few years since, has a passage showing how much an individual by a little bodily labor can do before breakfast, to gain remission of his sins; and from an acquaintance with the places mentioned, we can confirm the feasibility of the plan. "At sunrise he might kiss the Cross in the Coliseum, and obtain two hundred days' indulgence in a moment. He might hurry to the Church of St. Pudens and St. Pudentiana, and during a half hour's mass, secure to himself three thousand years' indulgence, and the remission of a third part of his sins. Returning by the way of Ara Cœli, he can recite the litanies of the most blessed Virgin at the altar of her who by Papal authority is called THE REFUGE OF SINNERS, and he has two hundred days more of indulgence, which he may either keep himself, or kindly give to one of his dead friends. If he has three pauls (thirty cents) in his pocket, he may exercise his charity toward that friend still further, by having a mass said expressly for his soul by one of the monks or any other priest, and thus deliver it at once from the torments of Purgatory. Crossing thence to the Mamertine prison he may gain twelve hundred years' indulgence, or on a Sunday or Festival morning, two thousand four hundred years, and the remission of another third part of his sins. Here, also, if he has another thirty cents to

---

[1] *Il Paradiso*, Cant. xviii. l. 50.

spare, he can pay for another mass, and liberate another friend from purgatory. Thus he may before breakfast, every day of his life, obtain for himself at least more than four thousand three hundred years' indulgence, and the remission of two thirds of his sins, with only a little bodily labor; and for the expense of sixty cents he may liberate two souls from purgatory."

While such corruptions exist, is it not natural that unbelief should be rife? The fear of the Inquisition may indeed prevent its open declaration, yet still it poisons the very fountain of faith, and changes men into formal hypocrites. The educated ask, Can this be the religion of Christ? It requires but a faint glimmering of reason to answer in the negative, and knowing nothing to substitute in its place, they fall into the coldness of skepticism. We believe that the external city well typifies the actual condition of the Papal Church. On every side we see decrepit, faded grandeur, the evidences of a mighty power which in past centuries had here its home, but which has now utterly passed away.

The most fearful picture of religion in Rome is that given by Mazzini. He writes indeed with the bitterness of an exile, and we should therefore feel inclined to soften some expressions and strike out some sentences of sweeping condemnation; yet as a whole, we fear there is too much truth in his view. "Conceive the state of a creed-distrusting people, curbed, domineered, overburdened by an army of priests manifesting faith only in force, who surround themselves with Swiss and Austrian bayonets, or, in the name of Christ, muster brigands from the galleys! Religion — I speak of Papal Catholicism — is, in the Roman States more than elsewhere, lifeless; lifeless in the educated classes as a consequence of the enlightened age; lifeless in the people as wanting a symbol — as wanting a something representative. Who in that country is ignorant, that the nomination of Christ's Vicar depends on ambassadorial intrigue, and that the direct or indirect *Veto* of Austria, of France, or some other power, throws into nonentity the so termed chosen of the Holy Spirit? Who is ignorant that long since the *King* strangled the *Pope;* that diplomacy masters theology; that the notes of foreign plenipotentiaries, have inspired Briefs to the clergy of Poland and the Bishops of Ireland? Which *motu-proprio* of a Pope but insults the *infallibility* of his predecessor? Who in the provinces but can point to the agents of the Prelate-Governors, shamelessly trafficking in all that can bring money to themselves or their masters? How, dizzied in this whirlpool of scandal, of hypocrisy, of dilapidation, can man preserve his faith intact? By a deplorable but too natural reaction, negation, materialism, doubt, day by day ingulf fresh souls. Nought of religion survives but forms, outward shows, and observances, compelled by law. It is compulsory that men should communicate at Easter; it is compulsory that the youth of schools and universities should be present at Mass each day, and communicate once a month; it is compulsory that public officers should take part in services termed religious. Such is religion in the Papal States."

This is the dark side of the Church of Rome, and we write it in sorrow that any branch of the Church of Christ should ever have given occasion for such comments. Very many, however, there must be who are not subject to these charges, and who in spite of their doctrinal errors and the dogmas of a perverted theology, seem to exhibit in their own characters the highest principles of faith. Their lives are marked by austerity, and self-denial, and ceaseless devotion. Unless it were so, they could not send forth works characterized by so elevated a tone of religious life — breathing a spirit of abstraction from this world, and a longing for the realities of that which is to come, almost unearthly in its nature. Nor can these productions be read by the people, and become familiar to their minds, without leaving some holy impress. Take, for instance, this little Latin hymn, with which they are well acquainted, and how lofty is its tone! It is ascribed to St. Francis Xavier, whose missionary labors in the East gained for him the title of Apostle of the Indies.

"O Deus! ego amo te:
Nec amo te, ut salves me,
Aut quia non amantes te
Æterno punis igne.

"Tu, tu, mi Jesu, totum me
Amplexus es in Cruce.
Tulisti clavos, lanceam,
Multamque ignominiam:
Innumeros dolores
Sudores et angores,
Ac mortem: et hæc propter me
Ac pro me peccatore.

"Cur igitur non amem te
O Jesu amantissime?
Non ut in cœlo salves me,
Aut ne æternum damnes me,
Nec præmii ullius spe:
Sed sicut tu amasti me,
Sic amo et amabo te:
Solum quia Rex meus es,
Et solum quia Deus es.
Amen"

We subjoin the following translation, without knowing to whom it is ascribed. It is, however, quite literal:

> "O God! my spirit loves but Thee,
> Not that in heaven its home may be,
> Nor that the souls which love not Thee
> Shall groan in fire eternally.
>
> "But Thou on the accursed tree
> In mercy hast embraced me.
> For me the cruel nails, the spear,
> The ignominious scoff didst bear,
> Countless, unutterable woes —
> The bloody sweat —death's pangs and throes —
> These Thou didst bear, all these for me,
> A sinner and estranged from Thee.
>
> "And wherefore no affection show,
> Jesus, to Thee that lov'st me so?
> Not that in heaven my home may be;
> Not lest I die eternally;
> Not from the hopes of joys above me:
> But even as Thyself didst love me,
> So love I, and will ever love Thee:
> Solely because my King art Thou,
> My God for evermore as now.
>   Amen."

That the mind from which such lines emanated must have been tuned to a lofty devotion, none can doubt; but when his words are adopted as a portion of the literature of a people, and sink into their hearts, we consider it an evidence that there are many in whose deep religious feelings the sentiments themselves have found a ready echo. With such it has been my good fortune sometimes to meet — men who, in their self-denying zeal and earnestness of spirit, might have stood by the side of Xavier himself. And I was always glad to avail myself of the opportunity to see and converse with those who differ from us so widely, to learn the extent of the gulf which separates us, and to hear their views stated by themselves.

This high character common report gives to Padre J., with whom I became acquainted in Northern Italy. He is a Jesuit, and, we were told, one of the most influential of his Order in Europe. Brought up in the army of France, he attained high rank under Napoleon, before he abandoned his profession for the priesthood. He is thoroughly versed in all the schemes of his Order, and is usually regarded as keeper to the conscience of the king in whose dominions he now lives. Yet everywhere I heard a tribute paid to his devotion and zeal; and if he is at times mixed up with the intrigues of states, it seems to be done without any sacrifice of those higher qualities for which we should chiefly look in the ecclesiastic. Although eighty years of age, " his eye is not dim, nor his natural force abated," and no one from appearance would judge him to be more than sixty.

The greater part of the morning before I left the city in which he resides, was spent in conversation with him. Meeting in the sacristy of the Church attached to his monastery, he invited me to his room. We went up through the long stone galleries, seldom trodden by Protestant feet, passing occasionally a monk who was walking slowly back and forth, apparently absorbed in the book he held in his hand. The cell of Padre J. contained only what was absolutely necessary. There were his little bed and table, the picture and Crucifix, the few books he used, and, besides these, we saw only naked walls and the hard stone floor. The day was cold, but there was no fire to warm the room — nothing but the little chafing-dish of ashes and of coals, which the old man held in his lap, and over which he spread out his hands as he talked. His face beamed with animation as he expatiated on his Church, and spoke of the cheering signs he discerned in France, which he trusted would strengthen until that land was redeemed from skepticism, although he himself could never live to see the consummation.

We mention this interview, because the conversation was a fair example of what such discussions must always be with members of the Church of Rome. They invariably turn upon a single point. The Padre quoted to me that declaration in the Athanasian Creed, "Whoever will be saved, before all things it is necessary that he hold the Catholic faith." This of course no one is inclined to deny, but it opens before us the wide inquiry, What is the Catholic faith? and this only carries us one step further back, which is to the question, "What is the *Catholic* Church?" Here at length we reach the separating point, on which we differ as widely as the poles. And this will always be found to be the gist of the argument. It will ever turn upon the inquiry, "Are we or are we not, a portion of the true Catholic Church?"

One claim by which the old Padre attempted most earnestly to fortify his position, was that of modern miracles for the Church of Rome. The occurrence of these he insisted on as proofs that she was *the* Church. He dwelt particularly upon one, with which he assured me he was personally acquainted. It was the recovery of the daughter of the governor of Nice, who had been confined to her bed for months with a diseased limb. At length mortification commenced and she was about to submit to amputation, when through the prayers of a friend offered up to a certain saint, she was instantaneously cured, and able to rise at once in perfect health. Of course, the only answer I could make was, "That all this depended on the question of facts." This, however, is a favorite argument with the members of the Church of Rome. The gift of miracles remaining in the Church is something tangible, and they are very apt, therefore, to bring it forward in support of their lofty claims.

Italy, of course, abounds with the records of modern miracles. Many undoubtedly are the effect of imposture, but many more owe their apparent existence to a more innocent cause. In this Southern clime the warm and glowing imagination of its children renders them disposed to receive impressions of the marvelous, with a facility of which the cold and cautious sons of the North know nothing. Their tendency also to figurative language and exaggerated descriptions, often induces them to clothe a common occurrence in language which conveys a very erroneous impression to the hearer. Thus the narrative of any event, seemingly strange, after passing through a few hands easily grows into a miracle, and is chronicled accordingly. This is in some measure the philosophy of the subject as I once heard it given by an ecclesiastic; and several of his illustrations were so new to me that it may be worth while to give them, as far as possible, in his own words.

"Many of these reputed miracles," said he, "are mere types of qualities which existed in the individuals to whom they are ascribed, and which are thus shadowed forth by sensible images, or they are figurative descriptions of actual events. For example, — in one of the towns of Italy a house is pointed out, in which, some half century ago, a wandering friar applied to the family for alms. Being rudely repulsed, he went into the kitchen, where a brace of pheasants were roasting before the fire. He made over them the sign of the Cross, when at once they slid off the spit, clothed themselves with feathers, and flew away. Thus, at least, runs the legend. Now, to you this undoubtedly seems a ridiculous fable; to me, on the contrary, it is a most edifying story. I strip it of the figurative language, and this history remains. That family was probably known to be deficient in the virtue of charity, and Providence brought misfortunes upon them. The pheasants represent the superfluities and luxuries of life, and by their departure we learn, that the riches of these churls 'made to themselves wings and flew away.' This was their retribution, and the narrative comes to us as an allegory."

"So it was," he continued, "often in England. St. Dunstan had a quarrel with Edwy, because that King had married Elgiva, his relative within the prohibited degrees. After a long contest the Saint gained the day, and the King was forced to yield. The common people, whose sympathies, in that rude age, were all with the Church, hailed it as a triumph. The King had been forced to overgo 'the lusts of the flesh.' St. Dunstan had conquered the Evil One. Thus they spoke of it as a battle with Satan, and in the next generation, by means of the figurative language in which tradition gave it, the conflict, in their belief, passed into a real and personal one. Their champion had actually encountered and routed the Devil. And, as stories which are thus handed down never lose, we now have the legend, that St. Dunstan ended the contest, by seizing the Devil with a red-hot tongs. So it is with all his life. Read the marvels which the old monkish chroniclers have given us about him, and you can reduce them all down to some such basis of common sense."

We give this exposition for its singularity, leaving the reader to decide on its value as elucidating the legendary lore of the Church of Rome.

And yet, amid all the ignorance, and superstition, which prevails in this land, there are reflecting minds sighing for a purer faith. They would not desert their Church, but they see her errors, and would have her remodeled in accordance with Catholic truth. They realize that she has borne herself too loftily, and would wish her therefore lay aside her temporal claims, and in lowliness of mind demean herself as she ought — changing, too, their Pontiff to a Christian Bishop, that he may no longer be induced, while the Lord tarries, to forget his duty to his fellow-servants, and to tyrannize over them. These are views which we have often heard expressed. On one occasion we travelled for some time with a gentleman from Milan, who had reasoned himself out of the errors of his Church, and into a Creed essentially Catholic. But, for the present, he did not dare to show that he had abandoned any of the old landmarks. And there were many, he said, who shared his sentiments.

May we not hope, then, that the time will come, when, within the bounds of their own Church, they will feel every aspiration gratified, faith have room for its exercise, and Catholic truth recognize her once more as its champion? How nobly would all that is pure, and holy, and of good report, advance in this apostate earth, if Rome could throw aside her errors, and lend her mighty influence to the cause! She still retains those ancient Creeds, which were acknowledged in primitive times, and are now held by all Catholic Christendom. The great truths she teaches are the truths for all ages — the awful verities for which confessors and martyrs, in early days, were willing to die. The errors she mingles with them are the dogmas only of her single Church — which particular times, and schools, have grafted on her, and which she has unfortunately retained. How earnestly, therefore, should we pray, that the hour of her awakening may come, when, leaving her relics to moulder in their forgotten shrines, putting from her all narrow sympathies, restoring her doctrines to the model of early times, and uniting at length with those who have retained the faith in its purity, the long separated branches of Christ's Church shall be able to go forth together to reap the harvest fields of the Cross! Then shall the Church become in reality that august spectacle which floated before the glowing vision of St. Augustine, when on the distant shores of Africa, and amidst the expiring throes of Paganism, he sent forth his "City of God," to hail, with all the treasures of his matchless eloquence, that universal dominion which he knew would be her heritage. This is the consummation which poor humanity is earnestly desiring. The world is wearying of strife, and more and more with hope, and love, and oft repeated inquiry, is craving the return of Christian unity. In every land we feel the mighty beatings of this intense desire with which the heart of our race is filled.

But we must close this chapter. We have, through this volume, spoken of the Papal Church, honestly and truly, as she seemed to us, expressing the admiration we feel for the many Catholic traits she retains; her charitable institutions for the relief of every kind of misery; her broad and expansive views, looking over the whole earth as the field of Christian labor, and the solemn beauty of so many of her services, appealing at once to the deepest cravings of the heart by their holy teaching, or raising the soul above this earth by the austere hymns received from early days. But the view is one of mingled darkness and light. We have been forced, therefore, to speak also of fearful errors perverting the truth, and of countless ceremonies marring the effect of her noblest services, till he who studies them in the Missal scarcely recognizes them when performed amidst the pomp of her old Cathedrals. We can have no sympathies, then, with Rome while she remains unchanged, but turn from her with renewed happiness to the stern purity of our own Church.

> "I love thee, nor would stir
> Thy simple note, severe in character,
> By use made lovelier, for the loftier tune
> Of hymn, response, and touching antiphone,
> Lest we lose homelier truth."

He must be unsettled, indeed, in the first principles of his own belief, who can decide otherwise, or gather from a study of the Papal Church any feeling but that of thankfulness to old English Reformers, because they were willing to peril their lives, even unto death, to defend the purity of the faith. "If first thou be well grounded," says Fuller, in his usual quaint way, "their fooleries shall rivet thy faith the faster, and travel shall give thee Confirmation in that Baptism thou didst receive at home."

But are there some who are unwilling to recognize anything good within her fold, and feel, therefore, as if we had not been thorough enough in our condemnation of Rome? We would say to them, It is not a pleasant office for the children of the Peacemaker to be widening those gulfs, which even now separate them so much from each other. We have, indeed, condemned where truth required it, but dwelt with regret on these portions of our subject, for we remember that we, too, as a Church, have our grievous sins, which might well hush every whisper of self-complacency. Widely, then, as we differ from Rome, we would speak of her with no feelings but those of the deepest sorrow, that such a mighty influence should be lost to the cause of truth. Let it be, as when in ancient Israel one of her tribes came not up in the day of battle, the prophetess declared, that for their defection "there were great searchings of heart." And should another reason be asked, we would quote to him who demands it, the words in which a poet of our own day inculcates the true Christian temper, and the remembrance of which has often restrained the pen, when we would have written words of bitterness, —

"*Thou* to wax fierce
　In the cause of the Lord,
To threat and to pierce
　With the heavenly sword!
Anger and zeal
　And the joy of the brave,
Who bade *thee* feel,
　　　Sin's slave?
The altar's pure flame
　Consumes as it soars;

Faith meetly may blame,
　For it serves and adores.
Thou warnest and smitest !
　Yet Christ must atone
For a soul that thou slightest —
　　Thine own."

CHAPTER XXIII.

FAREWELL TO ROME.

HE time of our departure draws nigh, and we must soon bid adieu to the Eternal City. Pleasant indeed have been the days of our sojourn here! Crowded with scenes which could not but awaken the deepest interest, they went by like the "Days of Thalaba." We have been living for a time in the shadowy Past. The remembrance of distant ages, whose traces are preserved only in dim tradition, came thronging on us at every step. It was moving back the shadow upon the old dial-plate of Time. It was summoning up from the depths of our own minds the memory, long indistinct, of deeds which moved the world, and here on the spot where they were acted, investing them with a reality and life. We look at what Rome has been in the days of the Republic and in the splendor of her Imperial sway, and then seek out the footsteps of these mighty Ages, in the fading greatness which still remains. And everywhere we trace them still uneffaced. The Mistress of the world indeed stands before us like Milton's Apostate Angel, whose —

> "Form had yet not lost
> All her original brightness, nor appear'd
> Less than archangel ruin'd, and the excess
> Of glory obscured."

We have been once more to St. Peter's to take another look at that unequaled temple, and from the brow of the Pincian Hill for the last time have seen the sun set over this array of domes and towers. How beautifully it goes down in the cloudless sky, pouring a flood of golden light upon the mighty city! Gradually the purple fades from the mountains, and the transparent azure above is exchanged for the deeper blue of the evening sky, gemmed by a thousand stars. We sat there, with no one near us, to watch the changing lights and shadows. A death-like calm, an air of dreamy repose, rested on the city at our feet. The idle loiterers had left the Hill, and we saw only its statues and obelisks, and works of antique art, mingling with the deep green of the foliage. As we looked upon the scene spread out in beauty around us, there seemed to be within our sight a glorious grouping of all that is exquisite, the loveliness of present nature mingled with the noble associations which the past has bequeathed to us from a remote antiquity. The fading light spread over it a bewitching softness, a mellowing and blending of every tint and color, which words cannot describe and which only Claude could have painted. And while the twilight deepened, there came faintly from the neighboring Convent the sound of solemn music, and the stillness around us was broken by the Evening Hymn to the Virgin: —

"Ave, Regina cœlorum,
Ave, Domina angelorum.
Salve radix, Salve porta,
Ex qua mundo lux est orta;
Gaude Virgo gloriosa,
Super omnes speciosa;

> Vale, O valde decora,
> Et pro nobis Christum exora "[1]

But what is to be the destiny of Rome? Is she to be the centre of Christendom, and age after age the place to which pilgrims from every land shall direct their steps? Is she entering on a new dominion — the third cycle, — in which she is to rule the world by Arts as once she did by her arms, and then by her faith? There is another thought which has in it something affecting and solemn. The malaria is increasing, so that large portions of the city which a century ago were famed for their salubrity, are now uninhabitable. At the Lateran, the Pope has been obliged to leave his palace, and the humble dwellers around him their abodes, so that the tall grass waves in those wide squares, and an unbroken silence has taken the place of the hum of busy population. The enemy is stealthily creeping on, its presence betrayed by no external sign, but there seems to be a fresh and delicious atmosphere, which they who breathe find to be death. No human sagacity can detect it in the transparent air, nor any human means arrest its progress. An invisible and mysterious agent, it expels man from the region over which its wing is spread, or he remains only to wither and die.

But if such continues to be the history of coming years, how strange must be the destiny of the Im-

---

[1] "Hail Mary! Queen of Heavenly spheres,
Hail, whom the angelic host reveres!
Hail fruitful root! Hail sacred gate,
Whence the world's light derives its date;
O glorious Maid, with beauty blest!
May joys eternal fill thy breast!
Thus crown'd with beauty and with joy,
Thy prayers for us with Christ employ."

perial City! Its people will gradually retire before this destroying spirit, and seek in other spots the safety denied them here, until once more the Seven Hills become as silent as they were before Romulus encamped upon their heights. Then it will remain, like the city of which we read in Arabian fable, whose inhabitants in a moment were turned to stone, so that the traveller wandered in amazement through palaces and halls, where none came forth to meet him, and no sound was heard but the echo of his own steps. Its mighty monuments will stand, like those of Pæstum, waste and desolate in their grandeur. Spring, and summer, and winter will pass over the forsaken city; the hoariness of age gather on its marble columns and stain its gilded walls; and Nature, spreading her luxuriance over them, and wreathing them each year with a thicker drapery, thus silently yet surely reclaim her dominion; until at last all on which we now gaze will only harmonize with the wild and dreary Campagna around.

But would not this be a fit conclusion to the long and eventful career of the Mistress of the World? There seems a strange and mysterious awe lingering about her which forbids the thought that she should fall by human agency. If, after surviving wars and sieges and conflagrations, she must at last be numbered with Nineveh and Babylon, and those cities of the Elder World whose names only live in history, let there be no proud conqueror rejoicing over her end! Let her not be crushed and humbled by the violence of man, but thus pass away "without hands," so that the hour can scarcely be marked in which she ceases to exist!

THE END.

WORKS BY THE SAME AUTHOR.

I.
The Lenten Fast.
Thirteenth Edition. $1.25.

II.
The Double Witness of the Church.
Seventeenth Edition. $1.50.

III.
The Early Conflicts of Christianity.
Fourth Edition. $1.25.

IV.
The Catacombs of Rome.
Fifth Edition. $1.00.

V.
The Early Jesuit Missions in North America.
Fourth Edition. $1.50.

VI.
The Unnoticed Things of Scripture.
Just Published. $1.50.

VII.
The Christmas Holydays in Rome.
New Edition. $1.75.

www.ingramcontent.com/pod-product-compliance
Lightning Source LLC
Chambersburg PA
CBHW030807230426
43667CB00008B/1105